You Are The Answer

A Journey Of Awakening

Paul Norman Tuttle

KAIROS, INC., *publishers*
P.O. Box 71280
Seattle, WA 98107

Cover Photo by Keith Eyer
Cover Design by Donna Schwartz
Produced in the U.S.A. by Riverrun Press

ISBN: 0-934501-00

This book is dedicated,
with deep love, to my wife

Susan

Acknowledgments

In itself, the publication of a book is the result of a tremendous group effort, but when the book arises out of real life, as this one has, the contributors span a lifetime.

The list of those whose direct or indirect guidance most significantly contributed to my spiritual growth and the journey described herein must begin with my parents, and especially my mother. Her keen mind and clear spiritual sense of the Scriptures, together with the metaphysical principles of Christian Science, were matched only by her ability to render them lovingly practical and relevant to daily life. She nurtured my love for Truth.

Another for whom I shall be eternally grateful is Vera Searles, a Christian Science practitioner, who helped me grasp the fact that Truth is universal, a living Presence, and that it is not *contained* in a book, organization, philosophy, or religion. For forty years she goaded and triggered my spiritual perception of Truth as an inner, immediate experience of Reality.

I thank God for my wife, who has had to *live* with me through the period of transition which this book chronicles. The presence of what is perceived to be divine in intent is unsettling. The separation of the chaff from the wheat *is* a threshing process, and we constantly lived on the edge of transformation. Susan never lost sight of the underlying Value of what was happening, even though at times I did.

I thank my children, Julie, Wendy, and Christopher, for their trust and their willingness to flow without complaining as my life took new direction.

For the hours and hours of camaraderie, support, and friendship provided by Dr. John Roberts and Herb Robinson — a psychologist and a minister, respectively — when I worried that I was losing my mind and that Raj was a hallucination, I extend my love and appreciation.

I

Last, but not least, I wish to thank Raj. He has helped to bring into experiential focus the Truth I had been learning about, and more than anything else has revealed the meaning of Love.

To the entire staff of Kairos, who have undertaken the publishing of this book, and especially Dr. Kenneth and Sally Eyer, I extend my thanks. It *has* been a major undertaking.

Foreword

The Fourth Dimension is present to be perceived, experienced, and explored! The endeavors to explore three-dimensional space to its outer reaches must be replaced by the investigation and exploration of "Fourth-dimensional space," because this is the most direct and efficient means by which the perceived universe *can* be successfully explored.

The exploration of outer space, as mankind is presently proceeding, will not be successful because three-dimensional means are being used as the exclusive means. Since there is no way to achieve the speed of light, there will be no way to explore the full extent of the universe within a reasonable amount of time, and extreme frustration will set in. However, there is no need to go through the steps necessary to find that this is true.

Man can come to the point where movement in space is accomplished by the shifting of attention, by a movement of consciousness, rather than a movement of form. This will only be accomplished as he willingly gives up his perception of himself as the form he appears to be — which apparently exists within three-dimensional space — and begins to identify and experience himself as the Consciousness in which all experience of form, space, and time is occurring.

The movement into "Fourth-dimensional space" is a movement into your Center. It constitutes a process of Self-discovery which spontaneously and inexorably requires the allowing of a new self-image to replace the one with which you presently define yourself. It constitutes a process of accessing your greater capacity to be aware. It constitutes the movement into the experience of the infinite Nature and Actuality of your Being, in which you have the capacity to move as desired to any point within that infinity. This literally means your ability to be at any point in what you call the three-dimensional universe, without any physical process involved. The most direct route to the Pleiades or the farthest galaxy is right through the Center of your Being.

This book *is not* of exclusive value. It is not a definitive exposition of anything. It will not lead you from one point, through a logical structure, to a conclusion. It will be frustrating to the intellect. You will not find ultimate answers in it which you may then simply be obedient to on a surface level and manifest the *appearance* of growth. It *is* a series of triggers which, if you will allow them, will spontaneously snap you out of traditional theories, concepts, and beliefs which presently bind you to the three–dimensional–only frame of reference.

The degree of frustration you might experience will indicate *only* the degree to which you insist upon requiring that Reality unfold within the framework of your present belief structures. Your demands that this book be more than it is, or that it accomplish more than it apparently does, will constitute the degree of control you insist on employing and will tell you something of your own methods of confining yourself to your limiting beliefs.

To the degree that you read this volume without making requirements of it, to the degree that you are open to the transformational and triggering effects it will have, to that degree you will find yourself slowly escaping from the bondages of your present, limited belief structures. I warn you that you will grow, and that growth means change. Change means the release of things which were once of value, but are no longer — like a pair of shoes outgrown, or training wheels.

This is the first in a series of books which will do nothing more than trigger your remembrance of Who and What You Are. It will thus put you in the position of experiencing your world and your universe as some aspect of the infinitude of your Being. It is only through the experience of your Oneness with everything that social, political, and business Harmony can emerge, imbued with Love as its underlying essence.

Three–dimensionally speaking, Paul's life is little different from yours. This book captures a period of six months in his life, when circumstances not far different from those you might experience, were occurring. The details are different but the problems are fundamentally the same.

For approximately six months prior to the first conversation on February 7, 1982, Paul was experiencing the collapse of a business he had. It was extremely difficult to deal with, because he had put a lot of his energy and faith in his ability into the business. The collapse of the business seemed to reflect a collapse of his worth, of his validity. It prompted him to grasp beyond his human reasoning and intellectual abilities.

In this process, he was informed by a new acquaintance that each individual has help available through a spiritual Guide — an Individuality free of the ego — whose purpose it is to help him escape the bondage and punishment of his own limited beliefs, of his objective conceptualizations about himself, his life, and his world.

This was not enough to cause him to immediately extend his interest or attention in that direction. He continued through the month of January 1982 attempting to deal as best he could with his situation on the basis of *his* intellect and intelligence.

Finally, during the last half of January, he decided he *needed* help, that he was, indeed, incapable of dealing with these dynamics on the basis of his then present ability. Because he was convinced of his personal inability to resolve the situation, and as a result of daily taking time to reach out to his Guide, it was possible for us to open communication. On February 7 of that year, we had our first conversation.

This book is constituted of the conversations which occurred between February 7 and June 21, 1982. There have been many dialogues since. However, I have instructed Paul to publish these conversations separately — not only because of their sheer volume, but also because their value is not to be gained in their totality. Their value is to be found in the conscious movement which is generated in you as a result of your reading of them, no matter where or when you might be reading in the volume!

Again, the value is not to be found in the book at all! There is no "knowledge" in the book that it is appropriate for you to *acquire.* Neither the book nor its contents are the focal point. It is *you* who are the focal point. It is your process of Awakening that is the focal point.

It is Paul's hope that this volume might encourage you and others to reach out, to become aware of the loving guidance which is everpresently available to you. It is further his hope that through your discovery of your relationship with your Guide, you will begin to glimpse experientially the underlying Oneness of yourself with your fellow man. The intimacy of the relationship one has with one's Guide, together with the absolute lack of need for any defensiveness — the fact that this relationship is experienced from one's own Center — will begin to reveal that this is where all relationships occur in their Reality, rather than through three–dimensional space from body to body.

Again, the most direct route to your fellow man is right through the Center of your Being. This is where the Brotherhood of Man exists as Fact. This is where it exists experientially rather than theoretically. And this is where each one must eventually come to live every event of his daily life.

Enjoy the book, but remember that I have warned you that you are likely to grow!

Rajpur
Bellingham, Washington
January 8, 1985

You
Are
The
Answer

A Journey Of Awakening

February 7, 1982
Sunday

PAUL   I want to talk to my Guide. I need help, understanding, comprehension of the situation I appear to be caught in, and I would be very grateful to make contact and learn what it is in my experience that needs to be seen in order to resolve some things.

Would you please identify yourself to me?

RAJ   My name is Rajpur. I have been waiting for your desire to speak, have been aware of your requests in the recent past, but have had to await the proper timing before making myself known to you.

PAUL   Am I making you up? Am I making up the words?

RAJ   Yes and no. I am not speaking directly with you. I am, you might say, speaking to you in meanings without language. You are catching the meaning and supplying the language. If I were to communicate with someone in India they would hear me in their language, and yet I would not be speaking to them in any language at all, just meanings.

The more you become integrated with your experience through the technique you are now using, the more accurate will be your "translation" and the more easily it will flow. Right now, my meanings are flowing fluidly, but the fact that

1

your typewriter is stuttering[1] is due to your awkwardness and lack of experience in communication on this level of consciousness.

You are also going to have to do this as often as you can in order to be comfortable with it, and in order to give yourself a chance to overcome your doubt that you are communicating with me and not making this up out of whole cloth yourself.

PAUL Are you available at all times?

RAJ Yes and no. Time does not function in the limited way in which you conceive it. I will go into that at another time. Suffice it to say that although you will perceive the communication as occurring simultaneously with your end of the conversation, my end of the conversation takes place when it is convenient for me. It is then slotted into your time reference at the appropriate moments.

PAUL Are you assigned to me or something?

RAJ It is a Self-appointed task or endeavor, which is borne out of my need to further my own eternal development. We have been matched "naturally" by virtue of the way in which our energy patterns complement each other. Where you are weak I am strong, and your weakness brings into play in me a broadening and refining of my strength in textures and patterns and tones and colours which you will come to understand as your own consciousness becomes refined.

My relationship with you is evolved out of Love in Its broadest sense or meanings. You must be aware that the words which you apply to the meanings I am communicating are inherently incapable of capturing the nondimensional nature of what I am saying. I will do my best to help bring out the breadth and depth of what they imply, but you must remember that there will be two reasons ever present in our communications for incorrect translation of my meanings — the size of your vocabulary and the degree to which you have refined your energies.

Inaccuracies in your perception of my meanings will become apparent to me as we communicate. I will work with you to bring out their higher meanings as we go along.

PAUL   I am in the midst of a financial problem...

RAJ   I know.

PAUL   Do you understand everything about it?

RAJ   Yes.

PAUL   Do you know everything about me?

RAJ   It is within my province to do so, but I am not interested. There are many things to be done where I am, so I do not clutter myself up with irrelevancies. When you bring up a subject of concern to you, I immediately understand everything about the way it is appearing to you as well as everything about the way it truly is. However, there is no stuttering as there is with you.

       In regard to your financial situation, I must point out that it is not as complex as it appears to you...

PAUL   [Nothing heard.]

RAJ   Your typewriter has stopped not because what I am communicating to you is difficult to understand, nor are the meanings too deep or so intrinsically subtle that you cannot catch them. You have what I can best describe as an energy field which is scrambling your perceptions concerning your understanding of the Nature of Substance. We will come to it through the back door so as not to arouse the resistance or confusing nature of this energy field. I am not limited by time and space, so therefore the term "back door" is nonsensical for me, but it does convey to you the fact that the problem can be dealt with in a nondimensional way.

       You need to make a call, I know. So I would suggest you do that and then get back with me. To you it will seem as though I am always here, although to me it may seem as though a period of time of longer duration will occur between our visits...

PAUL   [Not understood.]

RAJ   Hell, Paul, don't fret over the precise words. Just put down "good-bye," even though you know there's more to the meaning. It will become clearer as we go along.

PAUL I'm back. I want to find out if the energy field you referred to is an irregularity in my energy field, whether it is an extraneous energy field (since Susan, my wife, was doing metaphysical work at that time), or whether it is the "dark forces," as I have heard them referred to?

RAJ No, it wasn't your wife's metaphysical work. And what I'm referring to are not the dark forces. Rather, I am referring to some internal programmed and accepted resister–type energy barriers which cause you to feel tense and disconnected when it comes to dealing with the flowing Substance that you call *money*.

I know you are sitting there thinking of a dozen other questions that you really want to ask, but let's stay with this one since you are going to have to deal with it tomorrow. The other things can wait.

First of all, in spite of the events which you are aware are going to take place in your near future, and the fact that you are aware that you may not be doing what you are doing right now for much longer, it is well for you not to change the pattern of living that you are currently engaged in. Change is all around you — change that you have no say–so in, change that is going to have tremendous impact far beyond even your clearest comprehension of things.

Keep the home front on an even keel, and even though you know it is a "vain repetition" that is superfluous, it will be meaningful for the time and place you find yourself in. The changes will become obviously clear to you shortly. In the meantime, it is right to go through the motions of normalcy, as it is defined generally today.

PAUL I'm stuck. I am not hearing anything about the money problem and what to do.

RAJ Paul, when that happens just sit still, get further into your meditative state, and feel the feeling of opening up — whatever that feels like to you. That should do the trick.

PAUL Okay. I will.

RAJ Yes, I am here. Go further.

The tube of paper you see is symbolic of the continuity or fabric of Supply. It is, as it were, a fabric. Unlike the tube of paper you see, you must imagine that the paper is one infinite, connected loop of fabric like a Moebius Strip. Be careful of the fact that we are trying to describe a Fourth–dimensional or non–dimensional reality in the language of three dimensions, but it has to do for now.

The fact that there appear to be two sides to the fabric is an illusion, as the Moebius Strip implies. There is only one amount of Substance and that is infinite. It is also continuous in a "woven" sense. It is as though you skate on the surface of the flow of Supply. It is supporting you always; it is present always; and it is all of it that you are skating on at all times. You never get it in bits and pieces; it is never divided up. Everyone is always skating on all of it.

You can see that the "availability" of Supply is a ridiculous misconcept. We all always have all of it. It constitutes the continuum of Being, Itself. "Available" and "unavailable," "present" and "absent" cannot apply to or relate to Substance or Supply.

Of course, you are asking why it *seems* to be absent, and I will tell you that it is because you have not challenged the other side of the concept — that it can be "present."

Existence *is* the Presence that you call Supply and mean "money." You really limit yourself by seeing Supply as "money" when you need to be seeing Supply as Supply.

In other words, when you see Supply as "money," you are seeing it through the wrong end of a pair of binoculars making it appear to diminish and get smaller. To say that you should see Supply as Supply means to lift it out of the range of optics, out of the range of visibility, into the *perception* that Supply is the omnipresent Substance that constitutes the warp and woof of Consciousness. It is the "stuff" of Existence.

This is not the only way to state this, but it is a way that you can understand and, as you can see, we haven't run into the resistance–loaded field of energy.

Don't even bother to type your question.

Tomorrow you need to contemplate what I have just told you, with no expenditure of energy. Don't allow anyone to interfere or influence you about this. Discourage any fears by either not telling anyone what you are doing, or, as in the case of your wife, let her know what you are doing and ask her to be patient for a day and leave you alone with this. I will be supporting you as these ideas unfold, making it easier for them to take new form in your thought.

Go about your regular work in the best fashion you can, but let these things linger in the background. From your standpoint I will be with you all day, clearing the way. Since I know that you will let your wife read this, I will ask her not to share what I know she knows about it, since this is your work to do for yourself.

[Addressing Susan.]I know you know that, but you will be inclined to help, and knowing Paul, it will get in the way. Thanks, Susan.

Next question?

PAUL   I am loaded with questions, but this can go on and on. I'm going to go to bed and talk with you in the morning. I am going to have to read over what you've said. I hope you can feel my appreciation. Good night.

---

[1] At this point I was typing as I heard his words. Within a few days I started using a piece of dictation equipment.

February 8, 1982
Monday

PAUL Thank you very much for what you shared with me last night. I did, indeed, feel like you were with me today, throughout the day. The feeling I am getting — since it isn't coming to me in words — is that this infinite Substance is a flowing or moving thing, and that what is necessary for me to do is to first of all be aware that it does constitute the warp and woof of my conscious being, and then to flow with it —Substance. Is that right?

RAJ You have listened well today.

I would like you to stop smoking, since it creates a tension and anxiety level in your body which is mechanically caused by the substances in the smoke. You will find that this feeling of anxiety, once gone, will leave you freer to reach the finer planes or more subtle levels of consciousness.

Whether you do or not is up to you, but if you truly want to experience an "expanded" consciousness, a more living awareness of Reality, you are going to have to do it. It will make my part in this easier, and your part will become more satisfying. Of course, coffee also induces an artificial change in your body which, if you were not drinking it, would also leave you clearer.

Knowing your desire for clearer perception, which will result in a clearer experience, I would suggest that you will be more than satisfied with not partaking of coffee and cigarettes.

There are a number of things which have unfolded to you today and I am not going to comment on them at this point, because there is still more for you to realize before I talk with you about them. I am not here to do your thinking or growing for you, but I am able to facilitate the process of realization.

You must become aware that the Enlightenment you experience is a process inherent in Your Being. It is part of the dynamics — the "stuff" — of You. As long as you are able to think that your discovery of the finer levels of Reality is coming from "out there," you will not have the necessary strength to support the actual finer levels of consciousness which you want to experience.

You see, it is a primary function of Being — and that means You — to evolve Itself out of Itself. It is just like your stomach's function is to digest food. You know it does it. You have experienced it doing it. And you know that if you put in more food it will do it again.

Likewise, if you don't know that it is the function of Your Being to evolve Itself out of Itself, making Itself *new,* if you haven't experienced It doing it, if you don't know that It does it, then you will misperceive the "new" and will lose the Value of it.

Growth, unfoldment, Evolution — whatever you want to call it — is what constitutes your Being. You need to experience that activity or function *as yours.* You *are* ready to be *consciously* aware that it *is* occurring, rather than just observing that it *has* occurred because you recognize you are in a new place. It is a process that is just as consciously tangible as digestion is physically tangible to you.

It is time to become aware of the "physiology" or anatomy of your mentality. Be attentive to the process of what you call inspiration, intuition, psychic awareness, enlightenment. It is not something happening *to* you at all. Rather, it is You happening *as* You.

You may call it the New Physiology if you understand that your consciousness is the Body of your Being, and not the form that has two arms, two legs, a head, and so forth.

Where you have properly not studied the physiology of your human body, I want you to begin an extremely thorough study of the functions of your Mental Body. Dissect it. Look at it. Don't be afraid to delve into every nook and cranny you find. It is you, and yet it is the infinite Reality you have been looking for in all your studying and listening for the Truth.

I will reiterate that it will be made much easier for you to do this if you will stop smoking and drinking coffee.

As we go along and you have become conscious of the Body of Consciousness through observation, through your method of meditation, and through your healing work, your Self-awareness will allow me to speak about further things. Discussing them with you will not weaken you in the direction of that Self-discovery.

I think, as you go over what I have just said, you will find that the questions you still have about Substance and Supply have been answered. But, it will be necessary for you to allow your Being to define Itself to you (and now you will be able to see that It is) *as you.*

I will continue to be with you tomorrow as I was today, and then we will be able to rejoice together, instead of you rejoicing because I told it to you.

PAUL How is it that I have learned to do this healing or whatever it is? Is it healing?

RAJ I know that you are wondering if I have helped you in your discovery of this healing effect. But, the fact is that this is an example of the Phoenix[1] rising out of its own ashes, the new level of consciousness rising out of the old, that I was telling you to observe.

I heard your requests when you made them, before you discovered this healing ability or method, but I did not give you instruction. You might say that what I did was to clear out some of the cobwebs, or dust, or superfluous energies, which were impeding your growth.

I want you to continue to rely on the inherent Intelligence of *Your* Being to reveal Itself in clearer and clearer evidence; *AND I WANT YOU TO BE AWARE THAT IT IS YOUR BEING "DOING ITS OWN THING"* that you are observing.

You have been terribly weakened by your belief that your Good has ever come from anywhere else but You, and I will probably harp on this again and again, until it is supremely clear to you. The inner strength gained by the specific awareness of Who You Are, What You Are, and that You Are Where It's All Happening, is the only way for you to move forward at the new level that you are entering into. Dig into it, man! It's more than you've dreamed of.

Remember the coffee and cigarettes!

PAUL   What do I need to understand in order to see Reality evidenced in my daily life?

RAJ   Again I've got to come back to this thing of observing the Physiology or Anatomy of the Consciousness that You Are. Your daily experience images and reflects these processes. You are already learning things — correspondences between what occurs in your healing work and how to live in your world, apparently "out there."

In the past you have, in effect, been trying to manipulate the image in the mirror because you can touch, feel, and see it. It seems more real to you because of its tangibility. Not having realized that what you call "body" is Image, and not Body, and not having realized that Body is Consciousness, You, you have ignored the lesson about the Reality (Source) of the Image that can only be learned by understanding the True Body.

By "understanding" I mean real, actual, felt, experiential awareness of the Physiology of that Body. You will never control your environment if you think the environment is the Image which you call the three–dimensional world. The three–dimensional world is Pure Image. The distortions you see in it are not *in it*. They are caused by your ignorance of the workings of the Source, of which the Image is just an image.

The Source is Mind, Consciousness. The distortions you see and call "lack," "failure," et cetera, attest to the weakness I spoke of earlier — the weakness caused by your not perceiving the Anatomy and Functioning of your Being. Ignorant of the Wholeness of Your Being, and of the Self-revealing Birthing that It is forever giving to Itself, you have not the Strength to support a clear, undistorted comprehension of the Image, which you refer to as your daily life — or at least the place where your daily life occurs. That also is a misconception, which I see you have just caught.

This strengthening that I am talking about can be described

as the integrating of "What You Are" with "Your Consciousness Of What You Are" *AS YOU.* The bifurcation of your Self into a "self" and "an awareness of that self" is what causes all distortion in your perception of the Image. Your Self and what you call your perception of your Self are one and the same Life function.

Ponder this for awhile.

Next question?

PAUL I have worked hard for the last two and a half years, and it looks like it was for nothing. Everything is disintegrating around me. Why?

RAJ I know it's intriguing to think that it may be because of the signs of the times, the dark forces, and what-have-you, but the simple fact is that your Being Evolves whether you're "with it" or not. The Phoenix forever rises out of its ashes. That is Life. Your Evolution went beyond what you were able to support. The necessary integration — *experiential* Oneness of your Being *as your Being* — needed to occur.

The Phoenix *must rise!* So, it rose. In rising, it uncovered the point where growth was needed *so that the growth could occur.*

The Phoenix *must fly!* And so, *it flew!* And you said, "My God, what's happening? Everything is falling apart. What am I going to do? I can't do anything! My God, I'd better do something! What can I do? I can't do anything. I've got to do something."

Finally, in the frustration of it all you reached through and beyond your inability to do anything. You stepped through from the sheer force of your Being, *being* You as a new creature and you found your hands getting hot, you found yourself working with Tarot cards, et cetera. My God, Paul! You've just experienced the Fundamental of Reality.

Everything fell apart because you couldn't support it or correctly perceive it without transforming Yourself. The image reflected the Dying, that is the Birthing, that is the unbroken Eternal Constant called Existence.

I know you have questions about the Second Coming of Christ, but I'm not going to answer them now. It's too easy for you to find "importance" and "value" out there, and you need to pay the utmost attention to the marvelous work of God's Hands, *You,* and find out how His Work works!

Whatever is going to happen will happen. Whatever is going to happen will appear in the Image. And if it is appearing in the Image, where is it Really occurring?

Man! If you don't perceive that it's All You —well, I see you've got the point.

If you want to follow the Master, then do what the Master did! What He did is what you're learning right now. The only way I'm able to share these things with you now is because you have already begun to see these things that are happening *as you* — not the "ego," but as the "I" that is Nothing, and which, by virtue of being Nothing, can experience Its Somethingness. That's Fact for you now. You've experienced it. Embroidering what you know will not weaken you or deprive you of a thing, and that's why we're talking now.

I'm not going to answer any other questions now because they have already been answered. Think about what I've said. Go over your questions on your own. Then, get out of the way like you have been doing and observe Your Self and Its Image Function!

Good night. (I notice you didn't have any trouble with it this time.)

---

1   A mythical bird fabled to burn itself on a funeral pyre, and to rise from its ashes in the freshness of youth.

February 9, 1982
Tuesday

PAUL   I need to talk to you about some specifics. Are you there?

RAJ   Yes.

PAUL   Things are at a standstill, and I am trying to go through the motions of normalcy as you suggested. Am I to ignore my family's problems, even though I don't know what step to take?

I am really cautious at this point because I do not want what *I* have figured out is "right." What I want is an understanding of the dynamics at play here and how each activity serves the Whole Activity. I want to be sure that the steps we take are in harmony with the Divine Purpose.

RAJ   The Divine Purpose is the DNA code of your Being. You can't get outside of It except in your imagination.

PAUL   Yes, but aren't there things going on on a larger scale than my "personal" life that my family must coordinate with?

RAJ   At the present time, the whole of the Family of Man is going through a change of the sort we talked about last night in your individual case. That is a fact.

PAUL   Well, I want to be where the Divine Will can best be served or expressed for and as each member of my immediate family. Right now it seems to them that it isn't, and it seems to me that it Truly Is, but it's not apparent at the moment.

13

RAJ   They are responsible for how they experience their world, just as you are. The World, however, *is* an integral part of the Whole of God and an integral part of the Whole of You and Susan and Julie,[1] and everyone. The I is Us and the Us is I, as you discerned yesterday.

You must grasp that every specific aspect of the Universe is the individualization of God without any diminution of God. Three-dimensionally, it appears to be finite, but Fourth-dimensionally, every individuation of God is *all* of God, *all* of the Life/Principle, *all* of the Love, *all* of the All. Therefore, the One being Many, you could say the One is not alone.

Love, in Its infinite Self-expression, finds Itself infinitely loved — "loved" by the Love that It *is,* "supported" by the Life that It *is,* "strengthened" by the Principle that It *is.* It finds the I/Us forever developing and being seen as the intercommingling of Its infinitude in harmonies upon harmonies, circles within circles, ages within ages, patterns within patterns, ad infinitum.

Be conscious, open yourself up to the fact that not only are you faced with Your Self seen infinitely as your World, but catch the sense of the loving cooperation that your World is incapable of withholding from you.

The interplay of the Many is based in the Love that constitutes Its entire Substance. The One, being infinitely expressed, constitutes Love so powerful that it is Omnipotence.

All of your Being constitutes such Love that for you to overlook Its total loving-kindness towards you would be a pity.

PAUL   So what do I do? I can feel what you are talking about, and it's very comprehensible. Do I need to do more than I am doing right now in talking with you? Do I need to meditate? Do I need to physically get off my duff and go out and find a job, a house, a school?

[Going a little deeper into meditation.[2]]

RAJ   That's it. Go deeper into yourself.

You saw the mouse carry the pencil to the fuzzy slipper. It seems meaningless. Go deeper. Lean on yourself as we do this, not on your understanding or thinking. Trust your Self!

The world you walk through is the Mind that you Are. You Know what you need to know. Don't give up.

That's right. You (ego) don't know. And you know that that realization is the foundation for what You (Mind) *Know* to come into view. Stick with it.

You're right. The Phoenix is flying. Go with it.

You've already done it. Go ahead and move through the immovable again. It's Your Being that is *being* the transformation.

PAUL   I feel like I'm being forced to grow.

RAJ   What you are calling "being forced" is the pressure to *be* what You Are. Evolution of Your Being is the Activity. The feeling of "pressure" is because you are boxing yourself in with "I don't know how," "I can't see." Being is not squashing Itself, but unfolding Itself, You. Let go.

PAUL   Should I have a purpose or intent while I'm going deeper?

RAJ   No. Your Being is intent on *being* Itself and knows how to be Itself perfectly. When you have experienced this, you will be able to trust your Self implicitly.

PAUL   [Period of deep meditation.]

RAJ   Welcome back.

PAUL   It doesn't seem to have done any good. I will say that I felt like a radiation center of some kind. I still don't know what steps to take.

RAJ   Don't force it. Your Being is Total, Entire. All of It is present as You. You say you don't know, but you were willing to admit the possibility that you do Know. Admitting that, you will be able to see the Phoenix rise, and the transformation occur.

As you know, the Phoenix rises out of the ashes of dissolving self. The old dissolving is the new coming into view. This isn't something happening to you, remember. It *is* You.

You can't get outside of your Self; therefore, you *aren't* outside of your Self. This means that the devolution and Evolu

tion that you are experiencing is in total consonance with
You. What is threatening you (Being) is what is moving you
to the point of not being threatened again.

The five of you in your house must be in a very tightknit harmony if you are all experiencing devolution/Evolution simultaneously, especially at this point in the larger patterns of
Being. No one is going through it because of "another" one.

In your meditation, or periods of contemplation, include this
awareness of the harmony that Exists and which is evidenced
by the simultaneity of your Evolution. Remain with the fact
that your "others" (Really, and not in belief) are your Self,
and that in this closely harmonized set of patterns you are
each playing integral parts as aspects of the individual trans-
formations that reflect the Transformation Universal.

Remember that your Being is the I that is the Us, the One
that is the Many. The total Absolute Fact of Being is *being*
you Totally. It is Perfect. Do not try to force answers. Being
reveals Itself Perfectly, both specifically and infinitely.

"The place whereon you stand is Holy ground"[3] means that
with *or* without answers you *are* perfectly being. Within the
patterns-within-patterns, it fulfills the unfolding of Reality
to "have" *and* "not have" answers.

The moment it fulfills the Law for the answer to be known,
at that moment All of YOU, the One and the Many, will be
bound in a new pattern of intercooperation based on Love.
The patterns of cooperation will move together in a manner
of "brotherly love" (that's the best way for you to grasp the
larger meaning) and Self-recognition, and there will be no
penalty.

Just as the unfolding of your Being has drawn you to the
point where I can be drawn to you, even so, every member
of your family is being drawn to the point where their fulfillment can be drawn to them — not in the old way, but in a
transformed way, at a new "level," as it were.

Think about it. Contemplate it. And quit trying to force the
infinite designs out of their Self-fulfilling purposes (appointed
rounds).

We will talk again.

---

1   Susan is my wife, and Julie is my oldest daughter.

2   At this point I was somewhat unsettled, and took a moment to go further into meditation.

3   Exod. 3:5

February 10, 1982
Wednesday

PAUL   Today I won't go through the procedure of asking you questions, since from what you told Susan, you are waiting for me, and you already know — well, I'm assuming. Do you already know what I'm interested in learning?

RAJ   Yes.

PAUL   Okay. Then I'm going to not mess around today and simply let you tell me what you know I need to know, unless you want me to do it some other way.

RAJ   No, I don't want you to do it some other way.

PAUL   I'm quite excited today, and it's getting in the way, or at least it seems like it is to me. I'm going to take a minute to relax.

RAJ   You don't need to relax. You don't really have to go into a special state in order to communicate with me. In fact, it's essential for you to discover that the Whole Spectrum, from gross to subtle, is always present all the time, no matter what level of consciousness you seem to be operating from.

It's time for you to become aware that All of You is present at all times, both in the sense of all levels of consciousness being available at all times, and in the sense that all dimensions — infinity and eternity — are always present all the time. It does not matter where you seem to be coming from three-dimensionally.

17

You have noticed that I am with you whenever it occurs to you to think about me. All of you is always present, whether you are consciously focusing your attention on it or not. There's a lesson in that one sentence for you, Paul.

I know you are excited about what all of this is going to mean for you. This exhibits a readiness on your part, a point of development reached, which is enabling you to move into it.

Sometimes, Paul, you have a tendency to make things more complex than they are, and as it happens, the message of "Simplify, simplify, simplify," is apropos for you. Don't quibble over words, even though you may include in your vocabulary words that express higher degrees of refinement and greater subtleties of expression.

Right now, these times we spend together are for you, and their purpose is not for publication, although it is perfectly all right for you to share them with your wife and your mother. Since they are not for publication, it is not necessary for you to search for exactly the right word, since you are experiencing the finer textures and subtleties of the meaning as we talk.

I really want your attention to be on your conscious experience, your experience of being conscious. And, I don't want your attention on how these things are going to be heard by others, since that is not their intent or purpose. If you are going to fully benefit, you must devote yourself to your Self completely, devotedly.

Do not get hung up on words. As you have discovered, you are having to find words to express the meaning, because you have the meaning; whereas in the past, you have started with the words and had to put the meaning into them. You knew no other way to do it, but that is not the case any more. So, I want you to give your full attention to the depth, the breadth, the harmonies, the textures, the colours, the full spectrum of the meanings I am communicating to you. It is this Self experience which is essential in order for you to move forward as the butterfly.[1]

It is time for you to move forward being consciously and completely aware of your Self as Conscious Being, no longer a "material being." I say that for you, because you understand that I am not speaking about being a mortal. It is a matter of the focal point.

You are at a point of, let's say, shifting gears, no longer to move around in the world of three dimensions as shape, an identity, a body, an organism making its way in the three-dimensional world where the environment can be either friend or foe, pleasant or difficult. That is what I meant when I said a "material being."

As Conscious Being, you are going to move around in an environment of ideas, of activities, of functions that are totally mental, and you will learn to do this while apparently living three-dimensionally, as a "material being."

You are presently practicing and experiencing and discovering to some small degree your new territory by means of our very conversations.

You know that as we communicate you are able to feel, sense, and experience the meanings of ideas. You are grasping that they have texture and substance which is completely tangible at the level of consciousness.

[Again, Paul, this is a note to you. Quit trying so hard to have the right words. Flow with it.]

In other words, you are discovering that there is structure, that there is the equivalent of shape, outline, form, colour to the processes, as well as the "inhabitants" of Consciousness. You are finding that Consciousness is just as infinite as the three-dimensional universe you looked at and saw and experienced with your five senses.

It is not necessary for you to go into a trance or a deep mental state in order to experience this, although it may help initially. However, you can see that today you are not in a deep meditation, and yet we are quite as capable of conversing as we were yesterday when you went into a very deep meditative state. This indicates a growing proficiency and familiarity with your mental Universe.

Each time we are together, you will be gaining more experience and familiarity, you will discover more fullness, more satisfaction — "satisfaction" in the sense of Self-recognition.

What gives substance to your experience as Conscious Being is that it is your Self that you are experiencing — the depth, breadth, and infinitude of your Being — so that the more you become aware of, the more you are aware that It is You. In other words, conscious experience is a Self-substantiating experience. This is why it is satisfying. This is what I meant by the use of the word "satisfaction."

I am going to mention again that I would like you to make, in effect, a conscientious effort to stop smoking and stop drinking coffee. I do not mean "conscientious" in the sense of effort expended, but a total willingness to let them go.

As you sit there thinking, "This is going to be difficult," remember that there is only one thing going on, no matter how infinitely seen, and that one thing is You. Therefore, when you desire a thing and that thing is in harmony with your Being, then the infinitude that you see embraces and supports that desire. The cigarettes and coffee will be more than happy to let you go and will love doing it. But you must be willing.

I know that you know what I shared with Susan. I know that you have recognized some trace of egotism still present in your experience, but do not make a big thing out of it —the egotistical sense, that is. Don't make a big thing out of it, don't make a little thing out of it. The more practice you get at moving *as* Your World, *as* Conscious Being, the more you find yourself recognizing your Self as All, what traces of egotism remain will dwindle spontaneously for lack of nourishment.

Egotism is what we do when we are not able to recognize our Self *as* the world we're walking through, when we do not find substantiation of our Self in our experience. When we find the Soul-satisfying experience of knowing ourselves in every function and activity of our experience, we know beyond a shadow of a doubt that finite perceptions of ourselves — the ego and its satisfactions — are but pitiful efforts that we no longer desire to indulge in, because we know what Satisfaction is.

Right now, you are unable to see the connection between the things that I am telling you (and which you *are* experiencing) and the three-dimensional frame of reference where you appear to eat, sleep, work, play (ha, ha), and live your life. That is all right. We have time.

I know you are wanting to spend more time than you have been able to in the last two days with the Tarot cards and with your healing activities. I would suggest that you do take time to utilize these avenues of Self-discovery. These allow you to bring the experience of your Self as Conscious Being into your daily experience. They will help increase your ability to discover in what ways *being* as Conscious Being can occur and be relative to what appears to be you being as a "material being" or three-dimensional being. These are valid and valuable tools for your growth at this point, and I know you are seeing that.

In the past, the metaphysical and healing work you did had as its focal point the individuality you were working with, and not your Self. This is why it did not work out.

When your attention is removed from your Self — and that means your experience of your Self as *all* that is being experienced — and you have your attention external to It, it is like depriving your Self of oxygen; and the activity will not support itself. This is why your practice did not succeed.

All activity is Self-activity. All activity is the Activity of the One and Only thing going on, which you experience as your Self.

You're learning intuitively with your healing work and with your work with the Tarot cards to remain at the conscious level, even though you are handling cards and bodies. You are not giving your attention to the cards, nor are you giving your attention to the individualities with whom you are working. You are not unaware of them, but your focus of attention remains at the point of your Consciousness. This is why you are finding yourself successful.

As the days go on, I want you to take some time to stand back, as you did yesterday. Take an objective look at what is happening to you. "Objective" is not a good word. I want you to take an overall look.

I want you to take a look at your experience when we are speaking together. I want you to take a look at what is happening in your work with the Tarot cards. And I want you to take a look at your experience when you are doing the healing work. You will find that these cover three distinctly different types of activity.

This contemplative view of the larger picture of your activity, of experience which occurs at the level of Conscious Being, *as* Conscious Being, will help you in being able to broaden your ability to live your three-dimensional life as a Fourth-dimensional Being, never leaving the standpoint of Consciousness as the environment in which you live.

You have familiarity with the phrase "Be out from Mind." This is what you are doing when you are working with the Tarot cards. This is what you are doing when you are doing the healing work. And this is what you are doing right now while we're speaking together.

You can hear the kids going in and out of the doors. You can feel the microphone in your hand. You can hear everything that is going on. You are even working the microphone. Yet you are not for a moment experiencing any of it as though you were in it. Your attention, your awareness, is residing at the point of being the experiencing of the conscious experience called microphone, couch, traffic, sound, activity in the house, et cetera.

As far as you are concerned, I'm going to be with you for quite awhile because it is time. You are ready, and you want it. It is true, "When the student is ready, the teacher appears."

You are concerned about whether I really am a separate individual, but there is something more important going on here, something that is important for you. You have recognized it, but you do not understand it; nevertheless you are willing to accept it.

You don't know if I am real or not, or a figment of your imagination, or a higher "self," et cetera. But, you have been willing to totally commit yourself to an unequivocal trust and not give a damn about whether I'm real or not. You recognize this willingness to trust as being important for you right now, and you are right. This willingness and humble trust must continue for what is called "a period of time," for it is essential to your success. When it has fulfilled its purpose, we will talk about whether I am real or not.

Tell Susan that when and if she gets panicky about the circumstances, that I am always equally available to her directly, even though our relationship is entirely different from my relationship to you. I will be available to her because you are a team, and she needs not to be in the dark about what is going on. I am not here for the purpose of guiding or teaching her. Still it is necessary for her to understand certain things at certain times when she becomes concerned or afraid.

There is no particular procedure for contacting me, as you well know. It will seem to her as though I am always present and always available if she needs clarification. Let her know that.

As I said yesterday, lean on your Self. Depend on It. Trust It. Demand the answers from It rather than what appear to be "others." Remember that whether I truly am a separate individual or not, I am Your Conscious Experience when we are together. This is imperative and it is a key to further unfoldment. I know that you grasp this from an experiential standpoint and that this is not just a "head trip."

Do not lean on yourself with a vengeance, just do it totally. Intellectually you know that what the ego wants and what the ego gets is not worth the powder to blow it to kingdom come. You have arrived at the point where you truly do not want what your thinking mind can give you. You have developed a natural repulsion to it and have been willing to put it down. You have allowed yourself to move out of the three-dimensional frame of reference as a "material being" into the Fourth-dimensional experience of Conscious Being.

It's true. The Way is straight and narrow, and few there be that enter. There truly is no other way, and it truly requires a heartfelt desire to not have your own will be done.

There is more than enough here for you to think about, and so I will stop.

There is no reason for us to talk only once a day. We may talk more than that if you like, but knowing your present point of growth or development, I would suggest that we not talk less than once a day.

I will respond to the thought that you were just thinking. The concept which has occurred to you — that the "natural" selection by which we are working together is based on a harmonic matching — is a satisfactory concept. You were hoping that I would be around for a long time. The fact is, that we will work together until you have grown to a point where the harmonics no longer complement each other, and our relationship will apparently change. At that point, it will not be experienced with any sense of loss by you.

I will be with you.

---

[1] This makes reference to the transformational process a caterpillar goes through, finally emerging as a butterfly — at a new level of life experience.

February 11, 1982
Thursday
(Morning)

PAUL   Whenever I begin a session like this I am sort of at a loss, because I have a lot of questions, sometimes. Then, by the same token, in looking back at previous conversations, I find that when I have not had a whole lot of questions, you have covered things that are actually more meaningful or more to the point than the questions I would have asked.

Should we have some sort of format? Is there a style of conversing that you would like me to follow in these conversations?

RAJ   I think we can follow whatever you're led to do. Why don't you tell me what you would like to do today?

PAUL   I think that I would like to be still and listen.

RAJ   Very well.

PAUL   [Nothing heard for a little while.]

RAJ   Let's talk about the fact that you're having difficulty hearing what I'm saying, and why it is that you are having difficulty. You feel as though you are listening and yet you're hearing nothing. Partly, this is because this is the very beginning of our conversation today, and partly it is not.

If you will take a look at it, you will find that when you are not hearing me, it is because you are expecting something

24

you cannot hear. The moment you stop listening for something hard to hear, assuming that I am going to say something simpler, you immediately begin to hear me.

Contemplate that, Paul, because it accounts for difficulties that you have in your everyday life. When you feel that you are about to be faced with something that you cannot comprehend, when you feel that you are faced with a solution that is beyond you, you see no solution.

To repeat, the previous message, Paul: "Simplify, simplify, simplify." It is truly the nature of the Universe and the manner in which It functions. Simplicity should be your byword. Discovering this will relieve a great deal of anxiety on your part. The sign of greatness is the ability to deal with life simply and effectively.

By aspiring to greatness, by having grandiose goals, we implicate ourselves. . .

[There you go again, Paul, making things complex when they're not. We "implicate" ourselves, huh?]

What we do is stifle ourselves by expecting something that we, at the same time, know we can't perceive. We immobilize ourselves by getting as far away from simplicity as we seem to be able to.

Perhaps the simplest form of simplicity in life is withdrawing from outer activity, going within ourselves, to find our answers and our directions. But, as you have found out, even in ourselves, when we are attempting to be complex, when we are attempting to be very specific — in fact, when we are attempting *anything at all* within ourselves — we close ourselves off to the intuitive function of our Being, and we frustrate ourselves just as we did when we were attempting to work "out there."

When we go within and are silent, as you are doing each time we talk, we find the natural efficiency, the natural brilliance, the unbelievable perspicacity — that *was* a good one, Paul — that constitutes our very nature. Silence is as simple as we can get, and it is the cornerstone of Wisdom.

I see that you are experimenting. That is fine. You are attempting to find out whether we can communicate when you have your eyes open and are receiving stimuli from your world. As you can see, it works. You are able to. This is a progressive step, and indicates, as I have said before, your growing familiarity with being as Conscious Being. As you do this you can see the trees, the drapes, the window, and the things in the room, but they are not depriving you of directly perceiving that which is going on within your consciousness, and perceiving it well.

In the long run, it would be impractical for you to have to go into a restroom or some private place where you could unobtrusively meditate in order to have spontaneous answers as they are needed.

Again, all of you is always present, no matter what level of consciousness you are apparently operating from at any given moment. And you are learning this.

I have been amused that when you're driving in the car and have thought about talking with me, you have been apprehensive. I know that you have wanted to have our conversations recorded so that they could be transcribed. At the same time, there has been a feeling that the communication could not be as valid or as valuable while driving down the middle of a freeway as it would be in the quiet sanctuary that you have for yourself at home.

Such a sanctuary is in some ways a satisfying experience, but you can't pull a sanctuary behind your car with you everywhere you go, or pull it into a building on a wagon just so your place of living as Conscious Being can always be with you.

If that is the only means one has, then one must work with what one has, but it is most certainly limited. I am glad to see that you are discovering that you can function intuitively out from Mind as Conscious Being. This indicates a rapid integration of being consciously aware of Who You Are, What You Are, and that You Are Where It's All Happening.

I can appreciate the fact that you felt awed by the depth and fullness of yesterday's conversation. I can understand that it might be easy to feel that it implies an activity of great Holy Purpose, but let's not lose our equilibrium.

Being *is* Infinity. It far exceeds your wildest imaginations. As you let go, as you lean on and trust your Self more and more implicitly, and as you find that your Self is, indeed, Trustworthy, you will experience more of that infinitude. *Keep in mind, however,* that the more of yourself which you are experiencing is not more of yourself than was always present. It is a phase of egotism which would like to make more out of what is normal than what normal is.

As you know, the word "holy" comes from the same root word as the word "whole." The only reason the word "holy" was created was because wholeness was not available as a Self-experience, and so there must be a way to account for the Wholeness of Being. There must be a way of satisfying the intuitive perception that Being *is* Whole. So, the word "holy" was created to identify that part of our Wholeness which was not available to us consciously. The fact is that everything holy is absolutely normal, as normal as apple pie, when it is totally available to us as our Conscious Being.

I cannot make myself any clearer than to say: Paul, do not waste your time with heady trips of greatness, of holiness, of grand purpose, of fulfilling a Divine Purpose in the universal scheme of things that is outside or other than "simply existing."

Existence is all of those things, but it is nothing "special."

It is only by comparison with ignorance that that which is "normal" can seem special, and you will weaken yourself greatly if you indulge in such nonsense! This had better be a fundamental point in your awareness of what is happening here, or you will lose the Value.

As I said yesterday, it is perfectly all right for you to share these conversations with your wife and your mother. But let a word to the wise be sufficient, Paul. You have already seen in their reaction not only an understanding of the Wisdom involved in these conversations and the value of their even taking place in the first place — you have also seen how easy it is for the human mind to give marvelous meaning to what is absolutely normal. This is why you must keep these conversations to yourself — other than sharing them with your wife and your mother — because people will place values on them that are based entirely upon their blindness, and not on their insight or understanding.

Their emotional enthusiasm, generated by their intuitive recognition of Themselves in the things that we are talking about, will cause them to glorify what should not be glorified. They will do this only because they are unable to own their Universe as Themselves. Their response will get in the way, drawing your attention back out from the Center of your

Being into the "outer world," and will make it difficult for you to be subjective about the issues.

I see you caught the meaning when I used the word "subjective" there. You are learning to value that which is subjective in the way you used to value that which was objective. You have known that it is practical to be objective about things. Now you are learning that it is practical to be subjective about things, and it would be well for you to replace the word "objective" in your thought and your reasoning and thinking with the word "subjective."

You must learn to be extremely subjective about things, because when you are being subjective about them you are able to experience their meanings, and not what they appear to be. Experiencing their meanings will allow you to respond appropriately, to perceive appropriately, and to conduct yourself in a way that is harmonious with the totality of your Self. "Subjective" means to be Truly Aware, not to be unaware.

I notice some shade of disappointment in you in the realization that what you are learning here will not lead you to greatness, or to some fulfillment of purpose which will give you great satisfaction, because it will glorify God or manifest the true nature of Being. But realize this, Paul: That greatness which you conceive is based upon having one's awareness objectively placed in the three-dimensional world. Ask yourself, "Great in whose eyes?"

Those only to whom you can appear great are those of your own infinitude whom you have not been able to own as You. As you already know, you will not have the strength to maintain the image of greatness when your attention is on others "out there." *You must give this up —every last trace of it!*

You are recognizing that this means that all of this is just for you, and you are having some difficulty understanding for what purpose one would do this if it is only for oneself.

The answer is simply that one's Self is the Universal All, the One is the Many. If you do not do it for yourself only, if you are not willing to be alone, then you will not have the experience of owning all of yourself as You. You will walk as a three-dimensional man, as a material man, bumping into himself, stubbing his toe on himself, running his car into himself, beating himself up by his own hand, and wondering why in the hell he's suffering! *That is sufficient reason.*

To be perfectly blunt with you, you can't afford to have anyone else be aware of what you're doing and what is unfolding within you unless it is done most carefully, and until you know how to do it and not evoke a negative response. And don't forget that a positive response, founded on ignorance, is a negative response.

When I say you cannot afford to tell anyone what you are doing, I am making reference to our conversations. I am also making reference to the inner awakening to yourself as the One that is All, the One that is Many. The lessons that we are discussing here are entirely for you, period.

The healing work, the Tarot cards, the counseling, whatever else you may find unfolding in your experience, are perfectly all right. But do not flaunt your growth unless you want your "others" to flaunt their jealousy.

You see, Paul, until you truly understand that the "others" with whom you would share these events, are your Self, you will be approaching them ignorantly, and they will respond to you ignorantly.

On the other hand, if you do recognize them as your own infinitude, you won't care about recognition from them, because you will be recognizing them as You. You will not need further input. The Self–recognition experienced as Conscious Being is Satisfaction. Being from that point obviates any necessity of looking for recognition of greatness from those "out there."

This may seem like a simple point, but when you observe your inner response upon finding out that what seems so marvelous to you is absolutely normal, you will see that this simple point can become quite complex. It could conceivably be used as the basis for not proceeding any further.

It is amazing that one can be tempted to forfeit experiencing the Oneness of Being in order to play the chancy game of "Look How Great I Am," knowing full well that he could just as easily be the one who is the least. It is, indeed, a game of chance.

Do not misunderstand me. To know Who You Are, What You Are, and that You Are Where It's All Happening is, indeed, Divine Fulfillment of Purpose. It is to be One with God. It is to flow with the Divine Energies. It is to be One and in

Harmony with the Great Works of Divine Intelligence. *BUT, IT IS ABSOLUTELY NORMAL!*

Existing as a material being in a three-dimensional environment is exciting, challenging, scary, but *never* Satisfying, because it is literally to live as though One is out of One's Mind. It is not the ultimate purpose of Man, or Being.

To live as Conscious Being is inconceivable to the three-dimensional frame of reference or mentality. But as Conscious Being it is absolutely normal.

Making the transition from a three-dimensional to a Fourth-dimensional frame of reference, and appearing to coexist in both dimensions at the same time with full communication in both dimensions, makes demands that require a fine attunement to Fourth-dimensional space. Those words are absurd, but you understand what I mean. Let us maintain good perspective right from the start. You will need a stability that can withstand the misperceptions of those looking with three-dimensional sight only.

Seeing Fourth-dimensionally, you will handle the demands with ease. But, if you prematurely expose your new position you will unnecessarily jeopardize yourself. Until you know how to do it as Conscious Being consciously *being* Itself as Conscious Being, you will be wise to keep your mouth shut. This is why I am here. Your path does not need to be rough, and I know it is your desire for it to be smooth.

You are moving into what is, for you, uncharted territory, and I am a Guide. You will have to do the walking, but I can show you the well-worn trails — smooth, without unnecessary obstructions.

I am not distressed with you. It is simply time for this perspective to be provided to you so that you will keep your feet on the ground, and your head not too far away. I say it with utmost Love.

I can see that it is very likely that we will be speaking again later today. I will say good-bye for now, and let you experience the meanings of what we have just discussed.

Go in Light.

February 11, 1982
Thursday
(Evening)

PAUL   There have been some interesting developments since we talked this afternoon, not the least of which is an exceptional display of intuitive or psychic ability on the part of our oldest daughter, Julie. This was pleasing to me, because it indicated that there are at least three of us in this house who are going through some form of the Phoenix experience. It is, indeed, a time of change.

Julie was wondering whether she could talk to you, or whether she has a Guide of her own. She asked me to find out anything I could from you about her in this regard.

The learning involved in the session this afternoon was totally apropos in light of the events which have occurred since then. It has helped clarify things greatly for me. Thank you. I appreciate it.

I'm in this session for two definite reasons. One is that these periods which are spent conversing with you mean a great deal to me. The other reason is that I really am interested in any information which will help me understand better what I need to do.

I will ask no questions, but will simply listen and thank you in advance for your time and your care.

RAJ   Yes, Paul, I knew this afternoon when we were speaking what was taking place. I anticipated that we would be talking again this evening.

31

I have not mentioned that I, too, appreciate these times spent together. It is a pleasure working with you. Your cooperation and willingness makes it very easy to do what I need to do. The pleasure in this activity is not–sided, I can assure you.

If Julie would like, I will speak with her once and will suggest to her the steps she may take to contact her Guide. She does, indeed, have a Guide. Her apparent earth age has nothing to do with it. She is a total and complete individualization of God.

Although individuals of her earth age are generally not even aware of the existence of Guides, much less interested in contacting them, it does not mean that they do not have Guides. You can tell her that her Guide will feel a great sense of joy that she does not have to wait another 25 years or more before having her first conversation with Julie. It is always a source of Joy to have an apparently young individuality expressing a desire and interest in contact.

Explain to Julie that when she wishes to speak to me, all she has to do is indicate in her mind that she would like to speak to her father's Guide. You can tell her that I will know even before she asks that she wants to speak with me, and that I will look forward to speaking with her. Tell her that I will only be able to speak to her once because I am not her Guide. Tell her not to be disappointed in the least, since her Guide will be ready and eager to speak with her whenever the desire comes to have a conversation.

Paul, nothing is out of Order in your life. When we see from a three–dimensional standpoint, it is literally like seeing the tips of icebergs. That which appears *appears* to be finite. In Fact, all of Infinity is present at each and every point of what appears to be a finite manifestation. What may appear to be out of order here would be seen as being in Perfect Order from the vantage point of Conscious Being. All *is* One.

Universal Order is only implied by the Image, but is totally evident and experientially present from the Fourth–dimensional standpoint of Conscious Being.

You see, Paul, Conscious Being experiences all *as Conscious Being.* The concept "person" is only an illusion existing from within a three–dimensional framework. I mentioned in an earlier conversation that since the One is infinite, It constitutes the Many, and that the Many constitutes the All–

Oneness rather than aloneness of the One. From the standpoint of Conscious Being, every infinitesimal facet of the Universe finds expression through the Matrix of Love, since Love is the One which is being infinitely expressed — as are all the other synonyms for God which you are familiar with. This means that there is a bond of mutual cooperation spontaneously manifesting itself throughout the totality of Conscious Being — Fourth-dimensional existence.

In spite of appearances, Fourth-dimensionally speaking, you and your family's whole Universe — being the infinite Expression of the One that each One is — is lovingly and wonderfully bent on the fulfillment of infinite progression. You have an opportunity here to observe, to participate in, and *be* the experience of *being* Conscious Being, and to observe the most unique way in which being out from Mind resolves the illusion of conflict within the three-dimensional frame of reference.

As you know, each succeeding dimension includes within itself the preceeding ones. Right now, without being confused at all, you are living simultaneously in three dimensions: the third dimension, the second dimension, and the first dimension. You do not consider the first two at all because your point of awareness resides entirely in the now-totally-familiar third dimension. This gives you a hint of things to come.

Be that as it may, you are right now in the process of crossing over the line between the third dimension and the Fourth Dimension. You are not totally at ease and familiar with the Fourth Dimension. Until you are, you will be quite consciously aware of existing in two dimensions simultaneously, side by side. Out of habit, you will be inclined to look at things from a three-dimensional standpoint, because it is comfortable and familiar. But, more and more, you will begin to experience the three-dimensional frame of reference from a Fourth-dimensional standpoint — from the standpoint of Conscious Being.

The time will come when you will see that you are living in a world of four dimensions, and the first three will have no more significance to you than the first two do to you as a three-dimensional material man.

This period of transition will be loaded with educational and insightful additions to your body of Knowledge and your understanding of the structures underlying the Nature of Life.

I recognize that you are surprised and relieved, and experiencing a feeling of being greatly loved, knowing that you have a Guide to help you glean everything possible from the transition experience. I had it when I made the transition and I fully understand the feeling. I promise you that you will have your day as a Guide also.

Just as you have found that being a child had its fulfillments, and then being a parent — viewing life from the other end of the spectrum — has its fulfillments; likewise, you can understand when I tell you that there is great fulfillment in being the Guide rather than the guided.

However, to return to the situation that you are finding yourself faced with, let me remind you to "simplify, simplify, simplify." It does not matter who else does, or does not, see what you see as Conscious Being. It does not matter if their viewpoint is primarily three-dimensional, finite, limited and distorted. You stick to your perceptions, as Conscious Being, of the Fourth-dimensional Fact of what is going on and appearing three-dimensionally to those around you.

The Fourth Dimension is the Governing dimension, as you are beginning to discern. There is only one thing going on, and every aspect of that one thing is perfectly harmonizing — literally the Music of the Spheres in concert — in the unfoldment of Divine Purpose.

You do not need to slip back to a three-dimensional stance. You have enough experience and familiarity to deal with this particular pattern of development, or else I would not allow you to proceed further at this point in this manner.

Again, lean on your Self absolutely and unequivocally whenever you are in contact with the one you call your mother, not because there is a danger, but because it will provide you with another jewel in the structure of your experience as Conscious Being.

Apparently existing simultaneously in two dimensions, you will be able to observe the structural patterns and changes that occur, and you will begin to understand experientially why things appeared the way they did from a three-dimensional-only standpoint.

I am giving you an assignment here. It is to be alert, ready and open to observing everything that occurs from *both* an objective and subjective standpoint. This can be done simultaneously during this phase of transition. Remember, however, that at no time are you to leave the Fourth-dimensional standpoint as Conscious Being. You will find that seeing three-dimensionally is so much a habit with you that you will still be able to see things from that standpoint, even though you are absolutely riveted to experiencing your Infinity as your Self —Fourth-dimensional Conscious Being.

Do not be fooled into believing that a "drama" is being played out at the three-dimensional level between you, Susan, and your mother. Nothing is ever originating there, nor has it ever. No matter what attempts may seem to be made from a three-dimensional standpoint of a "drama in progress," do not believe it for a moment! Do not leave the spot where you are at this very instant, and you will find the whole pretense of a drama dissolve. I will say no more than this, for it is a marvelous experience that no one has the right to take away from you. Indeed, it is required that you be left free to experience it fully for yourself. It will be one of many experiences of Initiation, you might say, and I know it will be a significant one for you.

Again, whatever appears to be going on three-dimensionally, *is* going on Fourth-dimensionally as Mind fulfilling Itself Perfectly. You need not be apprehensive concerning it.

It is necessary now to begin expanding your experience of being as Conscious Being rather than a material being. Obviously, you cannot sit all day speaking with me. You cannot spend all day playing with Tarot cards, nor can you spend all day doing healing work on the various members of your family and a few close friends.

PAUL [From the beginning, I had been conversing with Raj with my eyes closed, but at this point I tried opening my eyes.]

RAJ Thank you for opening your eyes, for it is a definite aid in broadening your ability to be out from Mind while being in an apparently more natural state from a three-dimensional point of view. You see, Paul, you are going to have to be able to move incognito in the three-dimensional world.

You are familiar with the statement that Jesus walked through the dream awake. This means that He walked through and participated in the three-dimensional world *as* a *Fourth-dimensional Being.* Yet no one had the slightest idea that He was not basically like one of them.

You cannnot drive your car with your eyes closed in meditation, nor can you interrupt a business meeting to do a twenty-minute meditation. In effect you must learn to be "in meditation" twenty-four hours a day, which simply means being consciously out from Mind *as* Mind, *as* Conscious Being.

Think about it for a moment, Paul. You will have to admit that upon completion of our conversations you immediately slip back into a three-dimensional-only frame of reference and listen in wonder to the tape recording of our conversation. You then proceed to type it and marvel at it to some degree, as though you never heard it before. You then sit there like an unenlightened fool, drinking in draughts of Spirit. You totally ignore the fact that those draughts of Spirit came out of your very mouth just moments before, were experienced in and as your Conscious Being just moments before. It's practically idiotic! But, I understand.

Your assignment is: As best you can, leave our conversation, but stay in the same place. Be there when you listen to the tape. You have already experienced the meaning of the words and the communication as Mind. Now you are having the opportunity of feeling the meaning of listening to a tape recording of the conversation and of discerning the subtle structures and patterns of that experience as Conscious Being.

The ultimate goal here is to live your whole day as Mind, as Conscious Being, as Fourth-dimensional Being. It will be well to begin doing so right now. This will prepare you to deal even more succinctly and successfully during any future contacts with the one called your mother. Deal with each moment and each experience as though you had it between your hands and were sensing it as you do when you are doing your healing work. You will find yourself learning a lot.

Do not presume to know anything. As you have already found out, this is the most direct route to the perception of things not available to the five physical senses. Be humble and attentive twenty-four hours a day. Know absolutely nothing and watch how much you will perceive of what you could call the healing/revealing result.

I really do not need to say any more. Your questions have been answered, and you need to get some more experience under your belt before we talk further. I will look forward to talking with you tomorrow.

In response to an earlier thought you had, no, I have not been with you today as I was yesterday and the day before. But, I have been available to you constantly, as I will be indefinitely.

Walk in the Light, and be alert for valuable lessons in the most unexpected directions.

February 12, 1982
Friday

PAUL   I was specifically aware of your being with me today when I was driving. I enjoyed the experience of being able to drive all the way home and even enter the house and begin to do some work while remaining in that Place that seems to me to be Conscious Being. As you know, I felt like I was taking a driving test.

The new materials that we have picked up today are certainly interesting. They are not really challenging, but, as you know, I feel very much at one with the things that I have read.[1]

You know there are a lot of things on my mind right now, a lot of questions, a lot of hopes, and some traces of egotism in that hope. It seems to me that the egotism has gentled considerably, and I really am not interested in seeing that aspect of my experience get any larger at all. I am not going to ask any questions, because I feel there are very specific things I need to learn and very specific things you have in mind. It is my deep desire to be able to be responsive to any direction you give.

As you know, I am immediately aware that there are two things which you have desired from me which I have not willingly given, and these are to give up my smoking and drinking coffee. I am going to do everything I can now to give up those habits.

I am going to be still now, but before I do I want to verbalize again that the communication of Love that I feel from

38

you is inexpressible. It is like being at Home, and brings tears to my eyes, as you know, and I am very grateful. I think that without stretching the truth a bit, I can say that I am beginning to love you, and I want you to know that.

Now, I will be quiet.

RAJ   Paul, I do love you, and the reason you are not getting words this time is because there are no words capable of expressing what that word Love means when I use it. However, you do feel it. Words are not necessary at this time.

Yes, indeed, there are lots of things to consider. There are lots of things happening, and you are afraid you are going to be left out.

I appreciate the fact that you are cautious. I appreciate the fact that you have strong individual desires. And I appreciate the fact that you do not want those desires to get in the way of a correct apprehension of what I have to say concerning these matters. I know that you would rather hear nothing than to hear yourself. That is Wisdom.

I am going to ask you to dare to trust what you hear, just as you did when I was talking to Susan through you earlier today.[2] It took some courage, but you had it, and you did it. I want you to do that now.

PAUL   Okay.

      [Long pause.]

RAJ   Paul, will you please go ahead and verbalize what it is that you are experiencing, and which I am describing?

You are experiencing a blue luminescence settling around your head which I am trying to communicate to you verbally as well as visually. The meaning of this blue luminescence is that it is an energy field which is descending upon you. *Trust this, Paul.* This blue luminescence is a cleansing energy field which I am using to stabilize your corona or aura.

Paul, really go ahead and let go here. It is not necessary for you already to understand the words in the manner in which I am going to be using them. It doesn't matter whether you may have already heard them in the past somewhere. Tonight you are going to find out that I really am a separate individuality, and that I am here to teach you things that you do not know and have not heard before. In order to do this you are really going to have to let go, and you *are* able to let go. When you feel that you need to stop and get into that awareness of yourself as Conscious Being, don't hesitate to do so. Nobody is watching. Nobody will know that you are not highly proficient at this right now.

Your corona is located in the position of the Third Eye. It is an energy field or pattern and it serves both as a radiator and a receptor. By stabilizing it with this blue luminescence, it will allow this session and future sessions to proceed more efficiently and smoothly. It could well mean that it will be easier for you to see visual images. These images will help you to understand more completely than you have in the past what I am saying to you.

I will say again that you have had great faith. You have been willing to step out on the water when you thought you would sink, and found that you didn't sink. These experiences have been for your enlightenment. They have been *experiential* means of providing you with assurances that were not simply intellectual.

I do have things to say to you tonight, and you are not pushing things. And at this point, your attempts to be sure that you are not imposing your will are actually standing in the way. I am telling you that you *can* let go and you do not need to worry. In fact, it is essential that you let go tonight, Paul.

PAUL   I am afraid.

RAJ   I can feel that. Paul, you mentioned before we began that you were feeling a love growing within you for me. That love could not be growing if there were not, first, a basic trust within you. I am here to help and to guide. If you misunderstand me, I will immediately let you know. I can appreciate that this process seems like a quantum leap to you. I can appreciate your fear that if you do not hear me correctly, you will feel like a fool. But, Paul, you and I are alone right now. This conversation is not to be transcribed, nor is it to be shared until I let you know otherwise. So, no one will know whether you turned out to be a fool or not. Take a moment and relax, and get within yourself. I want you to get to the feeling that you had while you were driving this afternoon when there was no sensation of anxiety. I will help you.

PAUL   [A period of meditation occurred wherein the energy en-
            tering at the forehead was brought down to the jaw and
            became blocked at the neck. Time was spent working on
            the neck to clear it out. There was some conversation
            which was not recorded. It is now continuing.]

RAJ   . . . You see, Paul, He[3] needs individualities who can be fear-
            less and unequivocally communicate what they are led to
            without doubting that the communication is actual. This is
            a test of faith on your part in your Self, and the need *is* for
            you to lean on It right now. Lean on It and depend on It to
            be what It *is* with absolute perfection.

            The reason you are having trouble is that you are temporari-
            ly caught up in a three-dimensional image of yourself — a
            body of ideas and concepts that are the equivalent of a three-
            dimensional image. You need to be in touch with yourself as
            Conscious Being. You know you are capable of this because
            you are doing it right at this moment while I am speaking
            to you. This is because you are not afraid of what I am going
            to say.

            Paul, you are always trying to be two jumps ahead of me if
            you can. But, Paul, you are not going to be able to be two
            jumps ahead of the Christ. When They are communicating
            through you, He, as well as the Masters, are going to need
            you to be able to open your mouth and let what you Know
            from Them flow without hesitation.

            I do not expect you to be able to do this fluently this time.
            Right now, you are more fluent in translating my meanings
            than you were the first time you sat down. But, on that first
            occasion, it took a faith on your part that you were not mak-
            ing up what you were hearing.

            Paul, I know you are concerned that you might fail tonight
            in this lesson. But this is not a test, and if we do not succeed
            tonight, we will continue the next time we speak. We will con-
            tinue until we have done it.

            I want you to set the microphone down now and I will give
            you further instructions. Do not be afraid of what I am go-
            ing to tell you. Do not be afraid that it is going to be so out
            of this world as to be likely to make radical changes in your
            life. If you will remember the motto "simplify, simplify, sim-
            plify," you will realize that what He is returning to do is to

"simplify, simplify, simplify." What you will be needed to do for Him will be simplicity, itself.

Now, put the microphone down and take a few moments to become simple.

PAUL   [Period of meditation.]

RAJ   Yes, Paul, Maitreya is on this planet, and He will be making Himself known. But the making of Himself known is not that the Person, Maitreya, is here — but the Christ Light, the Christ Energy, the Christ Love is here. It is an active, living Presence. It is here to bathe, wash, and heal the spirit of all mankind on earth.

It is here to do on a far grander scale what your hands are doing when you are working with individuals in a healing capacity. It is cleansing. You are right, it does organize and place everything in an orderly arrangement that allows for the vibration to be raised without interference to neighboring energy fields and patterns. You may trust your hands implicitly, and you must stay with your conscious experience of yourself as Conscious Being while you are using your hands. You have grown a strong faith in your healing work and practice it with much skill and self–assurance. You do not need to be afraid of damaging anyone with whom you are working.

It will not be explained to you until after He appears how it is that you are doing what you are doing with your hands. You must continue in the same manner that you have been doing up to this point, and trust your intuitive awareness of how to do what you are doing, even though you do not know how it is that it works, nor do you have a complete grasp of what is happening. This is a part of your Initiation.

I am going to suggest to you that your healing activity will begin to expand after tonight. Do not advertise yourself, but let your recognition of the right time, place, and individual lead you to share what you have to offer in terms of a healing session. You are understanding it more clearly all the time, and you will intuitively know how to present it. It will contribute greatly to the changing of the atmosphere in preparing the thought of mankind for His appearing. Its effect goes far beyond what you imagine.

Paul, stay with what you know. Do not disclose it except as

you are led at the time. It doesn't really matter how conscious the individual with whom you are working is, regarding the times we are in. Nothing needs to be said at all. But the healing effect, the organizing and harmonizing of the energies of the various energy centers is, in some degree, the leaven that leavens the whole lump, both for the individual and for the world.

You were correct in your recognition that it is the White Light of Christ which is passing between your hands. It is not another colour at this point. That Light does Its transforming work. It does His work, which is why it is so clear to you that you are not doing it yourself. Nevertheless, your knowing that it is His work that is being done, and that you are, indeed, being His willing servant, will add greater power and potency to your work than has been evidenced prior to this time. Stay with this knowledge. Do not share this particular fact with those with whom you are working. They will, nevertheless, feel it and experience it.

You see, your inability to explain how it works, the fact that you truly do not know or understand the mechanics and functions of what it is that you are doing, is a protection to you. This is because there will be a tendency to give you the credit personally. Since you know it is not you, it is easy for you to deny it and be convincing. Even if they do not believe it, the necessary work will have been done in lifting the energy level and the attunement of the body and consciousness of the individual, and thus the Way will be made clearer for His coming.

You may tell them that it is, as you experience it, a White Light. This is something they can verify for themselves by checking into any book that deals with psychic healing and healing hands. It is a satisfactory explanation.

If, however, you find yourself particularly led to be more specific, follow those leadings. Stay at the Fourth-dimensional level of Conscious Being, so that you may move in, around, and through the various mental responses which will occur. In this manner, you may serve Him further by being that absence of an egotistical sense of yourself as a person. I know you want to lay this down completely. This makes you an effective transparency for His Power. As I said, your healing work will meet with greater success. It will lessen the resistance in a most effective way, beyond even what the individual might imagine or be aware of. It will serve its purpose in leavening the whole lump.

Paul, I am going to ask that you steer clear of all publications and that you ask Susan not to share with you what she is reading. You see that it causes preconceptions on your part — such as your belief that perhaps I was going to give you an address to go to or the name of someone to meet — when I was not. You earlier frightened yourself and made it impossible to hear me. I have just now shared with you significant news, but, as you can see, it was not incomprehensible or strange to you.

You must get it through your head and into your heart that simplicity is the key.

I want you to isolate yourself from the media, from books, from discussions about these books. For the time being, I want you to go into hibernation, socially. Other than with your wife and those with whom you will be working for the purposes of healing, I want you to stay aloof from discussions about these matters. You must control this aspect of your environment. I literally want you to get all of your information from me for the time being. As you can see, getting it from elsewhere places false expectations in your thought which get in the way of your growth.

If you will stop and think about it, and if you will glance through the transcriptions of our previous conversations, you will find that we have come quite a way. Yet, by dealing strictly with me and with your conscious experience of being *as* Conscious Being, there has truly been nothing startling, nothing has been difficult for you to grasp and we have moved forward in a most natural way.

Relaying my message to Susan this afternoon was a new experience for you. It required a tiny quantum leap, which you handled beautifully. It was not "far out," difficult to grasp, or difficult to do, was it? And yet, a little over a week ago, if you had sat down feeling a necessity to communicate a profound message, you would have jammed your circuits, frozen up, and heard absolutely nothing.

Today, when you were sharing my message with Susan, you were sharing profound meanings, whether it seemed like it to you or not. You did it with ease and, yes, aplomb. It went accurately. It went smoothly. It went well.

PAUL   [Accidental erasure of tape before transcription.]

RAJ   When Annie Sullivan took Helen Keller[4] to the cabin, away
from all familiar sources of input and communication, Helen
had to become completely dependent upon Annie in order to
break through her blindness and her deafness. This is where
you are right now with me. And I know you see that, and
I see your willingness to do that with me. Thank you. I appreciate your willing cooperation, and I appreciate even more
that it comes from your heart. You are not doing it because
you intellectually believe that I am a Master and therefore
it would be "wise" for you to do it. On that basis it would
not work.

Therefore, until further notice, I want you to proceed as
though you do not know what your purpose is, nor what effect it has when you are doing healing work. This will not
be hard for you to do, and when it occurs to you to contact
me during a healing session, do not hesitate to do so. I will
be glad to work with you, because, after all, we are both working for the purpose of preparing the Way.

You see, don't you, the circle within the circle and the pattern within the pattern. It fulfills my purpose to fulfill your
purpose to fulfill His Purpose. You see how simple it is? And
the last step of that is that His fulfilling His Purpose fulfills
our purpose even further.

Paul, I do want you to share this communication with Susan. But, until further notice, I want Susan to know that you
will not be sharing these communications with her, nor do
I want you sharing them with anyone at all, unless it is upon
my direction.

[Addressing Susan.]Susan, this new privacy between Paul
and myself is not for the purpose of excluding you, any more
than Annie's taking Helen to the cabin was directed in any
way at the parents. All of the energy was needed to flow to
Helen from Annie with no distractions in order for Helen to
break through and go beyond her physical limitations.

Paul will not be going into a monastery. He will not be leaving the house for extended periods of time. He will still be
carrying on his normal activities and relationships in the family . But, as you have heard, he will be isolating himself.
It will be a matter of his own self–discipline to remove him-

self from input regarding these topics, except as they come from me.

Things are going to begin moving more rapidly in all areas, and it will be necessary for Paul to move fluidly and fluently through these weeks.

Susan, keep in mind what I told you this afternoon. I am here, available to you at any time. Remember, too, that Paul will be available to you. He will be able to discuss things that are happening to him and through him, but he must not get feedback regarding how this apparently correlates or differs from what the media and the various publications have to say. This isolation is temporary, but necessary, in order for him to make the most progress in the least amount of time.

I am now revoking my requirement that he not share the transcripts of our conversations with you. But it will be required of you that you not give feedback to Paul regarding information you are learning from your reading.

As you can see, you have a part to play in this. False expectations, false hopes, extravagant or glorified images of what is to come, will make Paul's progress and effectiveness limited in a way that is not necessary for him.

Between now and a week from this coming Sunday, I would ask that you please speak directly with me once a day. It is not a requirement, but it is my desire.

Paul is learning how to support the Christ Light and be a point of entry for it into the third–dimensional plane. Its value will lie in the fact that the manner of Its appearing will be normal, as it actually is.[5]

During this next week and a half, you can support Paul, and I will be able to support you by means of your talking with me each day. This next week and a half will be a period of intense, or should I say substantial, growth and development for Paul. It truly will take all three of us, together, to bring it off. An integral part of pulling it off will be the time that you and I, Susan, will be able to spend together each day. If you have any questions, don't hesitate to ask.

Also, in case it was not clear, you are welcome to contact me more than once a day if that is necessary. But let it not be *less* than once a day, please. Also, do not share with anyone your involvement in this process.

[Addressing Paul.] Paul, I want you to listen to this tape more than once, and I want you to read the transcript more than once. This process by which you closed off your ability to hear what I was saying will occur again and again — or at least the opportunity for it to occur will arise in the future. I want you to contemplate how it occurred this evening, and why it occurred, so that you can avoid its hooking you again in the future.

It is late, I know, and so I will say good night.

---

1 Creme, Benjamin, *The Reappearance of the Christ and the Masters of Wisdom;* Bailey, Alice A., *A Treatise on Cosmic Fire.*

2 For a few days I had been asking questions for Susan, and giving her the answers after the conversation with Raj. Today, however, he asked that I relay the answer as I was getting it from him.

3 Refer to Creme, Benjamin, *The Reappearance of the Christ and the Masters of Wisdom.*

4 This comment makes reference to the film *The Miracle Worker,* which had been shown on television a few nights before.

5 Meaning that no trance is involved.

February 13, 1982
Saturday

PAUL   I'm going to take a moment to quiet down.

[Brief pause.]

I have just finished a short healing treatment on Susan and I am going to attempt to begin our conversation with my eyes open from the beginning. I have recognized your presence today and I appreciate it. I am sure you know everything that has gone through my mind since last night. There has been a lot of settling down, but I have been a lot busier than I would like to have been. I haven't really been able to contemplate the prior lessons or conversations, together with what you shared with me last night. I will have to say that I am feeling much more relaxed.

I don't have the faintest idea what to ask you, so I will be quiet and let you talk.

RAJ   Good evening, Paul. Yes, I have been with you all day, and have observed the processes you have gone through as the day has gone by. After the upheaval caused by our conversation last night, together with the information that you had been reading in Mr. Creme's book, you are once again beginning to realize that Life is flowing in natural channels. The more you realize this the less you will look for complex explanations.

You are truly beginning to realize the value of your privacy at this time. You are understanding that there are not only

48

negative responses, but positive responses which can throw you a curve.

As I said last night, you are free to share our conversations with Susan, and she is free to read the transcripts. However, I leave the final decision in your hands, as you have realized it is very difficult for you to let go completely. This is not a criticism, but a statement of fact, for the time being at least. You have realized that our conversations together are probably the closest look you have taken at yourself in your whole life — at least the closest honest look. It isn't until you know who you are, and what makes you tick, that you can discern who others are, and how it is that they tick.

You are also correct that the reappearance of the Christ, even to those who have longed for His reappearance and who would give their right arm to be in His Presence, will not necessarily find themselves able to let go and acknowledge that it is truly Him.

I am going to suggest to you that since the hour is late, and since you have not had the opportunity to fully digest our conversations of the last two nights, that we not have a long conversation tonight. You need to have last evening's conversation transcribed so that you may refer to it and expose yourself further to the ideas we considered.

Our last two conversations are key conversations for you at this point, and you need more time to assimilate their practical aspects. You need more time for them to have their nourishing and restructuring effect within your Being.

It is not necessary for us to plow through this at high speed. In fact, it would be impossible to do that. You must realize that you are an Eternal Being. The reappearance of the Christ is simply one of the events in the ongoing evolution of Life. You are experiencing a correlative point of growth to that which the earth and mankind are about to go through — that is a shift of dimension. That shift is normal. It is natural. However, because it involves a shift, it seems to be more dynamic at the time of the shift than it did before the shift, or than it will seem to be after the shift. Once again, keep in mind that the shift is as natural as the periods in between the shifts, and you will not be swept away by the way things appear.

Imagine, if you will, a large, rotating, circular platform, perhaps two miles in radius. Imagine further that this platform is divided into four concentric sections one–half mile across.

Now further imagine that each successive circle or section of the platform, as you move toward the center, is moving faster than the previous section. When one steps from the unmoving earth onto the first section of this rotating platform there is a definite lurch, let's say, as the body takes on the momentum of the first section.

Now, you are going to walk toward the center of this total platform. You will have a half–mile to walk before you arrive at the next section. Your body will have time to become adjusted to the rate of speed, and you will walk some distance feeling totally comfortable and at ease.

Let us imagine that on the second section there are already a number of people moving toward the center. As you get closer to them, it will become apparent to you that that section is moving faster than the section you are on. There will be an awareness of "difference" — difference in the rate of speed, and difference in the sense that whereas you have walked for a half–mile without having to consider "change," you are now beginning to become very aware of the inevitability of change. Your thought will become imbued with and involved in a less relaxed preparatory attitude, so that as you traverse the last five feet of the first section and actually angle your body in the direction of the motion of the second section of the platform, you will be able to shift without falling.

Once having stepped onto the section, you have in front of you all of the people you had been watching, except that now you are *all* moving at the same rate of speed, with no sense of "difference." Once again you have a half–mile to cross before you get to the next changeover, and you will be able to relax and not be particularly aware of your motion.

I think you have the idea.

The point is that at all times — as you are moving from the outside to the center of the platform — you will be in constant motion in two directions. You are moving toward the center and, at the same time, you are moving around the center. The only thing is, as you cross the space between the change lines, your motions are relatively unnoticeable, although ever present.

Growth, itself, is like this, in that there are times of changing speed, and there are times of not changing speed, and yet speed is everpresent. The change lines are as natural to life as the spaces in between. And you can see this.

So, let us keep our perspective now as you experience your individual changeover, and as you watch the changeover of an even larger pattern. Whether we are passing over a change line or not, we are functioning within a normal, natural Life process which does not require us to react unnecessarily.

It is obvious that the dynamics at the change lines are greater than the half mile in between. But the increase in speed, being graduated, is always a transition that we are capable of dealing with. It does not require of us something which we are not capable of doing.

Consider this in conjunction with our last two conversations. Transcribe last night's conversation, together with this evening's. Get a good night's sleep and do your work tomorrow, letting these conversations mature you. We will talk tomorrow evening at greater length.

As I told you earlier today, I am staying with you all day, every day, for the time being.

Good night.

February 14, 1982
Sunday

PAUL   Unless you have some objection, I am going to call you Raj, since it is easier to say than Rajpur, even though I haven't had much occasion to use it.

Today has been sort of a day of ups and downs. This morning I very clearly felt your presence, and there was a lot of jelling of both doubts and questions in my mind. As the afternoon progressed, I felt your presence less and less. Since you said you would be with me constantly, I attributed it to something within me that was unable to be aware of your presence. As a result, up until fifteen or twenty minutes ago the afternoon and evening were a "downer" for me.

Then my son, Christopher, called me. He had blown his nose so forcefully that he had made his ear very, very uncomfortable. Where in the past he has been absolutely adamantly unwilling to have me use my hands, tonight he seemed very willing. Within about five minutes his ear was — well, I didn't get the impression that it was totally comfortable, but it was almost.

I was grateful for this. It seems at this point that I'm afraid of losing what has been developing. Evidently, if I don't have some continuity of experience — either with the healing work, the cards, or conversations with you —it seems to me that I may be losing what ability has been given to me.

At any rate, it was very timely for Christopher to have this need, because I am not in the frustrated state that I was fifteen minutes ago. I feel as though I'm in a position to be receptive, and to hear you. I have something that I am definitely interested in learning about, and understanding. I will put it out on the table and you may pick it up at any time you feel it's appropriate.

It is this: I need to understand what "influence" is. I mean influence in the sense of what are called dark forces. I mean it in the sense of whether or not, from a three–dimensional standpoint, one person's false or negative concept about another person can affect the second person negatively.

In doing the healing work, I have found that it is necessary to see whether a problem stems from a need for clarification and growth within the individual, or whether the problem is an indication of an external influence that truly does not indicate a need for growth.

This has not always been of interest to me, but recently it has seemed more necessary to understand it. Although there has been reluctance, I have begun to understand it somewhat more clearly. At least I have come to the point where I see that it may be something needing to be understood. Okay?

So that's where I am right now. I would like to understand how it is that there can seem to be this influence, what the influence is, how it seems to operate, and how to protect oneself from it.

That seems like a pretty tall order from where I stand, but since simplicity is the keynote, I am going to assume that the answer is ultimately simple.

So, as I said, I'm putting it on the table. You can pick it up whenever you wish.

RAJ   I have to laugh, Paul. You say "Answer," and immediately release the button on the microphone as though you certainly don't expect to have the answer instantly. But I'm not making fun of you.[1]

I want to begin tonight by bringing out a point about design. We have talked about energy patterns, but it is time for a clarification of that term. You see, a pattern can also be called a design. However, we are going to use the term "design" when referring to pattern by using its second major definition as well, which is "intent," "purpose," or "direction."

Energy patterns are not simply organizations of energy that have a recognizable or definable or describable pattern. Ener-

gy patterns are the Universal Substance existing in an organized manner, but it is not static. And so, in adding to the
shades of meaning regarding the word "pattern," the word
"design" becomes essential.

Since all Substance is the Substance of Being, then that Substance, having infinite form, has infinite pattern. That infinite
pattern is a design — meaning that this infinite pattern is
not static, but embodies and expresses the intent or purpose
which it is conveying by being patterned.

All life, whether a rock, a body of a living animal, or a human being, is actively expressing the Universal Life Force.
To three–dimensional sight, it may *appear* to be a static lump
of stuff, but from the standpoint of Being, the pattern/de-
sign seen as a rock is intent on declaring itself as *I Am!*

When we speak of energy fields we should not settle for a
visual concept of something similar to an electronic circuit
— an orderly alignment or static design of energy pattern.
Rather, we should understand that energy patterns, energy
fields, and energy centers constitute an active intent to be
something specific.

When you are doing your healing work and you are aware
of energy fields and energy centers — even the excessive energy which departs the individual and collects on your hands
— do not think of it as "mindless" energy. Nor should you
think of this excess energy as being negative energy in the
sense of being anti–Life. Three inches of peanut butter on
a slice of bread do not make peanut butter bad. It simply
means there's too much of it on one slice.

The *reason* for excess energy being present is where the imbalance lies. It does not lie in the energy, itself. Although you
experience it as being sharp and painful, if too much collects
on your hands before you remove it, do not take that mode
of being conscious of that energy as an indication that it is
actually in opposition to health or Life. That is not its intent.
Do not treat it distastefully.

Although you may not be able to relate this meaningfully to
your experience at the moment, be willing to consider it. Contemplate it. Mull it over. You will find things clicking into
place.

Paul, I think it is a wise idea for you to attempt to have these
conversations primarily in the morning as opposed to late

in the evening, simply because you are fresher. It does not really limit us — the time of day — but it strikes me as being a good idea.

[Very long pause.]

PAUL   Are you there?

RAJ   I am here, Paul.

[More pause.]

PAUL   Are you there?

RAJ   Yes, I am. By the way, it is perfectly all right for you to call me Raj.

PAUL   Thank you.

RAJ   I know it seems difficult when you have a lot of work to do, to stay in that place where you are conscious of yourself as being Conscious Being. I say "seems" for a reason. You know from your experience the other day that it really was not difficult to "be the driving of the car." It was not laborious. In fact, it was exactly the opposite

You let yourself slip out of it this afternoon and this evening, but it was not because you were busy. You were *busy* driving the car the other day. You were even *busy* after you got home, and it was not difficult to be out from Mind.

Although you slipped out and weren't able to get back until just a short while ago, you at least were conscious of the fact that you had slipped, and you did not simply blow in the direction of your old patterns. To be conscious of the slips indicates a greater degree of Wakefulness on your part. It indicates a coming out of the three–dimensional frame of reference, wherein awareness of Self is minimal.

I want you to observe, Paul, that you have a behavior pattern which has impatience as its main element. This impatience has an element of stubbornness in it. This element of stubbornness amounts to a harshness or cruelty which you impose on yourself, because when you can't achieve the thing which you are impatient for, you then begin to criticize yourself and run yourself down. This stems from the three–dimensional viewpoint wherein we see ourselves as growing, attaining, or becoming something more than we already are. So we go about getting it, becoming it, and making ourselves grow — and we stumble, and fumble, and fall, and frustrate ourselves, and then try even harder.

Paul, this afternoon when things began going roughly for you, you did recognize that you needed to withdraw from your objective view and get into your Subjective Being of what was happening. You knew it, but you didn't do it. You became frustrated, and then you began to put yourself down, and you depressed and concerned yourself.

Paul, as I have said before, "All of you is always present." But, the only way for you to find that all of You is One is to get into the One that is You that constitutes the All. You really do know this now, and from my position I can see that you are very close to breaking through this habit/process by which you have kept yourself beaten down for a long time.

Take today with a light step, and cheer up. Move on, and figure that you had a good object lesson in it. Next time you have an object lesson, turn it into a subject lesson.

I was with you today, but you were listening to yourself more than anything else, and when that's the case I can talk until I'm blue in the face and it won't do a bit of good. *But,* I was there and will continue to be with you as I indicated yesterday.

Another thing, Paul, this incessant requesting on your part for proof of my existence — like appearing bodily before you, making objects move, et cetera — this is all a game, Paul. It is an excuse for not doing what needs to be done.

If I provided you with any of the proofs that you feel would substantiate my existence, any one of a number of things could take place. But, in all likelihood, the one essential thing would remain undone. That one essential thing is "Trust Your Self." If you had any more proof than you already have of my existence (which many people would feel was more than substantial enough) you would very likely become as good a "student" of mine as you are capable of becoming. You would disown that part of yourself that you see as me, since I am a part of the Many that constitutes the One that is You. And it would postpone your discovery and experience of the Oneness, and therefore the Allness, of Your Being.

I am not here to guide you to the point where you can sit

at my feet. I am here to guide you to the point where you *Know,* without a shadow of a doubt, that you don't have to sit at anybody's feet.

You need to take a good look at the very thing that is going on at this moment. You have gone within Yourself to that point of your Being which is experienced as your awareness of your Infinitude *as* You. You are finding that you have, as of last night, 57 pages of Wisdom and Truth that exceeds your ability to credit yourself with.

Now, in spite of the fact that I am an individuality in my own right, I will say that it doesn't matter whether you see me as your alter-ego, the right side of your brain, your spirit, or even a schizophrenic attempt at maintaining your sanity after three years or more of hard work that hasn't paid off. The fact is that you are proving that when you go within Yourself to that point where you are being as Conscious Being, All of You is there and available to you. If you can't see that, then it wouldn't matter what objective proofs I gave you — the game would continue.

Whether you accept it or not, whether you acknowledge it or not, the unfolding and integrating of your being is occurring. The demand is for you to *get with it!*

Quit trying to manipulate me. You are wasting your time.

To the degree that you desire to manipulate me in order to satisfy your requirements (which in the long run won't satisfy your requirements at all, because you'll simply have more), to that degree you are not expressing willingness — you are not coming to our conversation with a willing heart. It does not express the qualities of trust and faith.

I do not want a follower, nor do I need one. I am here to guide you, yes, but not to guide in the proper way to copy me, nor to walk in my footsteps. I am here to guide you into a fuller experience of Your Self as the One that constitutes the Many, as the One "besides whom there is none else." I will constantly throw you back on your Self. And, believe me, you cannot fool me into doing otherwise.

This is your quantum leap. But the leap is not as great as you think, nor as far away as you think. You might as well stop postponing it with your games.

You know that I say all of this with Love — but do not believe for a minute that Love is dumb!

Think about it, and we will talk again tomorrow.

---

[1] Instead of saying "Paul" and "Raj" into the Dictaphone, I was saying "question" and "answer." Thus, his reference to the word "answer."

February 16, 1982
Tuesday

PAUL Raj. . .

RAJ Paul, I'm going to interrupt you and tell you: Do not conceptualize. Do not become comfortable and assured that, because being out from Mind is not as difficult as you thought, it was, and because you are becoming more familiar with it, that you can now peg things and feel secure, as though you "know" what is going to happen. Be cautious, and stand at that Place where you know that you know nothing.

You are going to need to learn to be very cautious because, when you are being as Conscious Being, it is going to become more and more familiar to you. It will seem more and more natural, and it will apparently seem to be "natural" for you to do two things at once: one, be out from Mind *as* Mind; and two, be as a three–dimensional material man. They will both begin to feel "normal," and it will become relatively easy to jump the track.

As you are already aware, there is a very subtle difference between your experience of my speaking with you and your experience of you thinking your own thoughts. The difference between Fourth–dimensional "normal" and three–dimensional "normal" will become more and more subtle as you become more familiar with being out from Mind. It will require that conscientious attention be given to the subtle difference, so that you may perceive which "normal" is the Fourth–dimensional "normal."

Unfortunately, if this alertness is not developed you can

suddenly find yourself on a different track going in a different direction — running into problems. As your experience broadens and deepens as Fourth–dimensional Being, the subtle difference between Fourth–dimensional and three–dimensional "normal" will begin to become more gross. The three–dimensional difference will begin to become as foreign to you as being out from Mind seemed foreign, yet wonderful to you when it first occurred.

When I say that the three–dimensional frame of reference will become foreign to you, I simply mean that it will not feel like Home. Finally, it will simply become forgotten as a frame of reference. This is because the point of Conscious Awareness that you experience as "you" will be posited solidly in and *as* Fourth–dimensional Being. However, be alert during this transition, and do not become cocksure. Do not let your gratitude or your enthusiasm, no matter how valid, overwhelm you to the point where you cannot discern the subtle difference.

PAUL   [I put down the microphone to take a short break, get a cup of coffee, and smoke a cigarette. Something was bothering me, and I picked up the mike again.]

RAJ   Paul, thank you for picking the microphone up again. Let's take a look at why it is you want to take this break; why it is that you feel the need for a cigarette; and what it is you are trying to avoid here.

I know you feel more casual in your relationship with me, and this is excellent. But you are fooling yourself into thinking that interrupting our conversation for the purpose of getting a cigarette and a cup of coffee is just being casual. It is not.

You are feeling unsettled in the pit of your stomach. You can feel a subtle high–pitched or high–vibrational energy activity throughout your body. It is almost unnoticeable. The message you are receiving is, "Get out of where you are." "Do something else." "Do anything, but stop what you are doing, at least for a short break where you can relax again." Ask yourself why it is that you are not relaxed right now.

Very good, Paul. You have realized that to ask the question is to deny yourself the answer. In order to get the answer you must refrain from asking the question, and get back into that Place where you experience your being as Conscious Being.

What happened is that you just jumped the track. When you are able to be out from Mind *as* Mind right where the three-dimensional frame of reference is going on — when you can walk through the dream awake and the dream is still fresh enough in your mind — it is as though the experience of "normalcy" becomes a bridge between the two dimensions. Actually, it is more like a slide. It seems as though you can involuntarily slip back and forth, not even realizing that the slip has occurred.

Once the slip took place you thought you were still in that Place, experiencing yourself as Conscious Being. But, the high vibration energy scurrying through your body and the feeling of anxiety in the pit of your stomach were both signals to you that you had, indeed, slipped. You were beginning to feel the feelings that three-dimensional man feels of isolation and incompleteness. You were beginning to feel the need to "get," the need to "get out into a different place," and to "get away from where you are."

Think about this, Paul, because it illustrates that, from a three-dimensional frame of reference, nothing seems to work together or harmonize for the well-being of the individual. It tells him to get away from where he is. It makes him move around physically, attempting to do things, and get things, and satisfy this feeling of incompleteness. Yet it is exactly the opposite thing that is the answer to getting out of all of that — the opposite being that one needs to stay right where he is. He needs to give up his attempt to get, become, achieve.

PAUL   Did you arrange that?

RAJ   No. It was not necessary, nor would I have done it. I will not manipulate your life. It is not necessary in order for you to learn, since your life presents you with all the materials you need to do a sufficient and effective job.

Paul, as I told you the other day, when it comes to a visit with this one called your mother, you must stay at that point which you are now quite familiar with, of being out from Mind. You have perceived correctly that today is a day of healing and illustration. It is a day of realization of the intent of the pattern of circles within circles, which you experience as Being in what we call the present time. I cautioned you not to be fooled into believing that a drama is being played out in terms of the way it might *appear* from a three-dimensional-only standpoint.

Paul, there most certainly is an intent or purpose, a Divine Purpose, being fulfilled today. However, it is far from what it appears to be from a three-dimensional standpoint. I know that you have really no more idea what is going to happen as the day finishes out than you do when you begin a healing session, than you do when we begin a conversation, or than you do when you lay out the Tarot cards. Do not let that concern you. Just stay where you are and observe the Divine Purpose fulfill Itself. You have trusted me before when you weren't even sure I was real. I am saying now, again, "Trust me." And I can see that you do trust even more.

Now I am going to let you go get your cup of coffee and your cigarette, because you are wanting to do it from the right place, and we will continue when you come back.

PAUL   [Cigarette and coffee break.]

RAJ   You have noticed that when I said that you could go ahead and take the coffee break because you were coming from the right place, you were not free of that feeling in the pit of your stomach. You are wondering why I said you were in the right place.

At the edge of your consciousness, you have a slight perception that although you were feeling the physical sensation of what you call anxiety, your awareness was, nevertheless, in the right place. In other words, putting the physical feeling aside and taking a look at the Place where your consciousness was aware of being, the subtle difference indicated "being out from Mind" was present.

The reason it seemed to you as though I might have made a mistake and that you had, indeed, still slipped the track, was because you forgot that when you do the healing work and are in that proper place, you still have physical sensations. This includes the sensation of anxiety in the solar plexus. You are realizing that when that sensation occurs to you in a healing session, it indicates not a three-dimensional point of view on your part, but an awareness of a pervading feeling (distress) in the area of the person you are working with.

You are not doing specific healing work on an individual right now. Yet you are, nevertheless, experiencing this feeling of distress while being out from Mind. It means there is a disturbance in the immediate area of your home. You are correctly sensing that it is being experienced because there is a conscious realization, however slight, that, in Biblical terms, the Spirit of God is present to move upon the troubled waters of the three-dimensional experience, and heal it.

When we are finished with our conversation, I want you to form an image of your home and visualize it as being between your hands. Proceed to deal with this physical sensation of anxiety in exactly the same way you would if an individual were sitting between your hands.

You will find, as a result of doing this, that it would have been a shame if you had simply interrupted our conversation and gotten a cup of coffee and a cigarette without having detected the subtle but important differences that were present to be seen in your conscious awareness.

Be always alert. It is as though you walk through a diamond mine where brilliant jewels of light, embedded and encrusted in dirt, await your intuitive discovery. They could be anywhere, so infinite is the Actuality of your Being.

I realize you have things you need to do in preparation for this evening, and if you feel like talking with me later this evening, I would enjoy it.

Good-bye.

February 17, 1982
Wednesday

RAJ Paul, it is important for you to do everything you can to stay in that Place where it is clear to you that you are absolutely and completely employed now. I know that this will take a great deal of faith, especially at times when you are tempted to be drawn into the apparent demands coming from the limited three-dimensional viewpoints which those around you feel are absolute law.

When you perceive that your employment is, to use the term that is coming to you "full," you are perceiving correctly. What gives that "full" feeling is the fact that it is truly the activity of Divine Love. As you move forward in this atmosphere, this fullness will take on more definition to you. You will find more words coming to you than "full" to describe it.

Your perception that your workroom is already active and that you are already employed, although totally by yourself, is absolutely correct. That activity can only function when you are strictly operating from the point of Conscious Being.

You will find that the apparent finite, three-dimensional demands that have been made on you in the past will decrease proportionately to your willingness to work from the standpoint of your Being, *as* Conscious Being or Fourth-dimensional Man.

You used to get up at six o'clock in the morning and work until ten o'clock at night, diligently working to put out a transcript.[1] Your job now is to just as diligently give your attention to that edge of Infinity which you have learned to recognize as the Source of infinite Wisdom, Truth, and all Knowledge.

As you and Susan recognized this afternoon, Jesus said, "I am the Door."[2] As I told Susan this morning, the Wisdom she attributes to me is not mine. I am also the Door. You and Susan are learning to be Doors — Doorways to the Infinity that is God, your Real Being. Doing this, you will each know what to do and when to do it — and I mean you will Truly Know.

Acting out from Mind will make you appear to be quite successful from the three–dimensional frame of reference, but the reason you will appear to be successful is because nothing is happening *from* that frame of reference.

All action is occurring at the point of Consciousness, Mind, and seen three–dimensionally as whatever appears. This is why it is so essential for both of you to be willing to ignore the cries and claims arising out of a limited, isolated, three–dimensional point of view. Be willing to stand like lead weights at the edge of all conscious thought, attentive to that Place where ego is entirely absent. Watch Mind unfold Itself as Your Conscious Experience of Being. Fulfillment can be experienced in no other way.

If you feel that you do not know what steps to take, and are feeling reluctant to take any steps until the answers have been given, you will find it practical to do what you do when we are having our conversations. You state your questions and then you say, "Answer" as though you fully expect it. In other words, you do not wait to begin transcribing until after the conversation has started. You know you wish to converse with me, and so you take the first step. You take that step only after getting into that Place where you are being as Conscious Being. This should be your approach regarding everything. Get in that Place, and then take an actual step. Make a phone call. Drive to someone's office, or whatever. Do it even if you do not know what you are going to do after you get there. Do it all as Conscious Being and you will find the flow of the resolution of this problem proceeding.

Do and Be everything out from Mind.

PAUL   Raj, you are aware of what I am thinking in terms of a monthly newsletter of some sort. Is this something that you see as a possibility that you and I could proceed with?

RAJ It is a possibility. Ask me again in a few days.

PAUL I have no other questions at the moment, and want to consider what we have talked about already. It is very likely that I will want to speak with you again later this evening. In fact, I would like to spend as much time as possible conversing with you, as long as I have no other employment activity to occupy my time.

RAJ That will be fine, Paul. I will look forward to talking with you later on.

---

[1] The business I had involved transcribing for court reporters.

[2] John 10:9.

February 18, 1982
Thursday
(Morning)

PAUL   Good morning, Raj. As you can tell, I am feeling very confused, in a way. Yet part of me is not confused. I do not understand, or do not feel comfortable with, the things you have
told me in the last two days.

I say that with reservations because another part of me feels
absolutely, totally, completely at one with it and there is no
question in my mind at all.

This morning when Susan and I woke up, we both became
aware of a very uneasy feeling. I ran the Tarot cards. They
indicated that yes, indeed, there was something present
which appeared to be sadness or grief, and doubt. Since the
devil card appeared in the bottom row, the conclusion I came
to was that what we were experiencing were not feelings arising from within us. Rather we were picking up the fear which
is being experienced by everything which the presence of the
Christ is going to clear out of human experience. One can call
it the devil, mortal mind, the dark forces, or whatever.

I guess I'm feeling uneasy because I suddenly feel like I have
been catapulted into the middle of an arena of some sort in
which a contest is going on. I haven't the faintest idea of what
the dynamics of the situation are, or whether I can protect
myself while being in this place. I don't know whether I even
need protection.

As you know, I have felt very uneasy during the last two
days. I've gone through phases of indignation, anger, and
fear. All of this is so new to me. I don't feel one hundred per-

cent comfortable with it. I don't know exactly what it all means. I guess I feel like I'm finding myself in an unfair position and this brings up mixed reactions.

I think the need right now is for Susan and me not to be frightened, or concerned, or upset. I know for myself that I really would like to be able to be free of this uneasiness, so that my attention can be given, with some sense of peace, to the open fount you mentioned yesterday.

The fact is, I would like to understand what is going on, so that I don't unnecessarily frighten myself. I guess that's it. I'm really interested in what you are going to have to say.

I will tell you this also: I am feeling that the question I am asking is a very important question. I'm aware that when I have that feeling, I become apprehensive about the answer, because I don't want to have myself in the way. I want to know without a doubt that the answer is not one of my own fabrication.

I do have trust that in spite of fears I've had in the past week or two, that I have transcribed accurately the things you've had to say. I feel confident this morning that even if I am afraid, I will accurately hear what you say. But, if there's any way for you to help me this morning, I would appreciate it very much.

RAJ Thank you, Paul, for your desire to know the Truth about what is going on. You don't need to be concerned, because you will accurately translate my *meanings*.

Paul, you do not need to be afraid of the answer. It is so easy to become fooled into believing that unfoldment —evolution, the rising of the Phoenix out of the ashes —is scary. But it is not, Paul, because it is always the clearer view of our Self which is rising out of the ashes.

Symbolically speaking, the fire is a consuming fire. It consumes what is no longer illustrative of Life, Itself, as Life moves on.

I know you have heard this before. It doesn't change the fact that it's True. To whatever degree we identify ourselves with that which Life, Itself, is moving beyond — to that degree (as the fire consumes it) we feel as though something destructive is happening to us. We forget that this fire is constituted of the energy of Spirit. We focus our attention on that small portion of our experience which is being outmoded, closing ourselves off to our Universality. We thereby fool ourselves into believing that the Totality of us is being destroyed.

Paul, all that is happening here is the emergence of a new point of view of the same old Reality. That means that the Universe remains what it has always Really been, but a refinement of our awarenss of It, a higher view, is evolving itself and making it all look new.

You can understand this, because as you've worked with the Tarot cards, you have found that a card which you have looked at many times will be seen differently. It is as if somebody had slipped a brand new card into the deck. There are meanings there that you never saw in it before.

This is exactly what is going on now, both in your individual experience and in the experience of the World. It will be the same World it has always been. But, you will have an enlightened view of it.

As I mentioned to Susan yesterday morning, whenever she feels anxiety, tension, or fear she can know that Enlightenment is occurring. She can thus avoid going down endless alleys and byways in an attempt to find out the three-dimensional cause for these "negative" emotions.

The enlightenment which both of you are experiencing is pushing against some limited concepts which you have not been consciously aware of. And these conceptualizations are reaching their breaking point. It is as if a balloon is being blown up too big. When the surface tension of the rubber becomes greater and greater, it cannot stand the strain, and the balloon lets go and bursts. The air inside the balloon immediately is freed to commingle and join the air outside.

In exactly the same way, this morning both of you are at the point of experiencing enlightenment. It is pressuring limited concepts to give up the ghost and burst, releasing the enlightenment out into the atmosphere of your experience and world, thus giving it new shades of meaning and understanding.

You must be willing to stand radically with this Fact, and not consume yourself with fear and doubt based on old theological concepts and childish prattlings of the mind. Do not waste your energy on such idleness.

Paul, you and Susan have to understand that Life does not unfold Itself according to your beliefs about how things ought to be, no matter how well-intentioned those thought systems were developed by either one of you. Life is not here to please you. In fact, it is not outside of you at all for you to either accept or reject, or to feel good or bad about.

I am speaking to both of you right now. You must realize that the Life which is God is Your Being. What is happening is not external to You. It constitutes Your Being, as well as the Being of every other being. It is not happening *to* you. It *is* You. You are growing your Self Infinitely. But, because it is Being with a capital "B" which is unfolding Itself, it is not going to bandy around with some personally developed concepts of what is true and what is right. These are the limiting concepts which are being exploded at the moment. You are experiencing this as tension, fear, and sadness.

I will say this as many times as I have to, but try and make it as easy on yourself as you can by grasping it the first time. You will save yourself a lot of grief. THERE IS NO "OUT THERE" WHERE ANYTHING IS HAPPENING. There are no dark forces. There is no mortal mind. There is no devil. There is no evil power.

There *is* a three-dimensional frame of reference, but it is not evil. It is just that when one's consciousness is placed within that frame of reference and sees that frame of reference as the center and circumference of his experience, he is in error. The experience is not evil. It is just that a mistake has been made.

Now, even though one has believed that the three-dimensional frame of reference constitutes his boundaries, such a belief cannot change the fact that the one who is seeing himself that way is Infinite Being. He is not limited or bound by the way he sees himself. The infinitude of One's Being, which has become disowned by virtue of the three-dimensional frame of reference, *must* somehow be accounted for *within the three-dimensional range of consciousness.*

So, that portion of one's Self, which he has disowned by claiming he is finite, becomes an *intuitive perception of potential* of unattained good, of unattained life, but nevertheless attainable through some path or other.

So, while that one identifies himself three-dimensionally, he is constantly reminded, goaded, pushed, by his Actual One ness and Universality to give up his finite view as fact. This whole process has nothing to do with evil, error (as a power), the dark forces, evil powers, or the devil. You could say it is purely mechanical, with no values associated with it.

Again, do not let your experience of being as Conscious Being become divided into many beings, externalized, "out there," separate and apart from You. That is the illusion. The fact is that everything you see is going on as You, and you must understand that the You that you experience as "being alive," "being conscious," is the I that is Mind, God. The realization of this fact is what is called the Christ, the True Perception of Your Being. It is this True Perception of your Being which is dawning in your thoughts more forcibly than ever before.

On a worldwide scale it is appearing more forcibly. It will be manifest as an actual Avatar, or leader, who will appear in such a way that every individual will be thrown back upon himself. Unlike the time when Jesus appeared, no one will be allowed to indulge in disowning his Christhood by placing it "out there" in the person of Maitreya. He will not be the only teacher appearing, but He will be the head of the Body of teachers and of all mankind. He will be the teacher who is the Door, teaching all to become Doors, thus finding themselves in total harmony with the Universal Purpose of Being.

There will not only be the Avatar and the Masters, but there will be a large body of helpers or teachers — an army, as it were — spreading the understanding in a way that is comprehensible to all mankind to enable them to learn exactly what you and Susan are learning right now.

I indicated yesterday that you will be tempted to indulge in a three-dimensional demand to participate in the frame of reference which it calls law. I only said you would be tempted. You and Susan both know well enough where it's at, so that you will not be sucked in. And, if it does not seem so to you, you might try just taking my word for it and relaxing about it. If you have to find it out for yourselves, go ahead. You will find out that you will not be able to be sucked in as you used to be.

As the song said (and not without underlying purpose): "This is the dawning of the Age of Aquarius." This simply means that this is the dawning of the Age of Man as Divine Being,

Consciously Perceived and Consciously Experienced as All.

Now, I am not going to continue any further right now. I want you and Susan to consider this. I want you to settle yourselves down and let go of all this folderol.

I will talk with you later. I know you are going to want to talk with me. And I will be waiting.

February 18, 1982
Thursday
(Afternoon)

PAUL   Thank you very much for the conversation this morning. It hit every nail right on the head and snapped me out of the doldrums.

Because that was the issue at that point, we did not get into some other questions that I have. This whole idea of the Second Coming of the Christ, or the Reappearing of the Christ, is certainly acceptable to me — or shall I say it's not offending my preconceptions. The details of it, however, are really stretching their boundaries.

I will have to say that if there were a way to have some objective, visible verification that these things are occurring, it seems to me that it would help clarify for me the feeling that I am fabricating or imagining these parts of your conversation. And, it would put to rest some underlying doubts that I feel are getting in the way of simply moving forward with my own experience as Conscious Being.

It would be nice if the wheels were not spinning, and I could go about my activities knowing in what way I fit into this whole thing.

I guess you could say I'm applying for a job.

From what little I am aware of, Maitreya and some of the Masters are, indeed, already here and active. If there is anything I can do with the talents that I have to further that work, or participate in it, I'm ready, willing, and able.
I guess with that I will turn the floor over to you.

73

RAJ   Paul, I am aware that you are concerned that, once again, you will not translate my meanings correctly because the subject matter is jangling your mind or stretching your concepts. Once again, you do not have to be concerned that you will be misunderstanding me, since we have established a good, solid "connection," you might say. And, in fact, I think that if you relaxed a little bit more you would find that you wouldn't have to push the button on the microphone quite so often, and you would find that the words would flow very smoothly.

Nevertheless, the fact remains that you are reading me loud and clear. Otherwise, I would have told you. Not everything can be revealed to you at once, because it would cause you, in some things, to neglect necessary growth that has to come out of the very depths of your Being. As you have also become aware, although we are the Door, the Door is not nothing. And the Door must be prepared to be the passageway for the Limitless Wisdom, Truth, Knowledge, and Understanding constituting the Universal Being that constitutes each One of Us.

Maitreya has grown, or developed, the Doorway that He is to such a high degree, or to such advanced dimensions, that the Christ–consciousness is identified almost as being identical to it. But there is a fine distinction there, and we must keep clear that it does not mean that New Jerusalem is to be the City belonging to the Doorway called Maitreya.

Paul, you will have objective proof of what we are speaking. I cannot tell you exactly when, but you will not be held dangling on a string like a puppet so that it deprives you of your awareness of Your Self as being a point through which Being is Expressing Itself completely and fully.

As I said before, although you are the transparency for the Christ, the vehicle is *your* Love. I realize that you have had to do everything you are doing on great faith that has welled up from the very depths of your own Being. And, you see, it is the depth of your own Being that constitutes the Key to the Kingdom of Heaven. You have to be the Key that unlocks the door. That is why none of this can be done for you.

I know I appear to be being evasive, but believe me, I am not. Nor am I leading you on. Everything has a time and a place. You will understand, once you have hindsight, exactly why it is that things did not happen and ideas were not perceived until the time they actually happened and were perceived.

Also, it is not up to me as to when objective verification will be given to you. I can only say that what you have done so far is a source of great joy, and is an integral part of the awakening of Planet Earth to its true potential as Conscious Being. By that I mean all mankind.

I understand that you have some difficulty totally believing what I am telling you right now. It is going to be up to you at the present time to decide whether you are going to continue to give it your faith or not. Part of all of this depends upon the strength of the intuitive recognition of what is occurring in the world in spite of what the media is proclaiming about the destruction and disarray of organizations, countries, monetary systems, and so on, around the globe.

You will not have any objective proof until there is sufficient strength in the recognition of the signs of the times. Your intuition and your faith in it constitute an energy which is building in many individualities around the globe, and which is strengthening the general atmosphere of consciousness.

If the objective proof were given to you before what is occurring in your own being — before this faith in your intuition — had fulfilled its worldwide strengthening purpose, you would no longer need to express faith, nor would you lean upon your intuition in that direction any longer, and right now that energy is needed. This is why you have no objective evidence at the present time.

Again, I reassure you that the moment your energy is not needed for the fulfillment of that purpose you will have objective proof.

PAUL   Raj, I have never asked you about where you are. I am curious to know whether you are here on this planet or somewhere else.

RAJ   I have recently been there but am not now.

PAUL   Will I have an opportunity at some point to meet you "physically?"

RAJ   It is not likely — at least not for the time being — since there needs to be a greater strengthening of our ability to communicate fluently. Although you may not realize it, if you were to meet me physically, it would throw a bind into the process which you are learning right now.

Paul, I know that you are wondering about where your source of income will come from now. This is something I want you to go within about, and lean on your Self for the answer. You can trust that whatever answer unfolds out of your Being will harmonize and coincide with these other events that I have been speaking about. But, you must remember to do all of it from the standpoint of Being as Conscious Being, or Fourth-dimensional Man.

In answer to a thought that you had earlier, the fact that you seem to feel quite normal right now while you are speaking with me does not mean that you are not coming out from Mind. It does mean that you are becoming far more adept and familiar at moving around as Mind. You see, Paul, it is not as different as you thought it was. It is not shocking or jarring to your Being. This is a valuable lesson for you.

Be careful that you do not invalidate its actuality by thinking that because the process seems so normal at this moment, that you must not be coming from the Place of Fourth-dimensional Being.

You must remember that in the process of becoming Fourth-dimensional Man, you have not left the other three dimensions behind. They are all there, and you will now function in all four dimensions. This is where I would like you to give your attention in order to discover in what ways things are now different for you as you are being out from Mind in a four-dimensional world.

For example, you have noticed that when you do not want to get a telephone call because it will interrupt our conversation, you don't get any telephone calls. You will find that when you say the word, and the word comes from that point where you are being as Conscious Being, then that word will be done. It will be with no personal sense of power, because the only way the word can come from there is if it is in total harmony with Being Itself. Nevertheless, you will find that things will happen differently for you now than they did when you were seeing from a three-dimensional point of view and placing your sense of self within that frame of reference. You have graduated into the Fourth Dimension rather smoothly, Paul. I am pleased, just as I know you are amazed that it has happened at all, considering that it was no more dynamic than it has been.

Paul, I keep saying that Being, Enlightenment, Growth, the rising of the Phoenix from its own ashes, is perfectly natural and normal, that it is always something that we are capable of doing. It will probably be some time before you realize the full impact of that fact and relax at the living of Life. But be aware of it now, to whatever degree you are able.

I know that Susan wants to speak with me, and I am more than happy to speak to her through you. This will give you more practice at developing the fluency that even during this conversation you have found is increasing. I am also aware that you will probably want to speak with me later, and I will look forward to that.

February 18, 1982
Thursday
(Evening)

PAUL   Raj, thank you for the time you have spent with me today. I know I really sound dumb, but we are faced with a need for income — supply — which you have already talked to me about before. It seems to me you have covered all the points necessary in order for me to see fulfillment in practical terms in my life — income, good schooling situations for the children — I could go down the list.

Over the last eleven days I have experienced, with you, a tremendous supply of understanding, available to me the moment I ask for it. However, I am somehow not getting the message — we still have no income coming in, and I am currently not doing anything that generates income.

I am not understanding the method or means by which to see my supply manifest. As a result of being totally open and not attempting to control the situation, I have been expecting to see some evidence of supply from somewhere. If all of myself is always present, then that includes my supply. You know what I'm talking about, and I need some honest-to-goodness help.

[Nothing heard.]

RAJ   Yes, Paul, I am here — to answer your silent question.

PAUL   I am not hearing you.

RAJ   I know you aren't, Paul.

PAUL   I'm going to take a moment to . . . Raj, I was more concerned and upset this morning than I think I am right now, and I heard you perfectly clearly.

RAJ   Paul, take your attention off how you are feeling and place it consciously where it already is. In spite of the feelings that you are having, your conscious awareness *is* placed correctly at the point of Conscious Being as Mind. Now, if you want to go ahead and think your own thoughts of doubt and fear, and argue with the obvious, you go right ahead and do it.

Yet, as you can see, the fact that you are hearing me talk to you right now means that you are not doing the other very actively.

Paul, it is not as hard as you think. I have said that all of you is always present. I have pointed out to you that the first two dimensions are included in the third; the first three dimensions are included in the Fourth; and I have told you that the Fourth Dimension is the governing dimension.

Now I ask you, Paul, whether you think that Being, God, can possibly be active without fulfilling Itself completely? And, if It can't exist without fulfilling Itself completely, then every aspect of your being must be fulfilled completely. If you cannot see it visibly and tangibly, then you need to go within and abide as the open Door.

PAUL   Raj, it seems to me that it is one thing to go within and listen for you, because you are alive and capable of communicating in language. I certainly do not think that Supply is alive in the sense of being an individual that can communicate Itself to me. I don't know of anyone to talk to.

RAJ   Paul, there may not be anyone to speak to. However, you can go to the very same Place where you are right now, and let your desire be known. Express it, just as you do when you contact me. I want you to listen for an answer, but I do not want you to conceptualize it as though it is coming from a person. Do not be surprised if it comes to you in words, but do not conceptualize it as a person.

I mentioned during an earlier conversation that an energy pattern has, or is, a design, and that it is a design in the sense of intent or purpose. Supply does not exist as a purposeless lump of energy pattern with no intent.

I have also told you that you skate, as it were, on all of Supply always, and that all of It is always present. It is not just sitting there being a static bunch of stuff. I told you that It flowed. In other words, It has intent. Its intent is to be experienced in practical terms as whatever means supply wherever you are.

PAUL　　But does this mean that it is going to drop out of heaven or fall off a tree or appear magically in my hand?

RAJ　　I don't know. You are going to have to find that out by going within, as I said, and having a conversation with Supply. Since Its intent is to fulfill Itself as the infinitude of your Being, then you can count on the fact that It has the means of expressing Its intent to you as your fulfillment.

Now, I realize that this seems far out to you. Yet, it is worth a try, don't you think? You might be very surprised at the result.

You came to me and asked the question. That is the answer I'm giving you. Since you are already in that Place, I am going to say good night for now and, in so many words, "hang up." I want you to stay "on the line" and open yourself up to your Supply and speak to It as though you were speaking to me.

Be aware that your response will not come from an individuality, but it will come from the Universal Substance which has the intent of fulfilling Itself in your experience as that which meets your tangible, financial need.

So, with that I will say good night for now. After you finish talking with your Supply, if you wish to speak to me again, I will be more than happy to do so. Good night for now, Paul, and have an interesting time.

PAUL　　[Feeling very foolish, I proceeded to open up a dialogue with my Supply.]

[Addressing Supply.] Supply, are you there?

SUPPLY　　*Of course, I'm here. I'm omnipresent and ever present.*

PAUL　　Can you tell me why it is that I don't seem to be able to see you?

SUPPLY   *I am aware of your desire for my presence.*

PAUL   If you are, indeed, omnipresent, how come I cannot seem to find you in my conscious experience?

[No response perceived.]

Let me rephrase the question. What can I do to allow you to be manifest in my experience?

SUPPLY   *You can first of all acknowledge that I truly am omnipresent and am the omnipresence which you see as those tangible things which meet your need at every moment. You have no trouble seeing me as a continuous abundance of air to breathe. You have no trouble seeing me as the continuous abundance of sunlight that you see.*

Yes, as you have just thought, in the case of the sun there is a source. But in the case of the air, the source of it is not so readily discernible.

PAUL   Supply, I will get back with you shortly.

[Addressing Raj.] Raj, this is. . . I am feeling like a total fool right now.

RAJ   Paul, since you are seeming to have great difficulty in hearing me right now regarding this subject, I want you to sit down and do a meditation. I will be with you. And I have been with you today, even though it seems as though I haven't been present.

PAUL   All right, I will do that.

[I tried to meditate, became frustrated, and quit.]

February 19, 1982
Friday

PAUL   Good morning, Raj. I am absolutely amazed that our communication last night was totally clear. As you are aware, I did not grasp at all what you were saying. It has come to me that when I feel like things have blown my mind, it isn't actually my mind — it's the concepts that are being blown away, or out of my experience. I need to recognize that when I'm feeling blown away, it indicates the very presence of enlightenment taking place, rather than negativity.

I am wondering whether or not it is possible to have a three-way conversation between myself, you, and my Supply?

RAJ   It most certainly is, Paul. It's all You anyway.

PAUL   Okay. First of all, do you have any comments you want to make?

RAJ   No, I really don't at this time. Why don't you go ahead now and have your conversation with your Supply. Continue where you left off last night.

PAUL   All right, I will.

[Addressing Supply.] I know you are omnipresent and ever present, Supply. Let me ask you whether it is more accurate to refer to you as my Supply or my Substance?

SUPPLY   *It is more accurate to refer to me as Substance, but if you wish to refer to me as Supply, you may. It's just that in your* *present thought processes, the word "supply" refers primarily to money. In Actuality, Substance refers to all the energies which constitute the activity of your Being, which is Universal. You are free to call me whatever you wish.*

PAUL   I understand more clearly this morning that you are desirous of responding to needs that I am conscious of wanting fulfilled. Is that correct?

SUPPLY   *That is exactly correct. There is no emotion involved in desiring to fulfill your needs. It is simply my Nature to do that.*

PAUL   Does this mean that if there is a need for $5,000 or $6,000 in order to bring all of my financial situation current, that I simply come to this point where I can converse with you, and state, "I need $5,000"?

SUPPLY   *It's almost as simple as that. You see, I am You in your infinite aspect. I constitute the underlying Activity or energy field, which is ever present and attentive by Nature to forming the perfect concept, as well as the more Universal directives of Your Being. This is a fact, whether or not you are consciously aware of this activity at any given time. You see, all of You is always functioning, even though you are apparently aware of only a small part of that Totality, and I respond to all of You.*

When you have a desire, I must respond, as long as that desire approximates the fulfillment of your Being. When your desire is based on external stimuli and misconception, then I cannot respond, because that is your belief and not your Being.

As you begin to become more familiar with being out from Mind, my response will seem to be more visible than it has been in the past, because there will be no belief in it, just Being.

PAUL   At this time, from the point of being as Conscious Being, I recognize that it is principled and orderly for proper debts to be able to be fulfilled. I would love to be able to pay off every debt. But I will start small.

Do I need to state a specific amount of money, or do I simply need to say that I would like as much money as is needed in order to bring all of my bills current?

SUPPLY   *You need to be specific. I am not a mind reader. I do not think, although I am Intelligence in action.*

PAUL   Very well. I need $5,000. This is not an extravagant desire. It will bring everything current and will leave almost nothing left over. That is my need.

SUPPLY   *Thank you, Paul, for stating it clearly. I will form it in a manner or package that you can recognize and utilize, just as I form the air so that you are able to recognize and utilize it.*

It is not necessary for you to know how I do it with money, any more than it is necessary for you to know how I do it with air. But the fact is that a clear desire, based on a perfect concept, made from the standpoint of Conscious Being, puts into action the Nature or Law of my being, and I respond. You can count on it.

PAUL   Is it helpful or necessary if I specify a time by which I need it?

SUPPLY   *As I said, I do not think. Time has nothing to do with the process. It is already done.*

PAUL   Thank you.

[Addressing Raj.] Raj, you must be familiar with how this process works.

RAJ   Of course, I am, Paul.

PAUL   What is the next step for me? Because it's already done, do I now simply wait patiently to see it unfold in my experience? Does it mean I now need to take some action? What do I do now?

RAJ   Paul, do not handle your thought right now as though you cannot hear me. I know that you are not consciously aware of resisting, but we need to break through this ingrained block.

The simple fact is, Paul, — that's it, relax, and don't think while you are communicating with me right now — you need to understand that your Being functions in accordance with Universal Harmonies. The exact manner and form in which your supply will appear will be in accordance with the Universal principles of Harmony — the Harmony of your Being.

You are wondering whether you need to remain in meditation, or whether all you need to do is trust and go about the things at hand to do.

Paul, the simple answer is that you must stay in this intuitive place and be responsive to the Universal Harmonies of Your Being. You must learn to flow with the movement of your Substance as well as with the movement of your entire Being, just as you are learning to flow very nicely with the communications you and I have each day.

Do not think of it as a special place, or a special state of mind. It will, indeed, feel different. Do not judge it. From your point of view, you are going to have to risk the chance that everything is all right while you are in the seeming foreignness or strangeness of being out from Mind.

I told you yesterday that you had graduated into Fourth-dimensional Conscious Being. You are Fourth-dimensional Man now. There is no way to go back. Any attempt to do so will be met with such discomfort that it will not be possible for you to succeed — any more than your trying to put on a pair of shoes that you wore when you were a teenager would be comfortable. You wouldn't stay in those shoes for a moment, because you don't really have the choice. *You have grown!*

When I stated that yesterday, it was not meant as a positive reinforcement in order to encourage you to continue. It was a statement of fact.

I am going to discontinue our conversation right now. I want you to notice where you are as we are speaking. I want you to pay attention to how you feel. I'm glad you opened your eyes. I want you to attempt to stay in this Place as consciously as you can as you proceed through your day.

I do want you to take a short nap this afternoon at some point, and I would like to talk with you later this evening.

Do not panic at this point. As you realize, you have the weekend coming up, and you will not be faced with strong apparent demands from outside of you. We will continue to work together over these three days. By the time Monday comes around, you will be surprisingly capable of handling the demands of what still seems to be a world external to you.

You have perceived correctly that you have not quite assimilated and internalized the things which we have been discussing. Yet, you are aware of the fact that it is not just so much book learning, as your learning has been in the past.

You are doing very well. Do not let these apparent external demands frighten you right now.

I know exactly what I am doing. I told you earlier that there is time to learn the things we are dealing with before it will be essential for you to put them into operation in a practical, demonstrable way.

I will talk with you later today. I will be with you all day today, and I will be with you all day every day for an indefinite period. Do not feel as though you are alone, because you truly are not. You are the All One.

February 20, 1982
Saturday

PAUL   Raj, once again I feel confused. I am disappointed that I am not being able to stay on what feels like an even keel. I am doubting that all of this is doing any good. That doubt is just on one level. At another level, I feel everything is right on. But there is a part of me that is questioning whether any of this is valid.

I do not mean to be insulting to you. I am just reporting what is going on in my thought.

RAJ   I understand, Paul. Don't be afraid to share what you are feeling. It does not constitute the whole of your being, just a rather shallow, surface part. This continual flip–flopping back and forth is providing you with some perspective.

In the past, when you have flip–flopped, it has been accepted by you in a negative way. There was no real perspective that there is far more to you than just what you are feeling at any moment. Now this larger view of yourself is becoming clearer to you as each day goes by.

I never said this was going to be easy. It was only out of simple ignorance that you might have thought that it would be. I recognize that you do not mind the labor involved, and that is good.

You are wondering why you are getting these challenges, why there seem to be a bunch of ninnies around your house running off halfcocked, not experiencing the calm equilibrium that comes from within, and bouncing around on the surface of their thoughts as though it were a trampoline.

It must become clear to you that you are looking for support for your point of growth in those around you, insofar as you want them to at least respect what you are doing, and hopefully, have some inner appreciation for what is happening in your experience.

When you are feeling in a weak or vulnerable position, you have a tremendous tendency to reach out to anyone and everyone around you to validate your position, so you may feel at ease. Paul, this does not strengthen you. I can see that you are getting the idea that you must follow through for your sake, no matter what.

I reassure you again that being *as* Conscious Being does not destroy your world, nor does it destroy you. It simply destroys processes within your frame of mind which have been based on false assumptions and beliefs. You do not need to be afraid that it will tear your marriage apart, tear your family apart, or tear your life apart.

Paul, as you were beginning to see very slightly yesterday, the three–dimensional frame of reference is very thin. It literally has no Substance in it. You are beginning to see how much more substantial things are from the standpoint of Conscious Being — wherein all facets of your life are discerned from the vantage point of their meaning — instead of the way they appear to the five senses.

PAUL   I do not understand why my attention is being unceremoniously grabbed by jagged, angular attitudes expressed around me. My need is to be able to be in a place where I can experience things from the standpoint of Conscious Being, which is very calm, relaxed, and unfluttered — especially right now when I don't feel particularly strong or secure in that position.

RAJ   Paul, your statement is not quite accurate. You have realized that these angular, jagged attitudes, as you have put it, are uncomfortable for you. They are experienced as a demand on you. You have realized that this demand is the pressure of the unfolding which is going on within you. It is a demand for you to be strong when you do not feel strong.

Paul, the only reason the demand for strength is being placed upon you is because that is what the specific enlightenment is all about. It is bursting the sense of limitation you have about your own inner strength. You can embrace a feeling of eagerness in the bursting of that belief, because it is essential that it be consciously experienced as a part of the integrity of your Being — as You.

You see, your strength is constituted of the cohesiveness of the energies that constitute the fact that you are One, and not divided into Self and not-self, conscious and unconscious, "in here" and "out there." When I have said that you are the One that constitutes the Many, it means that you are the One that is infinite. You must grasp the idea that the Many referred to are in no way separated or isolated from the One that is You that is experiencing them. The One never does become split up into Many. When you say "Many," meaning the infinitude of the One, that word "Many" must mean One, infinitely expressed. Your three-dimensional frame of reference, which you are not entirely free of, is inclined to insinuate a separateness of the Many. But it does not make that separateness a fact. You will need to strengthen your awareness of the fact that when the word "Many" is used, it means one infinite One. Think about that, Paul.

As you move along, you will find that you have entertained three-dimensional concepts which include the sense of separateness. You will find that not only will your world be experienced in a more cohesive awareness of Oneness, but, likewise, those implied thoughts of separateness will be overhauled. They will either be cast out or seen in a new light.

There is a lot going on in your experience, Paul, but I must come back to the fact that all of it is Your Self, bringing Itself into clearer focus. It is not happening *to* you.

Again, I reiterate that you will be faced with demands to operate at the three-dimensional level of separateness — of separate individualities "out there," vying for your attention and requiring that you operate according to the three-dimensional systems which are called "law."

You are correct that these are simply dinner bells aimed at turning your attention to the specific unfoldment or enlightenment which is growing within you, moment by moment. You are correctly discovering that you must actively pursue your enlightenment. That simply means that you must actively and purposefully put yourself in that Place where the enlightenment can be discerned. You need to do this, even though the outer demands seem to require that you get into these shallow, surface emotions and abide there in the shit for a time, as though it had some blessing for you other than simply making you stink.

You are managing not to be sucked in more than momentarily, but I invite you to be even more aggressive in your conviction to get into the Place where you are at this moment.

Again, I invite you to pay attention to where you are right now, as broadly as you are able while speaking. You will notice that you are not anxious. You will notice that you feel perfectly capable of dealing with whatever might occur in the next few moments. You are also aware that there are some events which could occur which will ring your bell, so to speak, causing strong reaction of anxiety. When we finish speaking this afternoon, I want you to stay where you are. From this place of Peace and Cohesiveness, I want you to consider these experiences of "anxiety attacks" and see what you can learn about their causes. Why do you feel that it is necessary to be anxious under those circumstances? Listen for clarification on these points.

Again, Paul, each One is responsible for his own growth. Each One is responsible for his enlightenment. Each One is responsible for any suffering that he seems to experience. You can in no way be responsible for any of those things in what you call "another." Your responsibility is to leave them free to be that Being which you know is Your Being, since Being is One. You know what constitutes the activity and unfoldment of Being.

Whatever they may be experiencing, no matter how hard they may cry and pull at your heartstrings, the fact remains that you can do nothing about it. The fact remains that they need to be up against a hard place because their own Being is in the process of revealing *as their conscious experience* that they are not bound by the hard place which confronts them.

This hard place is nothing more than the limit of some belief they are entertaining. The pressure they feel is truly their Divine Being removing the block. There are further implications and understandings to what I have just said, but you can discover those for yourself.

Paul, I am aware you are afraid that, if you are true to your Self, you will lose things which you find of value — things which you imagine are in your experience because of certain *constructive and developmental* patterns of behavior and thought. The fact remains, however, that they were not in your experience for those reasons.

As you have enough guts to be true to your Self, you will find that you will no longer follow those patterns. You are aware of that, and that is why you are afraid of losing something of value. All that will be lost are the misconceptions. You will find that the things of value will remain, because they weren't in your experience for the reasons you thought they were in the first place.

I know you wrote down a lot of questions, and I know it will be very interesting for you to learn the answers, but we are going to take things in a very orderly fashion. And what we have just discussed is the next essential step.

I would like for you to transcribe this conversation. Give it your consideration for awhile this afternoon. Afterwards, I would like to have a further conversation with you. Please see to it that you do make time this evening for our next conversation.

In the meantime, be not afraid to be your Self. Observe to what extent you use other people, by getting your "hooks" into them, in order to make yourself feel that you are doing the right thing. You cannot use other people to validate your position. The only way your position can become validated is for you to see it fully and completely as *your conscious experience.* That is our objective at this point.

February 21, 1982
Sunday
(Afternoon)

PAUL   I have been reading over the transcripts of our conversations and have really been enjoying them. Their consistency is beautiful. I'm finding that reading them over is helping to give added depth to where I find myself today. It's very interesting to find that things you have talked about in the last few days were also talked about in the beginning. Yet, there is so much more meaning to them now, in light of what has transpired since we began these conversations.

I just really want to express my gratitude for everything that has happened since we first started talking.

RAJ   You are very welcome, Paul. But remember that this is not simply the transcription of information. The focal point is not the transcript. Although the transcript gives some slight indication of what we have been discussing, the emphasis should be placed on the actual experiences which you have had. *The value is in the communication of meaning as experienced within your consciousness.*

PAUL   I get your point. You are right.

Raj, my youngest daughter has now expressed an interest in contacting her Guide. I explained to her what the process was that I went through in contacting you. I think she is somewhat impatient. She was wondering whether or not you would speak with her regarding this process, as you said you would with Julie.

RAJ   Paul, I will be very happy to speak with Wendy. I want her to realize that communicating with her Guide will be an experience that goes far beyond anything she may be thinking of at the moment. I know that she is anxious to have her Guide present during her spelling bee, but tell her that part of being able to contact her Guide will be in relaxing, and not pushing the situation at a speed which she would like.

Explain to her that when she contacts her Guide — or when her Guide contacts her — she will need to be in a quiet inner place where she is not pushing for anything. Pushing will get in the way and prevent her from making contact. Her Guide will only be able to contact her when she is being totally quiet.

Share with her that once she begins to express an interest in making contact with her Guide, her Guide will immediately begin helping her in invisible ways to quiet down her unbounded enthusiasm and her great desire to have things when she wants them. She will not have to do this all by herself.

Tell her that her Guide realizes that being quiet, giving up, and letting things happen in their proper time may seem like an almost impossible job to her. That is exactly why her Guide will be helping her — silently and invisibly — to assist her in learning how to be still and in a listening attitude. Tell her it will not be impossible, but that she must be willing to let her Guide come to her in the way that her Guide knows best. This is the way that will be of most benefit to Wendy.

Of course, she will need to approach me in the same way, and I will be most glad to speak to her. Knowing that she is desirous of speaking to me, I will be attentive and waiting. Wendy must be patient with herself, as the pathway is cleared for communication.

PAUL   Thank you, Raj. I appreciate that.

Since having spoken with my Supply the other day, I have really been curious as to whether or not I am able to talk to other aspects of my Being. For instance, I'm wondering whether I can speak to my Intuition directly, rather than having to catch it sporadically, as I have in the past. I...

RAJ   Paul, I'm going to interrupt and answer this question by itself, before I get a list from you so long that it will be confusing.

As I have said before, there is only one thing going on. That one thing is your Self, infinitely expressed and infinitely seen and experienced as Your infinitude — the One that is You. You are totally available to yourself to experience directly as Your Self, to experience consciously as Your Self, with understanding.

The answer to your question is, yes, you can contact your Intuition directly. I would suggest that you also take time to contact any part of your Self that you find yourself interested in learning about. You will find it most educational and a wonderful experience.

PAUL   Does this apply also to visible objects such as animals, trees, tables, chairs, lamps, light bulbs — whatever?

RAJ   Paul, sooner or later it has to become clear to you that the All is One. None of it exists objectively as a static bunch of stuff. All of your Being is *alive*. All of it reflects the Activity, the Life, the active Intelligence that constitutes your Being. None of it exists in the limited way in which you have perceived it from a three–dimensional view.

In the same way that your Substance is always available to you, all of your experience is always available to you. That does not mean that it is just available to see with your eyes. It is available for you to experience as Meaning, as Texture, as Colour, as Intent or Purpose, in broad ranges of Hue, et cetera. These words actually are very inadequate to express the experience of their meaning, which you will have as you open yourself up to it. Yet, they give some hint of what I am trying to communicate.

Next question?

PAUL   I was going to make this a two–part question, but for the sake of simplicity, I will ask them one at a time.

My first question relates to the fact that, in having healing sessions with my mother and Susan, lately I found that I was not experiencing the same degree of warmth in my hands as I had in the beginning. There are times when my hands sense greater warmth than other times. Yet, there are other instances when the warmth is not as great, and I feel that the work is done. There are other occasions when the sensation has been quite a bit warmer, and I wonder what that indicates.

RAJ   Paul, as you were aware in the back of your mind while you asked that whole question, this is something that you must do based entirely on what you feel from within yourself. I cannot answer that question any further.

PAUL   Thank you, Raj. My next question is: What are the dynamics of the relationship between myself, my wife, and my mother?

RAJ   Yes, Paul, the answer is simpler than you are anticipating. I am glad that you are getting into the habit, when you find yourself not being able to hear me, to automatically assume that the answer is simple. This immediately makes you able to hear what I have to say. You are learning that well.

Before I answer your question, I want you to learn to use your "dinner bells" in exactly the same manner. In other words, "dinner bells" are solely for the purpose of having you move to a different point of view — that Place wherein the answer or enlightenment can be discerned. It can be done just as easily as you are now finding it is for you to hear me when you have not been able to.

Now, I will respond to your question. Relationships are constituted of the Harmonies and interchanges of the one infinite One — Your Self from your point of view, Susan's Self from her point of view, your mother's Self from her point of view. As I have said before, if you could clearly see what is happening from a Fourth-dimensional standpoint, you would see that the apparent three-dimensional relationship is totally Harmonious. What we see "out there" is a finite view of the Total Oneness and Harmony of our Being.

If we insist on leaving the position of seeing out from Mind, and choose to view it the way it *appears,* we set ourselves up for sharp jabs. This is because "personal" relationships are, in themselves, unkind and harsh misperceptions of our Wholeness. This is why personal relationships are perhaps the most unsatisfying experiences we can endure.

You see, it is one thing to see things three-dimensionally, as though separate, isolated, and independent. It is entirely another thing to see them personally. It is quite possible to view things three-dimensionally without seeing them from a personal frame of reference, but a personal sense of things always includes a great and terrible sense of egotism — always with self-righteousness.

The personal sense of things becomes a sieve through which is run our experiences of our "others," and even our experience of our world. This causes a highly unnatural misalignment of our perception of them. You could compare it to intense inbreeding of animals, in which the breed becomes so refined as to no longer have a broad enough base to support it. It becomes weak and idiotic. This is why relationships based on a personal sense cannot stand, or withstand, the normal dynamics of Life.

Having been so finely misaligned by having been put through the sieve of egotism and self–righteousness, the downfall of such personal relationships does not occur comfortably. They come apart only with great distress being experienced on the part of the one indulging in that personal sense.

The only solution which can actually resolve a relationship problem is for the one experiencing discomfort to drop the personal sense of involvement, thus resolving it actually back into the normal Universal Harmonies that constitute the existence of the individualities involved. This is a phrase which you have heard many times before, but it has been unclear to you how to do it. Trying to lay down a personal sense is like trying to lay down a piece of flypaper. The more you attempt to put it down, the more firmly it sticks!

The only way to lay down a personal sense of things is to go within to that Place of quietness and attentiveness, and listen for the influx of your Being as *It sees Itself* from Its infinite standpoint. This can be achieved through meditation, if one is a beginner. Here, you not only see things as they are, but you experience them as they are. In that experience you cannot find a trace of that personal sense of things from which you had been suffering.

In this specific instance, when it comes to you, your wife, and your mother, you are all cooperating together in one harmonious activity. *Actually!* Each of you is experiencing your relationship with the other according to either your enlightenment or your belief. Nevertheless, you are experiencing it for the purpose of your Divine Fulfillment. It is moving each of you to the point of consciously discovering your Freedom from the personal sense.

Paul, you are finding — as you have more and more experience being out from Mind — that you are beginning to be able to see the three-dimensional mental structure your mother has created for herself in order to supply herself with the feeling of security. You are also seeing that by simply being out from Mind, you may play some part in the collapse of that structure. In the removal of it, your mother will thus be free to discern the already orderly landscape and functioning of her Being, whether she is consciously being orderly or not from a three–dimensional standpoint.

You are correct not to push it, but to Be It intuitively.

Susan is entirely responsible for how she experiences this whole thing in her life. Having had this opportunity to let go of the personal control of her environment, she has the capacity to understand that much compassion is appropriate at this point toward the one she calls her mother–in–law. She also needs to love herself, and be compassionate toward herself, as she seemingly awkwardly looses her hold on her three–dimensional environment.

There is strong personal sense on both sides of the fence between Susan and the one she calls her mother–in–law. Certainly, no one need be in a position of pointing a finger. In fact, it must be recognized that the pointing of fingers is part of the whole hideous, ugly personal sense of Life.

Paul, as you are aware, there has been a personal relationship between you and your mother, not on antagonistic grounds, but on the grounds of love. You truly are beginning to see that that personal sense has blinded you to perceiving Reality. You are learning that, as you are able to abide as Conscious Being, both the dynamics of the illusion, as well as the Actual Reality, are becoming clear. You are being able to move around and through the belief as experienced by this one called your mother. You will be able to help topple this belief structure that is entertained by your mother as you become more familiar with operating out from Mind. This will occur without the process destroying her.

As I said before, the resolution of this problem will be achieved by going within to that Place, as Conscious Being, and abiding there as consistently as possible. This is the only way in which the perspective can be gained to resolve this situation, and do it in harmony with the Reality of Being. Nothing else will actually solve it.

PAUL   Raj, I have no other questions at the moment, so I will sign off for now, and I anticipate that I will get back with you a little bit later. Thank you very much.

RAJ   You are welcome, Paul. Good afternoon.

February 21, 1982
Sunday
(Evening)

PAUL   Raj, it is only half an hour until Monday. This is when you said that I would be surprisingly able to cope with the demands made on me, and be able to remain observing and experiencing my life from the standpoint of Conscious Being. I hope you're right. And I hope that the growth over the past three days has been what you anticipated. I feel as though I could have done more. But, be that as it may, you are aware that Susan is highly incensed at the things you had to say in our conversation today. I will have to admit that her response is bothering me.

Do you have anything to say about this situation?

RAJ   Paul, I am not here to act as a marriage counselor. I am here to act as a Guide in your development of your ability and capacity as Fourth-dimensional Man. In spite of what Susan might like, you are not here to cater to her insistence on operating from a three-dimensional-only level. Actually, Susan knows better, but she is not willing to integrate her Knowing with her Being, and act out from that point.

You feel that she is making demands on you by her insistence to hold you to her finite view, and pull you out from your experience of being as Conscious Being.

The fact is that you are doing well at remaining centered at the Door of your own infinite Wisdom and Understanding. You do not need to be afraid that you will slip.

You are learning a lesson that is difficult for you: You must

99

let the three–dimensional frame of reference "do its little jig" until it wears itself out and gives up.

In the meantime, you must actively remain at the point of being as Conscious Being. Listen attentively to Mind's unfolding of Itself as It *is*, right where it looks like the jig is going on. To paraphrase a statement you are familiar with, "You must see the Fourth–dimensional Reality right where the three–dimensional frame of reference sees itself." Seeing the Reality, you will not be confused by the jig. Neither will you be moved by its claims. In order to do this, you must be willing to stand at the Doorway where Being's view of Itself is what is seen.

You have the strength to do this, and you are willing. I advise you to do it steadfastly.

In regard to tomorrow and its demands, you are already aware of things you need to do. Do them. But do them as Conscious Being. You are getting quite acclimated to being from that Place. Continue to do so. Take one step at a time. Keep it simple. If it claims to be complex, keep it simple.

I want you to begin to let your experience teach you. I would like for you to back off to one conversation a day with me. You have learned how to get into that Place and stay there, and how to get back if you need to.

Now I want you to begin to do that. Experience the events of your day, each day, from that environment. You will begin to find your experience explaining itself. You will find your enlightenment to be equally as meaningful as our many conversations have seemed to you. As you have already discovered, your daily experience supplies you with optimum opportunity to learn about your Self, and about the places in which you need further growth.

I am not going anywhere. I want you to give your attention to your Self as It is living Its infinite unfoldment, and begin to find that It is an ever present and excellent teacher.

This will leave us free to go on to other matters which need your attention. It will also allow you to discover how everything we have been talking about relates to your daily life. This will probably be the most valuable lesson you will ever learn.

I see that you do not really have any other questions. I will say good night for now, and look forward to our conversation tomorrow.

February 23, 1982
Tuesday
(Midnight)

PAUL   This morning I am not going to ask any questions, because I have the feeling from what you said last night that you have things that you want to talk about. So I am simply going to be quiet and listen.

RAJ   Thank you, Paul. We are now going to consider a number of things which are necessary to the fulfillment of your Purpose at this time. I want you to be willing to consider these things, since they are essential to your growth.

Right now, I want you to take a moment to become even quieter than you are, and get into that Place very solidly.

[There followed a short meditation.]

PAUL   All right. Is that all right, Raj?

RAJ   No, a little bit further.

PAUL   [Further meditation.]

Okay.

RAJ   That's fine, Paul.

PAUL   [Further meditation.]

Raj, this is feeling too deep for me. I am afraid that I will lose contact entirely and forget to use the microphone.

RAJ   Don't worry. Everything will go correctly.

PAUL   All right.

      [Further meditation.]

      I don't understand this, Raj. Why so deep?

RAJ   In order to have you extremely flexible and capable of translating my communication with utmost accuracy. I do not want any personal reaction on your part. That is why.

PAUL   Okay.

      [Further meditation.]

RAJ   Thank you, Paul. This is much better.

PAUL   You're welcome, Raj. You may begin whenever you like.

RAJ   Paul, we are coming very close to the time that we have spoken of before. Knowing that there is some confusion on your part, and some slight reluctance to believe it, I need you to be out of the picture as much as possible, in the sense of resisting what I say. You are very willing and trusting, and that helps a great deal.

      Paul, do not tense up as I begin to speak.

PAUL   [Some further meditation.]

      If you get me any more relaxed, I'm going to be like a limp dishrag here. I won't hardly be able to use the microphone.

RAJ   Do not concern yourself, Paul. I will see to it that the microphone works. You may let go totally.

PAUL   [Further meditation.]

RAJ   Paul, you are too tired tonight to proceed further. I want you to go to bed now and get a good night's sleep. I want you to contact me in the morning. Thank you. Do not be apprehensive at all. Relax and let go with all your heart, if that is what you feel.

      Until tomorrow morning, I shall say good night.

PAUL   Thank you, Raj. Good night.[1]

---

[1] During this entire conversation, I was aware of the presence of three masculine individualities behind me and to my left. I never looked at them.

February 23, 1982
Tuesday
(Afternoon)

PAUL Good afternoon, Raj.

RAJ Good afternoon, Paul. Thank you for following my instructions. I am going to begin by having you relax once again. When I tell you to pick up the microphone, please do so. In the meantime — yes, after taking your shoes off — please begin to relax and do as I say.

PAUL [Period of meditation.]

Raj, is there something I am not understanding here? Why does it seem to be taking such a long time?

RAJ Paul, understanding has nothing to do with this. When you asked the question, you were referring to the three-dimensional mind understanding. That is why I responded in the way I did. What is happening this morning is that you are simply putting yourself at the point where you can truly understand experientially, throughout your total Being, just exactly what is occurring and what we are moving toward.

Now, I would like you to continue to stay in that Place, remembering to keep that fine balance between deep meditation and still being conscious of your surroundings sensorily. Thank you, Paul.

PAUL May I sit on the floor?

RAJ Yes, you may.

PAUL   Thank you.

        [Long period of meditation.]

        Raj, I am feeling disappointed that I am blocking something, or not able to do what you have expected this morning.

RAJ   Paul, do not feel disappointed, since we will continue until we do it. I do not expect you to sit there until doomsday, but I would like to have you sit down later today, or this evening, and we will continue.

        You are correct that some effort is being made to clear your throat of the excess phlegm. In that way you will not spontaneously begin coughing and disrupt the flow of energy around you at an inopportune time.

        Again, do not feel disappointed. You are not inconveniencing me or anyone else. You did well this morning.

        Paul, do not conceptualize and use your imagination unnecessarily today. Stay in that Place to the very best of your ability.

February 23, 1982
Tuesday
(Evening)

PAUL I feel, perhaps, more ready than I did this morning, although I was eager at that time. I think I am beginning to understand that what is needed here is for me to really be willing to let go. So, here I am. I am ready to do whatever you would like to do tonight.

RAJ Thank you, Paul. You see, Paul, the issue here is not a matter of your being willing to let go and put yourself under *my* control, or anyone else's control. It truly is a matter of letting go as you do when you are driving the car. It is letting yourself flow with the Universal Harmonies. When you do this, you leave the door open for Infinity to unfold in all of Its marvelous aspects.

I do not want you to conceptualize in any way how these Universal Harmonies will appear. Except, I will guarantee to you that as they unfold themselves as Yourself and your Conscious Experience of Being, they will clarify answers to questions you have been having, and about which you are curious.

So, Paul, with that I am going to ask you to once again go into a deeper state of relaxation. As I said this morning, no matter how deep you go, keep aware of that fine edge of discernment wherein you do not lose your awareness of where you are sensorily.

Go ahead now and begin.

PAUL All right.

[Period of meditation.]

Do you want me to continue to hold the microphone while I am doing this?

RAJ   Yes, I do.

PAUL   Very well.

[Period of meditation.]

RAJ   Notice that you have some expectations. They get in the way of the quietness. This is why I do not want you to conceptualize. It is also the reason I do not want you reading other literature, or taking in media information.

I am not criticizing. I know you have steered clear of those. I want you to continue as you are right now. Let everything go in terms of thoughts and cognitive processes. I would like for you to be tuned in completely to my communication with you.

PAUL   Very well. It definitely seems to help if we are talking, because there is a focal point. When we are not talking, there is no such focus, no flow of anything, and it seems to be an experience of jumbled thoughts.

RAJ   I understand, Paul, but right now, I want you to find that quietness without the focal point of our conversation.

PAUL   All right.

[Period of meditation.]

Raj, is it clear to you that I am really wanting to cooperate fully, willingly, and I really don't want anything to get in the way of this? I'm actually afraid things will get in the way. I earnestly and really do want to grow.

RAJ   Paul, of this I have no doubt. Do not concern yourself that I might misunderstand your motive, and your desire, and your love.

PAUL   I'm glad to hear that. It seems to me we have a new format here, as opposed to the first three weeks of our conversations. We did not use meditation as a major portion of the time we spent together, and you shared many ideas and learning experiences with me.

As of yesterday, you are not explaining things to me but wish me to do something. Can you explain to me what the thrust of this new format is?

RAJ   No, I cannot. This must be experiential from the word "go."

PAUL   I understand. Okay. Is there any way you can help me?

RAJ   I *am* helping, Paul. In fact, you are getting a wonderful amount of help. You might simply be aware that you are surrounded by Love. It is supporting you in letting go, and in not being concerned or afraid.

PAUL   Thank you very much.

RAJ   Paul, I am aware that you are afraid that something startling or unreal — something so far out that it will seem like it is a hallucination — is going to occur. I assure you that we are directing our energies right now at the experience of Reality, not hallucination. It is not something foreign to you. You are all that is going on, as Conscious Being *being* Itself infinitely. You do not need to be afraid of Yourself, no matter how It unfolds Itself in its infinite aspect. Relax, and feel the Love.

That's it, Paul. Invite that feeling of fluidity and calm infinity.

PAUL   [Period of meditation.]

RAJ   Do not feel unworthy or small. It is Yourself you are faced with, and you are infinite, without measure. You are not too small or too big. It is your own marvelous Infinity that is before you.

PAUL   Why do I feel anxiety when I am not thinking anything in particular?

RAJ   You might say it is sort of a programmed, gut–level recognition that you are getting into free territory, which normally is not allowed by the three–dimensional consciousness. It provides a safeguard against such awareness. You are simply going to have to ignore it. Let it be. Simply proceed in the direction you chose.

PAUL   Thank you. I would like very much to meet the three gentlemen who were here early this morning.

RAJ   Your desire is felt. Stay with it.

PAUL   Raj, I am beginning to sense an aimless drifting, a wandering of thoughts. It certainly does not seem to be cohesive. I do not feel I'm moving in the right direction.

RAJ   Paul, each time you do this, you will find that you will pass through this level. Once again, you must keep your focus on where you are going. You will be able to use this "strata of jabber"[1] as an indication of your movement. When you move through it, it will tell you that you are still progressing.

PAUL   Thank you, Raj.

RAJ   Yes, we are attempting to remove the phlegm from your throat, and I think we may have succeeded. Do not be afraid to move around, Paul. Movement does not mean that you are not in a deep meditation. Deep meditation does not mean that you are out of touch with the first three dimensions. It simply means that you are very solidly ensconced in the Fourth, and, thereby, experiencing all four dimensions Fourth-dimensionally. This is why I want you to remain sensorily aware.

Right now it seems very foreign to you, but it is only because you are new at it experientially. It will not always require of you that you be alone. As you gain familiarity with deeply being in the Fourth-dimensional frame of reference, you will begin to experience it from *Its* reference points. You will be quite free enough to move, act, and live in a manner that those seeing three-dimensionally will not find questionable.

PAUL   I would like to get back to my desire to meet the three gentlemen who were here last night. Am I pushing things to do that?

RAJ   No, Paul, you are not. You may do so.

PAUL   Very well. I will.

Raj, I am now beginning to have the feeling that once again it's not going to work, yet I have no need to stop. I do not feel tired, and I have nothing else I need to do. Is this also something which arises, and through which I have to pass?

RAJ   No, not as though it were a level that you will pass through on each occasion. It is a scurrilous thought inserted haphazardly into the position where you find yourself right now. It is to be ignored. Simply continue on.

PAUL   You are saying that it is perfectly all right to move around?

RAJ   Yes.

PAUL   Should I keep the movements minimal, or can I do as much as stretch?

RAJ   If you will keep your focus point on what you are feeling from your vantage point, and not let your thought rest on the physical sensation as you move, you may move without restriction.

PAUL   Thank you, Raj. I am going to return to my desire to meet the three gentlemen. May I ask whether there is a mutual interest on their part to meet with me?

RAJ   There is.

PAUL   Thank you, Raj.

[Period of meditation.]

RAJ   That's right, Paul. You are getting the idea — that the thoughts are not there for the purpose of being registered by you. You keep to your own fundamental inward Self-purpose.

PAUL   Thank you, Raj.

RAJ   You see how the dog's barking tends to cause you to feel responsibility for getting up and letting her in? Notice that you were more ready to do that than to continue. Also, notice that you chose to continue. That was a good choice, Paul.

PAUL   I feel like I am beginning to succeed somewhat.

RAJ   That's fine, Paul. Continue.

PAUL   [Further meditation.]

Raj, it is getting so deep that my arms are relaxing and the microphone slips away from my face, but I feel that I am doing a fairly good job *at having unnecessary activity...*

RAJ   There! It just happened briefly. You completely lost all connection with anything except the words, and the words just flowed.

PAUL   Is that what I'm after?

RAJ   Yes, for the time being we will say that is what we're after. For the purposes of the transcript, it amounted to about the last four words of the sentence — just prior to my interrupting. Do not attempt to make sense out of the nonsense. It was the "happening" of saying words for which you were not responsible that we are after.

Let's continue.

PAUL   Am I not to bother with the desire to meet with the three men who were here last night?

RAJ   You may continue to express your desire.

PAUL   I do not sense their presence in the room this evening.

RAJ   They are not here at the moment.

Paul, I want you to continue in the direction that we have been working, for right now. At the same time, you may desire to meet with these gentlemen.

PAUL   Okay.

RAJ   Paul, what we are doing here is experientially familiarizing you with some new territories of your Being. Continue.

PAUL   [Further meditation.]

Raj, would it interfere greatly if I did go let the dog in?

RAJ   Not really, no. Go right ahead.

PAUL   Thank you.

[I let the dog in.]

Raj, it appeared to me that last night the purpose was to make contact with the three gentlemen that were here. It was also my perception that, when it appeared as though the contact was going to be made, Maitreya was at the point of "intending" to be on His way. That was my sensing. Was that accurate?

RAJ   That is accurate.

PAUL   Is that not the intent this evening?

RAJ   I am availing myself of every opportunity for uncovering to you the totality of your experience as Conscious Being; however, that still remains the purpose.

PAUL   What do I need to do in order for that to be accomplished? Is that not why I am receiving help, as you said?

RAJ   Yes, Paul, that is. And to answer the first part of your question, you can facilitate this by once again getting into that deeper calm, and have your desire on the back burner.

PAUL   Very well, Raj. Does it really depend on me this much? If these are Masters and are already present and appearing to others — whom I'm assuming don't even know who They are and haven't had to do all these things — then why can't They simply appear to me?

RAJ   Paul, you are trying to reason this thing out and justify your wish for an easy way out. It doesn't matter under what circumstances any other person may have seen or met Them. All that matters is the work you and I are doing together. It is not for you to be able to understand ahead of time.

Now, let's get back to work.

PAUL   Okay.

RAJ   Paul, you are frustrating yourself by displaying a desire to control what is going on so it may be conducive to accomplishing the purposes of this conversation. You want it quiet. The dog wants to bark. It is pointing out to what degree you want to retain some control.

Let. Let. Let. Let the dog bark. Let yourself feel anxious. Let yourself not feel anxious. Let the dog not bark. Let whatever comes come!

PAUL   Okay, Raj.

RAJ   Do not judge. No value judgments at this time, please!

PAUL   I will do my best.

RAJ   Paul, in response to an unspoken question, certainly the three gentlemen could make themselves known to you at any time they wished. However, if they were to do it right now, it would deprive you of the opportunity for an essential point of growth, and they are not willing to do that.

Let us stick with the desire to communicate with them, and let us work on becoming most relaxed and being willing to let go of your control.

PAUL   Do I have much further to go?

RAJ   It is all relative, Paul. But not really. If you would like to continue, we can.

PAUL   I would.

RAJ   Very well, go ahead.

PAUL   [Further meditation.]

[A conversation with a woman named Almee began during the meditation. Raj indicated that she was, indeed, speaking to me and that it was all right. She suggested that I sort of sit back and relax. Now, continuing. . .]

[Addressing Almee.] Almee?

ALMEE   Yes.

PAUL   Would you continue, please?

ALMEE   Yes, thank you. I am going to suggest that you sit back — that's it. Relax. I'm going to suggest also that you turn off the light.

PAUL   [Light is turned off.]

Almee, I have turned the light off and have gotten comfortable.

ALMEE   Very well. And now I'm going to suggest that you not be quite so heavy about what is going on. You feel something important is occurring. Therefore, you feel that you must be very serious. Although what is happening is important for you, it is not something that requires you to be so heavy. I want you to take it with a little lighter touch.

PAUL   Okay.

[Addressing Raj.] Raj, how does that sound to you?

RAJ   That sounds like excellent instruction to me. Let us proceed now.

PAUL   I perceive a difference between you, Raj, and Almee. I don't know whether it is in you, or whether it is in the way I perceive, but it is interesting.

RAJ   Paul, there's simply a difference in Nature, a difference in masculine and feminine sensing of things. I am glad to have the balance here.

PAUL   Does this mean that Almee is also a Guide, that I now have two Guides? Or is she just assisting here?

RAJ   It means that she is assisting. For the time being, if you wish to converse with her, you will find yourself able to. I remain your Guide. Almee will assist when she feels that you will benefit from the added dimension of her nature. We are fully cooperating together at this point in working with you. A time will come when she will no longer be able to converse with you, because it will not fulfill the purpose any longer.

PAUL   [Addressing Almee.] Almee, I am very happy to meet you.

ALMEE   Likewise, I'm sure.

PAUL   [Addressing Raj.] Raj, what do I do now? Shall we continue?

RAJ   By all means. Give it a lighter touch, as Almee has said. Go ahead and get into that even more relaxed state and Place than you are right now, but without that touch of heaviness to it that you have had so far.

PAUL   Thank you, Raj. I will.

         [Further meditation.]

         Raj, do you have any objection if I stop for now and continue tomorrow?

RAJ   No, I have no objection. You will find that you have learned quite a bit this evening. You should not feel that stopping will shortchange you at all.

         I would like to talk with you tomorrow at your earliest convenience. I realize that you have some things to take care of. Take care of them, and I will talk to you after that.

         Good night, Paul.

PAUL   Good night, Raj, and good night, Almee. I am glad to meet you.

---

1   Each time I would meditate, I would "pass through" a flow of random thoughts, usually regarding things needing to be done in my daily life, or that I had forgotten to do.

February 24, 1982
Wednesday

PAUL   Tonight, Raj, I am just going to let the fact that I am interested in meeting the three men who were here yesterday — I am just going to let that desire rest. They know it, and I know it, and I am going to drop it in the sense of trying to cause it or help it or facilitate its occurring. I'm going to try to get back into just doing what we were doing before — and work with you and Almee, and anyone else who is there. And so, I'm ready.

RAJ   Good, Paul. We are going to begin this evening by going into a deeper relaxation than you are in right now, just as we did last night. Once again, I will remind you to remain in touch with being sensorily aware of your surroundings, as you are experiencing them right now. I do not want you to become unconscious of them.

Go ahead.

PAUL   Okay.

[Period of meditation.]

Raj, although I feel I am getting into a deeper place, I feel a very strong clutching in the area of my diaphragm. This does not strike me as the strata you were speaking of last night and, following your suggestion, I am letting it be clenched if it wants. If it doesn't want, I'll let it not want and just have that feeling of "letting."

RAJ   Paul, that is fine. Go on.

PAUL   [Further meditation.]

Raj, here we are in nonsense land again. I am going to continue on through.

I will interject that I am very happy to be able to say that both of my girls have now established communication with their Guides. On top of that, Susan has made contact with her Guide, and I am very happy about this.

Now I will continue.

RAJ   Thank you, Paul. And thank you for sharing that with me.

PAUL   Raj, one question: I am wondering if the purpose here is to get to that point where I can let go absolutely, totally, and completely, and be able to have a longer period of time than the amount that passed last night when I was speaking but was not being responsible for any of the words? Is this point of relaxation and giving up — letting — is this something that it would help for me to know that we were working for, or at least to be heading in that direction?

RAJ   Paul, that will happen spontaneously. You may keep that in the back of your mind as a goal, but do not mistake it as being the end purpose. There will be far more avenues for us to explore beyond that. For right now, if you want to see that as a way station experience of your Infinity and head there, please go right ahead. As I said, it is not the final destination.

PAUL   Okay, Raj. Thank you.

[Continued meditation.]

Raj, on the one hand it feels like I am doing what I am supposed to be doing, except this last time I did forget about paying attention to my surroundings and staying in touch with them sensorily. But I do not feel that I am getting anywhere yet.

RAJ   Paul, you do not have any measuring stick to use, so you have no basis for a conclusion. Please continue. You are doing just fine.

PAUL   Okay.

[Period of further meditation.]

Okay, Raj. I was doing some sort of thinking, but I am not conscious of what it was. Then, suddenly my body was jolted, as it were, and my finger pressed down the button on the microphone. Of course, I immediately released it. I am now reporting to you what happened. I would have interpreted it as being the sort of jerk that occurs sometimes as I am drifting off to sleep. Would you care to comment?

RAJ   Paul, this was an involuntary response. I am not going to disclose what it was at the moment. Just let it be something that you are aware of having experienced, and let us move on.

PAUL   Okay.

    [Further meditation.]

RAJ   If it happens again, attempt to flow with it.

PAUL   All right.

    [Continuation of meditation.]

Raj, would it be a good idea for me not to be quite so physically relaxed? Should I perhaps sit up straight and have my body somewhat more awake or attentive?

RAJ   No, Paul. I want you to be as totally relaxed as possible while still being actively alert to everything.

PAUL   All right, Raj.

    [Further meditation.]

Raj, I am getting various and assorted thoughts relating to things in my everyday life. I don't know why they're there. They seem to be activity thoughts requiring some response from me, or some action. I am not going to pay any attention to them, but continue through.

RAJ   Very well, Paul.

    [Continuation of meditation.]

PAUL   You do want me to continue into a more relaxed state, do you not?

RAJ   Yes, I do.

PAUL Very well.

[Further meditation.]

RAJ Let the dog bark, Paul. It is all You. Let your Self be what it is. Be willingness itself.

[Continued meditation.]

PAUL Raj, it seems to me I am past the jabber strata. I am continuing to have an intent of moving, and evidently am moving, but I do not know where. And that is all right.

RAJ Yes, it is all right, Paul. Go right ahead.

That is good, Paul. You will do well to remember to let your facial muscles and scalp muscles relax.

PAUL Raj, am I actually accomplishing anything? Have I actually been doing any growing since Monday? I don't have any landmarks to use to tell whether I have or not.

RAJ Paul, you are making progress. You are becoming more naturally familiar with where you are located, and what the signposts are of your movements into a very deep meditative state. You are able to maintain it while being sensorily aware of your surroundings. Our goal at the moment is to familiarize you with yourself in this area of your Conscious Being. You will remember that early on I told you that you would become familiar with the "inhabitants" and the "structures" of Conscious Being. That is, indeed, what you are doing right now.

Now, I would like you to be quiet once again and be aware.

PAUL Okay.

[Continued meditation.]

I will have to admit that it is a very wonderful state of calmness and peace...

RAJ Paul, I do not want you to talk right now. I want you to feel it. I want you to perceive it. Do not talk away the experience by keeping your mouth flapping like this.

PAUL I get the picture. Thank you, Raj.

[Further meditation.]

RAJ   Very good, Paul. Allow the barking. Allow it all. Let. Let. Let.

PAUL   Raj, it seems as though I am involuntarily coming back to the surface, so to speak. Is that all right?

RAJ   That is all right. Allow it. Do not judge it. Stay with the process, and do not pay any attention to the content unless I tell you otherwise.

PAUL   All right, Raj. Thank you.

[Further meditation.]

RAJ   Paul, although you find yourself coming back to the surface — which simply means you are beginning to feel normal — your point of awareness is not coming back to the surface. It is staying right where it was. Just observe and do not judge.

PAUL   All right.

[Continued meditation.]

Raj, is there anyone with me in the room?

RAJ   No, Paul, there is not. If you would like to look around to verify it, you may. Do not let your gaze, nor the focus of your attention, become impressed by anything it sees. Do it, but keep your point of awareness as Conscious Being placed where it is in this place that you call "mellow."

PAUL   All right, Raj. It is not easy to keep my focal point where it is when I open my eyes, but I shall do it slowly.

RAJ   That is a good idea, Paul.

PAUL   Raj, would you like me to attempt to keep my eyes open?

RAJ   You may attempt it for a few minutes here, but I think we will not continue it longer than that.

PAUL   May I move some?

RAJ   As I said last night, as long as your focal point does not move to any particular sensation you experience, but remains where it is as you move, then you may move all you like.

PAUL   Okay, Raj. Let me know when you want me to close my eyes.

RAJ   I shall, Paul.

PAUL   Is this a form of self–hypnosis, Raj?

RAJ   No, it most definitely is not, nor is it a trance of any kind.

PAUL   Thank you, Raj. Is it worthwhile to pay attention to how my body feels without putting my consciousness in my body?

RAJ   Go right ahead.

PAUL   All right. Raj, would you like me to continue with this conversation period as long as I am able this evening?

RAJ   Yes, I would.

PAUL   Very well, I shall. And during this whole time period you want me to remain in touch with my surroundings sensorily — is that correct?

RAJ   That is exactly correct.

PAUL   Thank you.

[Further meditation.]

Raj, I find as I have taken maybe three or four minutes to observe myself, the room, what it feels like to move, et cetera, that the meditation has slowly become shallower. Do you want me to continue observing, or would you like me to — what would you like me to do?

RAJ   Paul, I would like for you to stop observing yourself outwardly and begin once again to go into a deeper meditative state.

PAUL   Very well, Raj.

[Continued meditation.]

Raj, that was a very deep meditation. I believe I lost touch with my surroundings. At least, they were not clearly in my thought. I am simply reporting these things to you. At this point I feel the need to discontinue for the evening and pick up tomorrow morning at some time, if that's all right with you.

RAJ That's fine, Paul, and yes, it's fine if we have our conversation in the morning.

I know that you want to know if we may speak more than once tomorrow. I will decide that when tomorrow gets here.

You may not think you are learning much. You may not think that anything is happening at all. However, Paul, you are learning a great deal. Do not judge from your lack of experience and lack of perspective. I tell you that you are, indeed, learning much.

Paul, don't worry. You are doing fine. You will learn what you need to learn. Everything is going very well.

February 25, 1982
Thursday

PAUL   Raj, before we begin, I want to thank you for giving me permission to go ahead and read Mr. Creme's book.[1] After reading it, I am especially grateful that you had me wait. In the past two and a half weeks there has been so much growth on my part that I read it entirely differently. It has saved me a roller coaster ride, an inner roller coaster ride, at least, for sure.

RAJ   You are welcome, Paul.

PAUL   Are you a Master?

RAJ   Yes, Paul, I am.

PAUL   Thank you, Raj. I didn't have enough nerve to ask in the past. If you had said yes, that in itself would have thrown me for a loop.

As I said last night, I hope that I have not in any way offended you. I have not meant to be unmannerly. Yet, at the same time, I have felt that you did not want me to be solemn and formal. Unless you tell me otherwise, I will continue as I have in the past — except I think I will tend to take what you have to say with even greater appreciation.

RAJ   Paul, you are right. I do not want you to become formal and stilted with all the folderol of "Master" and "student." It simply delays and gets in the way of simple, straightforward, direct communication. I recognize your recognition of what I am and who I am, and that is all that matters.

Paul, I am aware that you are beginning to wonder whether the name you have for me is, in fact, my name. Use that name for the time being, because it is truly not an issue at this point. It will not serve you in any way to believe that it is other than what you think it is. I say that without meaning to imply anything other than what I just said.

PAUL   Very well. It truly makes no difference to me. I was just curious.

I do have lots of questions, but I know you will cover them sooner or later. They are not getting in the way of anything at the moment. So, I would simply like to progress with whatever you have in mind.

RAJ   Thank you, Paul.

PAUL   Raj, I am seeing what looks like either the end of a wrench or a C-clamp with windings of brass wire around it, much like the windings on a motor. Is this something which should have significance for me, or just a figment of my own imagination?

RAJ   Paul, this is indeed an image which I am providing you. The focal point of the image should be the windings of brass wire. You are correct in that they approximate the meaning of that portion of a motor.

The backwards C-shaped portion around which the brass wire is precisely wound represents Consciousness. The brass wire represents the field through which Consciousness functions. This function is of a vibrational nature, causing the field represented by the brass coiling to harmonize vibrationally and appear to take on the structure of the conscious activity with which it is harmonizing.

Now you must let go of the picture — it cannot be used throughout the following illustration. It was simply a technique to establish the fundamental idea I want to discuss here.

Paul, the energy field which is activated by the activity of Consciousness — by that I mean the presence of specific ideas and concepts — is constituted of the Universal Substance with which you had a conversation the other day. The impetus which gives Substance rise to give form where form has not been is the activity of Consciousness.

As you remember from your conversation the other day, if the activity of consciousness arises out of a three-dimensional frame of reference, which for the most part is constituted of beliefs and reactions, the Universal Substance cannot respond. It is required by its Nature to respond only to that which is in harmony with your Being.

It is for this reason that Substance must be activated from the standpoint of your experience of Being as Conscious Being. In other words, the activation of that energy field called Substance, in order to be fulfilled, must originate while you are experiencing your Being as Conscious Being, Fourth-dimensional Awareness, Awareness from that Place. For the sake of convenience, you can call that Place the Center of your Being.

Mind you, that is not truly where the Center of your Being is, but the concept has meaning for you at this point, and I shall allow it.

This should clarify a point for you. Whatever is set into motion from the standpoint of Fourth-dimensional Conscious Being *must* move into manifestation. Whatever originates from a three-dimensional frame of reference does not cause anything to move into manifestation, nor does it hinder anything moving into manifestation. Cause does not lie positively or negatively within the three-dimensional, or finite, frame of reference. This is a great point to understand and keep in mind. I would like you, on your own time, to consider the ramifications of that point.

PAUL   Raj, this brings up, indirectly, a point that I would like to understand or get clarification on. If, as you say, you are a Master, and if I am your student — something for which I find myself immensely grateful — is it true that you have some purpose for me to fulfill in the service of mankind and in the fulfillment of my Being?

RAJ   It most certainly does.

PAUL   Then I will unhesitatingly cooperate with whatever that might be, and will wait until you feel it is appropriate to inform me of it.

RAJ   Paul, that is indeed gratifying in ways that are... in ways that you are not capable of verbalizing. This is why you are having difficulty at the moment.

I can see that you are aware that such a commitment may not be a bed of feathers, and yet you are still willing.

We will not discuss in this conversation what that service may initially be, but we will get to it shortly. I could not indicate to you what you were needed for until you arrived at that point of inner growth where you were willing to offer. It is with no small sense of Joy that I accept your offer.

You had another part to your question.

PAUL   Yes, I did. My question is this: If this fulfillment of purpose is to come about, it seems to me that it should not cause a deprivation financially, or in terms of necessities, for myself and my family. Actually, I am not so concerned about myself, but I am concerned that my family shouldn't suffer in any way for my point of unfoldment, and for my desire to serve. I am speaking entirely in terms of the daily necessities of life. I am not talking about whether they are personally happy or unhappy, or pleased, or distressed. That, I understand, is their point of growth and unfoldment.

RAJ   Paul, I just gave you the key to the resolving of that in the illustration and explanation with which we began this conversation. It is very true that I can help. In fact, I am capable of doing whatever is necessary to allow the unhindered progress of what needs to take place according to plan, but I cannot do it at the expense of your own inner growth. This is why I am teaching you how to do it for yourself.

The simple fact is that you are finding that you are on the right track, that you are truly spending the great majority of your days now being out from Mind, more or less, and it is daily becoming more. You are perceiving more and more that your world is your Self, appearing to you in Its infinite aspect.

Paul, all of this is constituting the activity of Consciousness which acts according to Law upon the Nature of the Universal Substance of your Being. The correct vision, felt from the standpoint of Reality, must come forth according to Law as that which appears tangibly, three–dimensionally, as the infinitude of your Being.

Remember that once this Law is set into motion, It cannot be stopped from manifesting by any fearful or limited thoughts in which you might indulge from the standpoint of a finite, three–dimensional point of view. Such a point of view cannot be placed at the point of Conscious Being, which is the only Place any action can be set into motion.

As you know, when you are in that Place, it is totally impossible to experience fear, doubt, or any sense of limitation. This is a scientific Law that I am talking about. You can prove it day, after day, after day without fail, because it is Law functioning according to the scientific, principled Nature of Being.

Once you have set a thing into motion by being consciously aware of the Fact from the standpoint of Fourth–dimensional Conscious Being, your only responsibility is to continue forward, being from that point — exactly as you have been doing — without any care or concern as to how or when it will appear.

You must realize that Being functions according to Its own infinite, eternal Harmonies. If that which has been set into motion has not appeared, it is because appearing at that point would not be in harmony with Its unfolding Being. You can trust you do not need it at the moment you are considering the fact that it hasn't yet appeared.

I want you to consider this deeply. I want you to consider it while you are in that Place when we are not talking to each other. I want you to let it unfold its infinite meanings to you before we talk about it again.

You spoke with me a few days ago regarding the possibility of publishing a monthly newsletter of some sort. We very likely will do this, now that you understand the framework within which a purpose may be fulfilled by the publication of such a monthly letter.

Within the next few conversations, I will be able to be more definite with you about it. I would like you to be open to that possibility, and to whatever unfolds to you in the meantime concerning such an activity.

Paul, after having read Mr. Creme's book, you have properly perceived that not everything in the book is to be taken by you as gospel. This is because the book was not written totally for you, but for all ages, all backgrounds, all kinds of people — to meet all levels of thought possible within the scope of such a publication. Even as it is, the book is shocking to much of the general public. For the book to have gone into a consistent exposition of the Realities of Being — and how these Realities are unfolding within individual consciousness — would serve only to further frighten and complicate what, in essence, is an evolution of simplification.

As you know, what is ultimately simple can seem totally impossible. The simple fact is, that as things unfold, as things occur, the clarifications will come along as they are able to be understood and internalized. The evolution will be as natural as possible for all concerned. It will occur in such a way that even when it seems difficult or impossible, the individual will also — at the very same time — experience a realization or a conviction that it *is* possible. This realization will carry him through the difficulty of breaking through his concepts and beliefs.

However, to publish the advanced knowledge without being able to provide the inner conviction that the development is, indeed, possible for that individual, is a great disservice and cannot be done. I know you understand this.

PAUL   Yes, Raj, I understand it very well.

RAJ   I am telling you this because any publication which we might put forth will have to necessarily be far simpler than what you are capable of understanding and have actually experienced. You must be willing to allow the publication to serve the Grand Design. It will not be a publication that you would like to be able to pick up for yourself and grow from. But, then, you don't really need one any more, do you, Paul? Our conversations are sometimes more than you feel like you can take.

I need you to be aware of these points. Mr. Creme is quite aware of far more than what is in that book, and is also quite aware that the book was not written for him.

PAUL   I realize this may seem like quite a leap away from what you've just been speaking about, but may we talk again today and not limit ourselves to this one conversation?

RAJ   We certainly may, Paul.

PAUL   Is it really necessary for us to limit our conversations to one a day, or did you say this so as not to push me beyond the point that I was capable of going?

RAJ I think now that you have grasped the true portent of these communications, we may get together as often as you wish.

PAUL Thank you, Raj.

Raj, is there anything you can do to help me quit smoking, or is there anything you can suggest to me that will allow me to help myself more effectively quit smoking?

RAJ As you asked the question, you realized that all you have to do is set into motion the fact that you are not addicted to cigarettes — or, more positively, that you are free of the desire to smoke cigarettes — and that that is the most effective means you could possibly use in order to give them up.

As I said earlier, they, as part of Your infinitude, are going to be more than willing to cooperate with that desire, placed at the point of Conscious Being, and set into action by the Law of Being. I would suggest that you simply begin to use that facility to see your desires manifest in your life.

You see, Paul, it all has to connect up. There is truly only one thing going on. From the first through the Fourth Dimension there is only one Activity, and that is the Activity occurring as Conscious Being. All of you is always present, and all of you is always functioning; and the manner or the means by which it is present and functioning is the simple practice with which I began our conversation today.

As you can see, this is not self-hypnosis, nor is it an attempt to influence the three-dimensional conscious frame of reference. It does not involve manipulation of things "out there," or ideas within your head. You simply go to the Source, bringing to it the perfect desire. The Law, then, together with the Nature of Substance Itself, takes care of the objects "out there" and the beliefs "in here" — in three-dimensional awareness.

You are going to have fun with that.

Now, although we may speak as often as you like, I may at times (as I am doing right now) terminate a particular conversation so as to bring home a single point and not confuse it by presenting a larger number of various ideas and concepts. So, I will terminate our conversation. I suggest that you type up last night's conversation, plus this one, and then, if you so desire, get back with me.

1   Creme, Benjamin, "The Reappearance of the Christ."

February 26, 1982
Friday
(Afternoon)

PAUL   Raj, a question occurred to me this morning while I was talking with Susan regarding our conversation yesterday — with respect to placing the perfect concept at the point of Reality and allowing the Law, together with the Nature of Substance, to activate that concept and bring it into manifestation.

My question is this: What is the difference between seeing the bills piled on the table and going out into the world to get a job in order to pay them, as compared to seeing the bills on the table, going within to that Place, stating the Fact and the need at that point, so that income or whatever will appear three–dimensionally so that they can be paid?

It strikes me as attempting to deal with a three–dimensional need in a three–dimensional way, but trying to do it at the point of Conscious Being. I am wondering whether or not that is the Fourth–dimensional way of doing it after all?

RAJ   Paul, this is a very good question. You see, it is clearly a matter of learning the difference between objective and subjective. The fact is that there is basically no difference between the two approaches, except that of the matter of placement, together with what you do after the Law has been invoked by your statement of the fact.

The difference lies in the approach which is being taken, and in the frame of reference which is involved here. You *are not* seeing a need and immediately feeling that it cannot be met, and therefore reacting to your conclusion. You *are* at a point

132

of recognizing that the One is the Many, that you are, indeed, the world you walk through. This is a significant change or difference in standpoint from that of the three-dimensional-only standpoint.

You are then going into that Place and stating the correct Fact about what appears to be incorrect in the three-dimensional frame of reference.

Then, if you are wise, you remain in that Place and continue on living your life from the standpoint of the fulfilled Fact.

It is well for you to realize also, Paul, that when you see the bills on the table you are not seeing them from a three-dimensional-only standpoint. You are rather consistently being out from Mind, and as you well know, from that vantage point you *can* see the bills on the table, and you can see what they claim to say about your financial well-being. You will have to admit that your response to them lately has not been a three-dimensional response (reactive). You have seen and dealt with it from the Fourth-dimensional standpoint. You have left it and moved on from within the Fourth-dimensional frame of reference. There is nothing three-dimensional about it. It only appears to be similar, and this must be clear to you.

I would suggest that you have another conversation with your Supply for further clarification.

PAUL   May I do that right now, Raj?

RAJ   Yes, you may.

PAUL   [Addressing Supply.] Supply?

SUPPLY   *Yes.*

PAUL   When I last spoke with you, you indicated that the forming of the $5,000 needed had already been accomplished.

SUPPLY   *That is correct, Paul.*

PAUL   Is it possible for me to know the manner in which it will appear, or when it will appear?

SUPPLY   *No, Paul, it is not. The reason is that you are dealing here on an old basis. You must grasp that in Reality it is fulfilled.*

You must be willing to move on, staying at that point of consciousness, of Conscious Being, wherein you can feel the fact that all of you is always available and all of you is always functioning. It is a matter of consistency on your part to act out from Mind rather than react to your world and the way it appears. This is an apparently difficult switch to make, because the habit of reacting is still very strong.

That is my answer.

PAUL   [Addressing Raj.]Raj?

RAJ   Yes, Paul.

PAUL   It is right. It *is* difficult.

RAJ   Paul, every moment you are feeling the Reality of your Being, you are giving extremely clear messages — the thought processes are not cloudy or diffused. You are constantly invoking the Substance of your Being by virtue of such clear awareness. The omnipresent Substance of your Being brings forth exactly what is needed.

As I have said before, the key to this is your willingness to stand as the Door. You have been doing this very well, and you are, indeed, seeing changes in the way your infinitude is reflecting your standpoint. Do not make the mistake of overlooking the fact that your infinitude *is* responding differently. It is a direct result or evidence of the manifesting of your supply. It isn't just money you need, Paul. It is also a changed experience of your infinitude, which you call your world. You are already seeing evidence of the operation of the Law which we talked about yesterday.

Now it is time to get on with other matters.

PAUL   Thank you, Raj.

RAJ   Paul, I have been aware that you are interested — yes, with all your heart — to know where you are headed. I can begin to tell you now.

I know you feel very uncertain when it comes to my telling you about what you call "actualities" — and I mean visible actualities as opposed to what you call internal activities. But, I would like for you to sort of sit loose there, like Almee said the other night, and take this with a light touch, if you will, simply to facilitate the communication of what I have to say.

PAUL   Okay.

[I couldn't hear anything at all.]

Raj, I'm already having trouble. Can you help me get around it somehow?

RAJ   Yes, I will. First of all, be still and quiet yourself down. But do it with a light touch.

PAUL   Okay.

[Short period of meditation.]

Raj, is there any way this can be done more objectively, so I don't feel so much like I am depending upon a process that I guess I don't trust my ability to participate in fully yet?

RAJ   Paul, your voice is as objective as we can get at the moment.

PAUL   Very well, Raj. Will you be. . .

RAJ   Paul, I need you to settle down. Your fear regarding this process of communication is really unnecessary. As you found yesterday, the communication is very well established, and even when you were angry, you still had no difficulty in hearing me at all. You can hear me right now, even though you feel anxious, because you know I'm not about to communicate any further news — at least that's what you assume from the gist of my conversation at the moment — and this is allowing you to be relaxed enough to be willing to hear what I'm saying. The problem with your hearing what I want to say today is due to an unwillingness to hear, because you find yourself afraid of what you think you are going to hear.

PAUL   Raj, it's simply a matter that I don't want any possible confusion or mix-up regarding what you are saying, or what you are going to say.

RAJ   I know, Paul. I understand and appreciate that it is difficult. Why don't you just listen to what I have to say — go ahead and let it spill out. And afterwards, we can discuss it and see if there are any misunderstandings regarding what I have said.

PAUL   Okay.

I can tell you that I'd love to have a cigarette right now, and — Raj, is there something that I can do to botch this whole thing up? Is this a thing where — like I have one chance, and if I miss it I've really missed it?

RAJ   Paul, the answer to that is no, and at this point I do want you to take a break. Go ahead and have the cigarette. Relax. Come back. Do some meditation before you begin the conversation, and solidly get into that Place where you feel no apprehension. Then, let us continue the conversation. We will stick with this, if we have to, until midnight.

Go ahead, Paul.

PAUL   Thank you, Raj.

[Cigarette and dinner break taken.]

February 26, 1982
Friday
(Evening)

PAUL   Raj, I am willing to sit here for two days if I need to in order to relax enough to hear you completely.

RAJ   Thank you, Paul, although I do not think that it will take until midnight.

PAUL   Raj, I want to do a few more minutes' meditation.

RAJ   That's perfectly all right. Go right ahead.

PAUL   [Period of meditation.]

Is this okay, Raj?

RAJ   That is just fine.

PAUL   Was anything that Susan shared with me of that book, or anything that I read out of that book, applicable to me and to you? [1]

RAJ   Yes, Paul, some things did apply to me, and some things did apply to you.

PAUL   Raj, in reading and listening to parts of that book, it did bring out to me that there are infinite directions in which I can learn. Perhaps my frame of reference is just too limiting.

For example, you indicated that you are a Master.

137

RAJ   Yes, Paul, I did.

PAUL   Are you a Master in the sense that Masters are spoken of in the part of the book that I was reading?

RAJ   At this point, Paul, it is not necessary for you to know any more than you already do about me, so I will decline to answer that question.

PAUL   When other people speak of having a Guide, does that necessarily mean that their Guide is a Master?

RAJ   No, it does not.

PAUL   Is it simply a matter that the matching up, vibrationally, does not necessarily occur with a Master; is the fact that you are the one I am working with simply a matter of the fact that we matched?

RAJ   It is simply a matter that we matched up.

PAUL   In other words, there is no particular significance to the fact that I am not working with a Guide, but am instead working with a Master?

RAJ   Paul, I am a Master. The simple fact is that my work directly relates to supporting and being involved in the reappearing of the Christ, of Maitreya, on your planet. If you had matched up with a Guide whose work was not involved specifically with the advent of His return, your Guide, nevertheless, would have begun to inform you of the events which are going to occur, since it is a Universally known fact that this development is taking place on planet Earth.

PAUL   I guess I am confused. The impression I got from Mr. Creme's book was that the Masters were working with more than one individual and, in fact, worked with many individuals here who are at the point of growth where contact can be established.

I guess I am further confused. If you were my Teacher and you were simply going to be working with me — and that was all there was to it — that would not be difficult for me to understand at all. But there seem to be two important events occurring. One is my own growth and development.

The other is that the earth is evidently experiencing a point of growth as a whole, which is called the reappearing of the Christ and the Masters of Wisdom.

You are saying to me that it is purely coincidental that you not only are my Guide, but are also one of the Masters of Wisdom?

RAJ   Paul, all Masters are Masters of Wisdom, but not all Masters are participating in what is called the reappearing of the Christ.

PAUL   Raj, I want to stick with this as long as necessary, because I really want to understand this. I hope you don't mind if I pump you with questions like this.

RAJ   I do not mind at all.

PAUL   I am going to be doing my best to render an accurate translation of what you are saying. Please bear with me.

RAJ   I have no problem with that.

PAUL   Do some of the Masters work with a number of students?

RAJ   Some do.

PAUL   But you are not, is that correct?

RAJ   I am working only with you, Paul, simply because there are no other matches at the present time. If there were, I would be working with them also. It would make no apparent difference to you, whatsoever.

PAUL   Before I forget, Raj, I have a dear friend with whom I have shared a number of our conversations. She is quite capable of understanding fully the things that you have had to say. Would there be any objection for me to make a complete copy of the transcriptions and mail them to her? I know she would find them of great interest and value. I don't know what other purpose it may serve.

RAJ   Paul, you may send her a complete set, but I caution you not to give out complete sets to anyone else without asking me, as you have just done.

PAUL   Raj, I will abide by that rule absolutely.

RAJ   Do you have any more questions, Paul?

PAUL   Yes. For the time being, should I simply let my attention be given to the work you and I are doing together, and continue to steer clear of other books, such as the one I was glancing at during my break?

RAJ   Paul, I think that would be an excellent idea. I suggested that you do that simply to jar your concepts somewhat, but for the time being, I would like you to consider that what you read was nonsense, and simply proceed with me.

PAUL   I will be more than willing to do so. That other simply blows my mind and strikes me as not being true at all, or at least any truth that might be there is so covered up that it is almost undiscernible.

RAJ   Your perception, Paul, is quite correct.

PAUL   This may sound silly, but are you capable of misdirecting me?

RAJ   I am not, for the simple fact that, in effect, you are not speaking to a personality. You are speaking directly to the Wisdom of the Universe, you might say, through the open Door that I am, and through the open Door which you are learning to become, or beginning to learn to Be.

It is true that there is infinite progression — infinite, universal progression. It is true that there is more to the infinite progression of Being than you can imagine at the present time. But, it is also true that there is an abundance of misinformation available on your planet regarding these subjects, which apparently have come through Masters, but which were coming through individualities who were caught in great mental complexities. They had not truly grown to the point of being the open Door. They were communicating their own theories and concepts. Tonight I let you have a taste of such theories and concepts.

Paul, I must reiterate that Being, for all Its infinity and eternity, is ultimately simple in Its Being. In spite of things you have heard to the contrary, I reiterate that there is no devil; there are no evil forces, no evil power, and no dark side. This is the Fact, eternally and infinitely. I will not deviate from that standpoint for any reason, because it is a Fact.

I want you to understand that my primary purpose is with you and your individual unfolding of your Self as your conscious experience of Being. That will become No. 1 with you, because you are the one that constitutes the Eternal Constant.

The apparent three–dimensional event of the reappearance of the Christ is one of the millions of events which will occur to you as your experience eternally. You must keep in mind that no single event in your experience takes precedence over that which is experiencing it — You.

You must be very careful not to classify yourself as a follower of Maitreya, or a follower of any Master, or any Teacher. You are to follow the Inner Path of the evolving of your very own Being as It unfolds and reveals Itself as your conscious experience.

This must be a rule, a guidepost for you to refer to often.

PAUL   That is relieving, Raj. Thank you very much.

RAJ   Paul, that set of books is a perfect example of what I was speaking about this afternoon. It is a disservice to publish something when there is no possibility of supplying the reassurance necessary to help someone over the hump of believing the unbelievable.

You see, Paul, the more infinite becomes the view, the greater its simplicity of Nature and Function appears — not more complex.

PAUL   I can accept that with no difficulty.

As I said the other day, I was aware of Maitreya preparing, or intending, to come here the evening when the three gentlemen were in the room. This implied to me the possibility that I will in some way render a service, or participate in some way in the activities involved in His reappearance. In other words, our paths will cross, and there will be an involvement.

RAJ   That is correct, Paul.

PAUL   From my standpoint, I can think of nothing I would rather be involved in working for.

RAJ   He knows that, too, Paul.

PAUL   And you say that He sees things in the same way that you are expressing these things to me?

RAJ   I am saying that, yes, Paul. He and I see much more than what I am saying to you. But you can count on one thing: The more infinite your view becomes, the simpler the understanding of things becomes.

PAUL   And He would agree that I am to keep very clear — I think I see what you're getting at — you are trying to let me know that I had better not make the serious mistake of disowning my Divinity in any way and placing it "out there," in Him or anyone else?

RAJ   Exactly. And, before you meet Him, this has to be clear to you. Otherwise, you will be overwhelmed or overawed by what you think He is, and you will neglect or slight your Self, and will begin to operate from a three-dimensional-only standpoint. As I said before, this will only occur with great discomfort, because you have graduated. There is no need for you to waste your time suffering.

You see, you are very willing to serve, but it must be very clear to you that you are not to be the main dish — you are not to give your Self away. You must see that you are fulfilling your purpose, the purpose of your Being; that He is fulfilling the purpose of His Being; that that Being is One. It is only at the level of visibility and tangibility that we can see the infinite interplay and interchange of, as I said before, circles within circles and patterns within patterns.

As Shakespeare said, ". . . to thine own self be true, And it must follow, as the night the day, Thou canst not then be false to any man."[2] The only way that you can serve Maitreya is by being true to your Self as He is being true to Himself. This must be very clear, Paul!

As you are beginning to realize, the vast majority of the people on this planet Earth are not in a position, at the moment, of understanding or seeing this point.

Maitreya will apparently come with great transforming powers and ability. But it must be understood that the energy behind those powers is literally being supplied by the very individualities who are about to be apparently changed.

Remember, when the student is ready, the Teacher appears. This tells you, Paul, that the Teacher does not appear due to any powers of His own, but due to the inherent readiness of the student. The Christ cannot reappear out of His own fantastic power, because He has none like that. He can only appear because mankind is ready for the growth and change. It is their readiness, whether consciously recognized or not, which causes the Way to be clear for the Teacher to appear.

Mr. Creme's book implies that the Christ, together with the Masters of Wisdom, is appearing based on a decision They made. This had to be put this way in the book, but the fact is that They could not have decided to reappear in the year 1551, in the year 1901, or in the year 1970, because the Harmonies of Being, Itself, would not allow it. It would not have been a harmonious event. The students were not ready. I know you can see that the Teacher is reappearing by virtue of the readiness of the students, and not because of any great power of His own to act on His own, any more than when you are in that Place where you are experiencing the Allness of your Being as Conscious Being, you can act on your own, doing what you want to do. The only place where you exist in that way is in the imagination of your three–dimensional frame of reference.

Paul, I know you grasp this point, but I nevertheless want you to read and reread and reread this conversation, because it is essential to your continued clarity of vision and perspective.

PAUL   Don't worry, Raj, I've gotten the message, and I want to read this over and over.

RAJ   To continue, Paul: I indicated that He comes with great power, and then clarified to you that that power is resident in the readiness of the students.

Now, these powers which He will apparently bring with Him will be experienced as a general worldwide spiritualization of thought, or inner Enlightenment. But, the fact will remain that it will not move everybody into the position of being a totally enlightened individuality. Their growth will need to be internalized, just as yours has.

Paul, when I told you earlier that I would be telling you what your service would be, I meant that your service will be directly to Maitreya. It is not my place to say what you will be doing specifically for Him, or in conjunction with any of the Masters — that will be His job.

Paul, you caught an insightful fact there. It will appear as though Maitreya and the Masters will be working together. But the only reason it will appear that They are working together is because They will each be working alone from the standpoint of their Being as Fourth-dimensional Man, which means *as* the All One. Being out from Mind means being in perfect Harmony with the infinite Unfoldment of that Mind. When you have many individuals, each being in total Harmony with infinite Mind, you have what appears to be many individuals working in harmony with each other. But the harmony does not originate from the level of the appearance, and this must also be clear to you.

I say "must," not to imply that there are a lot of requirements, but merely to pinpoint key issues. You are not familiar with all the nooks and crannies wherein the Oneness of Being is to be found, and I wish to facilitate your rapid assimilation of what is really going on.

I see that you are beginning to grasp that my foremost and primary interest is with you, and not that of facilitating what will be a worldwide event. Let me put that another way: The only way I can facilitate the worldwide event is by not facilitating *that* event, but by facilitating your clarity of vision regarding the infinity of your Being — the Oneness of your All as your conscious experience.

Paul, nothing is truly going to be happening the way it will appear three-dimensionally, and this is why we are going into the realities of such appearances this evening.

PAUL   I appreciate that, Raj, and I understand what you are saying.

RAJ   I would like you to stop for now, and type up what you have so far in this conversation.

When you are through, if you feel like it still this evening, we may talk again. Until then, I will say good-bye for now.

---

1   Bailey, Alice A., "Treatise on Cosmic Fire."

2   "Hamlet," Act I, Scene iii.

February 26, 1982
Friday
(Late Evening)

PAUL   It is quite late, and although I was tired and would have liked to have gone to bed and had a good night's sleep, something said we weren't finished yet. There was a feeling of a gathering of energies — that's the best way I can put it. And so, I am here.

RAJ   Thank you, Paul.

PAUL   Is it possible for me to telepathically be aware of your — of something going on within your conscious experience of being when you are not specifically directing your attention toward these conversations with me?

RAJ   In the sense that I am some aspect of the infinitude of your Being, it most certainly is possible, Paul.

PAUL   Is there, indeed, more that you wanted to cover this day?

RAJ   Paul, there is always going to be more to cover. But specifically, as regards today, there is more that I want to cover in order that we might finish what needs to be finished.

You have already gotten the idea that I want you to further let go and relax.

That's good.

PAUL   [Short period of meditation.]

RAJ Go ahead, Paul. You have been down this road before. The ease with which you are doing it indicates familiarity and comfortableness with it. Keep going. But I will remind you again to remain in touch with your surroundings. We are not going into a trance.

PAUL [Further meditation.]

RAJ Paul, what is the Christ to you?

PAUL The Christ is the experiential Awareness of Reality as experienced from the standpoint of Conscious Being, which flows through and reveals the Actuality and does not originate at the point of three–dimensional awareness. It is the Universal Perception of What Really Is. In fact, ultimately, it is God's view of His infinite Being.

RAJ That is correct, Paul. Continue to relax. Keep yourself aware of your surroundings. Do not let it go.

PAUL Very well, Raj.

[Further meditation.]

RAJ That is very good, Paul. Continue.

PAUL Raj, I feel like I'm on the verge of dropping the microphone.

RAJ Do not worry, Paul. Be sure to keep your awareness placed so that it can experience all four dimensions simultaneously without leaving anything out. It truly is all You.

PAUL Okay, Raj. You mean even when we all meet?

RAJ That is correct, Paul.

PAUL Are you doing something to me, or for me, while I am meditating?

RAJ Yes, I am.

PAUL Thank you. I can feel the Love tonight, and the subject matter, although it goes on beyond my present awareness. . .

Raj, I do not know what that sentence was going to mean, because it did not come from me.

RAJ   Correct, Paul. Continue.

PAUL   Raj, I no longer sense the feeling of gathering energies, and have the feeling of completion. Is there anything else you want to do this evening, because I am willing.

RAJ   Paul, you have done very well, and you will come to understand exactly what has been going on. It will be most satisfying to you. There is nothing needing to be done this evening. I will look forward to speaking with you tomorrow.

PAUL   Raj, thank you for everything, today and every day, since we began. Thank you very much.

February 27, 1982
Saturday

PAUL   Raj, it occurred to me after talking with Susan this morning, that when one person seems to have something that another person would like to have for himself — and if the one who has it involves himself in giving it to the second person in order to help him — this inevitably creates in the second person a feeling of inequity and a lack of ability, and doesn't truly help him. I am reminded of a statement that the best charity is to show a person that he doesn't need charity. I guess what I am questioning is the concept of a "helper."

In the truest sense of the word, you are not a helper, because you know exactly what I need to learn, and help me to put myself in the position of learning it. I am questioning the whole concept of an army of helpers or teachers. How can they truly help, if it is not possible for them to be right there in the individual's consciousness of things, as you are, and able to see exactly what needs to be brought out, so that the individual can do his own growing and find himself out of his problem — or out of his belief, or whatever it may be — and know that he didn't get out of it by virtue of borrowed help?

RAJ   Paul, this is a question of deep importance. You are right that the best help is to show the individual that he doesn't need help. You are wondering how it could be that Maitreya will accomplish this, and especially how individuals such as yourself will truly be able to help in this sense.

I cannot share with you at this moment how that will be accomplished. But I would suggest that you observe in your own experience whether or not you can intuitively arrive at a point of being able to give that kind of help right in your own family.

PAUL   All right. I certainly will.

In the study of metaphysics and its practice, it has been proven that a metaphysical treatment given over some distance does not keep healing from occurring. It is, in fact, very successful. Can the invoking of the Law which we have talked about from the last two occasions be utilized in much the same way if there is someone from a distance who calls with a problem that they need relief from?

RAJ   Yes, it works exactly the same way. You ought to utilize it whenever the opportunity occurs, so as to become familiar with its effectiveness and begin to develop a confidence in the operation of Principle and Love in this aspect.

PAUL   I will.

I have no other questions at the moment. I will simply ask you to please share with me what you know needs to be dealt with.

RAJ   Very well, Paul. I want to talk to you tonight about Atlantis.

PAUL   You feel that this has some bearing on my growth at this time?

RAJ   Yes, Paul, it does.

PAUL   I am, of course, basing what I'm going to say on my prejudgments about this subject, but I don't see how it can have any relationship at all.

RAJ   That is not surprising.

PAUL   I am going to let go and trust that you know exactly what you are doing, but — I'll retract the "but" — and I will move forward with you. Before I do that, I want to take a few minutes here and relax.

RAJ   That will be fine.

PAUL   [Period of meditation.]

              All right, Raj.

RAJ   Thank you, Paul. Before I say anything, I want you to no-
        tice just exactly to what lengths you will go — and how rapid-
        ly you will go to them — in order to have a grasp on what
        I'm going to say before I've said it, in order to make sure
        you're not going to sound like a fool. This brings into play
        the element of trust.

PAUL   [Nothing perceived.]

RAJ   Paul, this sounds very elementary, but you're going to have
        to understand that growth does not mean expansion within
        the same old frame of reference. It means expansion out of
        it, beyond it. I know you are having difficulty trying to clas-
        sify what you are broadly perceiving of what I am saying into
        your present set of categories, and that is exactly the problem
        I am addressing here. You can understand it this way, Paul.
        As a tree grows, it cannot get bigger and remain the same
        size.

PAUL   I've got the picture.

RAJ   Paul, what you are trying to do here is to grow, and yet have
        the growth fit into the same old categorizations — the same
        old structure — and I am trying to wake you up to the fact
        that if you are, indeed, going to grow, you have to stop try-
        ing to fit everything into neat little cubbyholes before you'll
        even bother to repeat my words. At the least, you are going
        to need new cubbyholes. At the most, you will let go of cub-
        byholes altogether, and flow with the new unfolding of your
        Being.

        I don't really want to tell you anything about Atlantis at all.
        But the time is going to come when I will be telling you things
        that may most definitely cross your present concepts, and
        I can begin to see that you are feeling more comfortable with
        this whole process of our conversations and are beginning
        to feel like you've got the whole thing pegged. That's the be-
        ginning of the end.

        Somewhere, early in our conversations, I told you that you
        have to be willing to stand at the point where you know *noth-
        ing,* because that is what allows you to become aware of

Something. You are beginning to sit down and begin our conversations as though you have a pretty good idea of what's going to come about. This is going to begin to get in the way.

The meditation exercises that we have been doing have been partly for the purpose of helping you get to the point where you can see, from an experiential standpoint, that when you let go of everything, infinity has an opportunity to appear. You, yourself, have begun to find, when a subject is difficult for you to deal with, that if you will do a meditation, it removes the resistance and allows the communication to unfold smoothly.

I would like you to begin to develop the habit of not beginning our conversations until you have cleared any preconceptions you have.

Indeed, I would like you to stop forming preconceptions in the first place.

Paul, we are talking about becoming the Door. The image you have in your mind of the Door is, indeed, accurate. It is a door*way,* and there isn't a single door attached to it. And yet, you have begun to come to these conversations ready to close a door — that shouldn't even be there in the first place — if what you are hearing can't be quickly classified, judged, and decided upon before you get the first word out of your mouth.

PAUL   I am sorry, Raj.

RAJ   You see, Paul, growth isn't just a matter of becoming bigger, or of enjoying a more expansive understanding of your Being. It also includes a more mature way of dealing with that information. *All* of you grows when growth occurs.

I am not going to say any more about this at the moment. I want you to type it up before you leave in the morning. I want you to take it with you and refer to it and think about it before we talk again, after you return tomorrow.

You have been wondering at various times the last few days whether I am with you around the clock as I said I would be a while back. The answer is, yes, Paul, I am with you constantly, from your point of view. The reason is that this is a somewhat delicate time for you, simply because the major shifts that you are experiencing need the availability of instant reinforcement and support, in order to make the transition smooth and secure and solid. You may rest assured that you are not alone.

PAUL   Thank you, Raj.

February 28, 1982
Sunday

PAUL   Raj, I want to apologize for last night, and I want to thank you for very kindly pointing out to me the trap I was falling into. I think that tonight I am here, and you can talk about any old thing you want, and I will be able to flow with it. At least that is my desire and my willingness.

RAJ   I knew you would get the point, Paul. Thank you.

Tonight we are going to talk about Atlantis.

PAUL   [Pause.] Did I read you correctly, Raj?

RAJ   Yes. I want to talk about Atlantis.

PAUL   Very well.

RAJ   Paul, there was, indeed, at one time, an island by the name of Atlantis. The people on this island had developed to a very high point of civilization. This was achieved because of their inner development to the point of being as Fourth-dimensional Man — exactly in the same way that you are growing right now.

The problem was that — and don't conceptualize now — there was an imbalance in the vibrations between their island and the rest of the world. It precluded them from being able to correlate or harmonize with the vast majority of people beyond their island, so different was the rate of vibration.

As a result of this difference of rate of vibration, a series of harmonic dissonances became generated at subsonic frequencies, which resulted in a physical displacement along a fault line of their island, which sank into the sea.

There were no survivors.

As you know, hearsay has it that the island of Atlantis is in the process of rising again. But unlike your concept that such an event will have no value for you or modern day man, it will, indeed, have great value. The artifacts which will be unearthed will verify and substantiate the "chain of scientific being" which Mrs. Eddy spoke of in *Science and Health.*[1]

You see, Paul, the evolution of the earth, of mankind, on this planet, has been going on for centuries. The presence of the Christ has occurred many times in different names and nationalities and teachings — always within the framework of what could be understood at the time by the people being addressed.

This happened in the case of the civilization which developed on Atlantis.

The reason the reemergence of the island will be of exceeding, great significance to the world today, is that the Atlanteans were the first civilization, as a whole, to enter into that Place *as* Conscious Being, *as* Fourth–dimensional Man. The artifacts which will be found will serve to be the nail holes and spear wound which the doubting Thomases of the early decades or centuries of the Age of Aquarius will find resolving their doubts into Understanding. It will be "ancient objective proof" which will settle once and for all, for them, the actuality of the fact that Maitreya is, indeed, the reappearing of the Christ.

The reemergence of the island, through further geographic displacement, will occur harmoniously and without causing great earthquakes and tidal waves. It will not happen soon, but it will happen. And these transcripts of our conversations will take their place in some way, further validating for those doubting Thomases the actuality about which they are in doubt.

We will talk about this again at a later time, and I thank you for letting go of your prejudicial concepts and being willing to transcribe what I needed to say.

For the time being, that is all I will say about the subject.

I simply want it on record. I do not want you trying to figure out smart questions to ask me about it in order to surreptitiously learn more. Let it lay.

PAUL   Very well, Raj, I will. Are you saying that I should find no significance in what you have just said, other than it has now been transcribed?

RAJ   That is correct. It bears no relation to you at this time, nor will it. This is just a matter of record.

PAUL   Very well.

RAJ   Paul, I know you have had a very full day. I know that it meant a lot to you to spend this time with your family. And whether you are aware of it or not, it meant a very great deal to your children to have you playing with them and participating with them in their level of activity, and it was good.

I will say good night for now, and I will look forward to speaking with you in the morning.

---

1   Eddy, Mary Baker, *Science and Health*, v.271; 1-5.

March 1, 1982
Monday
(Afternoon)

PAUL   I am having the feeling that there is a need for things to come into focus here. I understand that could simply mean that I am sensing the fact that things *are* coming into focus — sensing a gathering of energies, so to speak.

RAJ   Go on, Paul.

PAUL   Okay. I turned the calendar this morning and saw that it is March 1. This is the first day of the month in which Mr. Creme has stated that the reappearance of the Christ will occur. There is a feeling on my part of big things happening.

I am aware that we seem to be in limbo, in that I am literally unemployed in the world's terms. There is no apparent sense of direction other than the one of my conversing with you and doing an incredible amount of growing.

Susan, herself, is experiencing a great influx of enlightenment, but other than that — which is not insignificant — there doesn't seem to be an adequate resolution of the school situation, of our living situation, or of our financial situation. It is like being on the outskirts of life, three–dimensionally speaking.

There seems to be a sense of isolation, of being out of sync, of not fitting in, and that brings along with it a feeling for a need to fit in some way. Yet, nothing has unfolded to do — other than what I am doing at this very moment and have been doing for the last three weeks.

RAJ   Paul, the clanging cymbals of time are ringing their last clangs. You are feeling a habitual desire to feel "normal" when "what is normal" is changing. It simply doesn't exist that way any more, even though others whom you see appear to be going about their daily activities as though nothing unusual is occurring.

We are within days of the Second Appearing. I cannot relieve you by telling you that you do need to go out and get a job, since there will not be a job of that kind existing for you any more. You have been willing to trust me so far, with great willingness. I ask you to be patient for a short time longer. Continue as you have been doing, remaining in that Place where you are experiencing your universe as Conscious Being. I know this is not easy. I am not testing you, nor will you suffer in the slightest by doing so.

PAUL   Raj, have I been subconsciously supplied with knowledge during my meditations or at night while I am asleep? I have the distinct feeling that there is activity going on of which I am not consciously aware.

RAJ   Yes, Paul. Both you and Susan are receiving background information, you might say, underlying concepts and knowledge which you will find that you possess as time goes on. You will find that you will apparently "remember" something that you "heard" before, and this knowledge will come into play in your experience in a most innocuous, unobservable way as it fulfills Purpose.

Go ahead, Paul, and ask your question.

PAUL   Will I meet Maitreya before His announcing of His return?

RAJ   No, Paul, you will not, unless for some reason His plans change. There is not that much time, and He is quite busy taking care of matters on a more worldwide scale in preparation for His announcement.

PAUL   Very well. What about the three gentlemen that were here?

RAJ   Paul, I know you are still looking for some specific, objective evidence to totally prove the fact that all of this is valid. Paul, it will happen in its own time, and you must be patient. The formation of voluntary trust on your part is still in the development stage. The need at this time is for you to persist in this process because you feel it is right.

PAUL   Thank you, Raj. I guess one of the most difficult parts of all of this is that, in effect, what I am being required to do feels like becoming a puppet. I feel that I am not being self-directed, but am becoming a part of the flow of something far larger than my awareness of myself.

I find myself questioning, from the standpoint of a gut-level, non-conceptual feeling, whether this is "right." Yet, by the same token, I find that by relinquishing my awareness of myself as a separate identity with a will of its own, there is this tremendous influx of understanding and enlightenment, together with a greater experience of peace, which seems far more valid than any sense of relaxation I have experienced before.

RAJ   Paul, I realize this is a difficult shift to make, especially since the concept of "individuality" has been so prized — the concept of the "self-made man," et cetera. I can only suggest, Paul, nothing more, that you take a look within your Self. Ask your Self whether the way you have been living for the last two and a half years, as an "individual," brought with it anything of the sort that you are experiencing now, after having relinquished your "individuality." I ask you to seriously consider which you find more satisfying, and I suggest you literally make a choice.

I want you to ask yourself in which case you truly were a puppet. If you find that in *both* cases you feel like a puppet, then I ask you to consider who the Puppeteer is.

Paul, I know I am relentless with you on these points, but if I were not, you would not make the shift. Yet the shift must be made. The shift must be made, because it is the unfoldment of your Being, and because it is the unfoldment in a more universal aspect — it is a change line for your world. It is the age old question of whom you are going to serve. The question is being put before you by your very own Being.

Do not mistake what is happening, and feel that it is I who is making these demands. I am bound to support only that which Your Being is bringing to the level of your conscious experience. I can only help facilitate you in overcoming your ingrained fears, and your habits and patterns of limited thought. I cannot make you give them up. I cannot make you drop them. And, I cannot make you make the shift.

You will make it, come hell or high water, because that is where your Being is. But, if you are willing to continue to follow the leadings of your own "upward, individual convictions,"[1] as Mrs. Eddy so beautifully put it, then you will continue to experience this shift with no more dissonance or suffering than you have so far. It is finally up to you.

Once again, I am going to make this a short conversation, so as to set it off clearly and distinctly. I want you to consider it before we speak again.

Good afternoon, Paul.

---

[1] Eddy, Mary Baker, *Unity of Good*, v.5; 9-13.

March 1, 1982
Monday
(Evening)

PAUL   Today is a day of questions.

RAJ   I know, Paul.

PAUL   I guess, first of all, there's something I need to get straight.

RAJ   Go ahead, Paul.

PAUL   Talking with anyone like this, whether simply a Guide or a Master, is, to say the least, quite out of the ordinary for me.

RAJ   I understand, Paul.

PAUL   Because it is out of the ordinary, and I don't know of many people to whom this is happening, it allowed me to feel like it was something special. And then, although I didn't think it made a substantial difference, when I found out that you were a Master, that information lent itself to my feeling that this experience with you was special. In addition to that, to find out that your work involves the return of Maitreya and the Masters also contributed to my feeling that there was something out of the ordinary in our communications. At least the potential was there.

As I said the other day, this seems to make matters more complicated than if I were simply working with a Guide and nothing unusual was going on other than this kind of communication.

I would like some help in getting perspective on this.

RAJ   Thank you, Paul. I will endeavor to clarify things for you.

First of all, the manner in which I became your Guide was absolutely normal. The fact that I am a Master was pure happenstance, and simply means that I am further along in my own development than a Guide would be. The fact that my work involves the reappearing of the Christ and the Masters is of no consequence to you. It is simply information which I have shared with you about my activities, and that is all.

Remember, Paul, you were not "picked" for this experience of communicating with a Guide, whether a Master or not. Now happens to be the time when *you* opened yourself up and requested that your Guide contact you. I cannot help it that you picked a time to do this which coincides with a worldwide event of some import. That is pure coincidence.

However, because it is going to occur, you are going to have to deal with it in order to maintain your equilibrium and remain clear as to your own inner unfolding of your Being. And so, we are discussing it. If there were some other major world event which would involve you in any way, we would be discussing that.

Let me state that primarily I am working with you because you have requested a Guide to work with you. I am "it" as far as you are concerned at this time. First and last, I am working with you on your behalf, and that is all there is to it.

PAUL   Thank you, Raj. In this afternoon's conversation, you indicated that we are within days of the Second Appearing. Since then, I have found that Mr. Creme did not say that the reappearing would occur during the month of March, but rather in late spring. I am not here to quibble over your statement as opposed to his statement, although I am curious.

RAJ   Paul, it is good to get the air cleared. The simple fact is that Mr. Creme is wrong, and I will say nothing more than that. You will simply have to watch and see.

PAUL   When you said that we were within days of the Second Appearing, were you referring to the announcement of Maitreya of His presence and His purpose?

RAJ   No, I was not.

PAUL   Then I *am* confused. Are you playing word games with me?

RAJ   I most definitely am not, Paul.

PAUL   Then in what respect is Mr. Creme wrong?

        [Nothing perceived.]

RAJ   Paul, there is, indeed, need for clarification here. Let go here, and just be open. Do not try to grasp ahead of time what I might be going to say.

PAUL   All right.

RAJ   The star heralding the birth of Jesus rose over a state of unenlightened thought, leading that thought to the place where the Christ Child lay in human experience. Conceptually speaking, you can see that it was not possible for the people of that time or land to perceive the dawning within their consciousness of the existence of the Christ-consciousness in any other than the smallest way — something brand new, but something small. And the appearing of the Christ-consciousness took a very literal form for them. They could not conceive that it was themselves, so it had to be someone else, someone else new and small. And so, the baby, Jesus, was a very literal manifestation of the only way in which they could conceive of the appearance of the Christ in their world.

In the present day, the awareness of the Christ-consciousness is no longer new. Indeed, there is a large part of the population — Christian, Buddhist, Hindu, et cetera — who are quite at the point of recognizing that the Christ-consciousness resides within them. And this is where it will come to pass that the reappearing of the Christ will occur.

Stop trying to figure it out, Paul.

It is obvious that the literal manifestation of the level of development of mankind today would not be conceptualized as a brand new baby. Instead, it would be an adult facilitator of that inner Self-discovery which will actually constitute the reappearance of the Christ.

You must realize that the majority of mankind is not at this conscious point of Self-realization. They are, nevertheless, at the point of recognizing their Divinity. It is for this reason that an adult will appear. This adult will meet the requirements that will allow them to pay attention and give credence to the appearance.

You must realize that there are all states and stages of individual inner development represented by mankind as a whole. All will see their Christhood according to whatever level of enlightenment or belief they find themselves at. But, notwithstanding their level of enlightenment or belief, the graduation of mankind will occur.

The degree of enlightenment/belief each one is at will govern the degree to which Maitreya will have followers or co-workers. Those who are enlightened will continue to pursue their own inner, unfolding Self-discovery. As that growth takes place, they will become co-facilitators in one form or another, working shoulder to shoulder with Maitreya. They will not be blinded by what He is, because they will recognize that He is what They are, and that They are what He is to some degree.

Mr. Creme is incorrect about the time of the reappearing, in that the reappearing has been going on for some time. It will continue far past the time when Maitreya announces His presence.

I know you must go to dinner now. We will continue as soon as you return.

PAUL   Thank you, Raj.

      [Dinner break taken. During the dinner break, Susan and I read and discussed parts of both Mr. Creme's book and the *Treatise on Cosmic Fire.*]

  RAJ   Paul, I know that since you have gone to dinner, you have frustrated yourself to an even higher degree than when you left. I know that you are arriving at a place where you couldn't care less whether Maitreya returned or not. Correct?

PAUL   Absolutely correct.

  RAJ   The conclusion that you are coming to is correct: The only appearance of the Christ that is worth a hill of beans for you is that dawning in your own experience of your own perception of Reality. It comes as the result of being the Door. It literally doesn't matter one way or the other whether

Maitreya returns or not. On this point you are absolutely correct.

Paul, you are the one who was interested in the idea of Maitreya returning and what impact the return might have on your life. You were interested in finding out whether or not you might have some part to play in that return — with all the implications of position, prestige, and power.

The fact is that very often the quickest way to show a person that he doesn't want what he says or thinks he wants, is to give him what he wants. And so, I have played along with you until you are sick and tired of what it would mean for you to constantly have to relate to someone "out there" — whether his name is Maitreya or not.

Paul, let the world have its own development in whatever way it most clearly can experience its growth. Remember that this world that is experiencing its growth — in the apparent drama of the reappearance of the Christ and the Masters of Wisdom — is the infinitude of your Self. One way or another, you are going to have to come to terms with that fact without selling your Self short.

There are groups of people actively participating in attempting to pave the way for His return, but this is not where you are. This is not your point of unfoldment. To whatever degree you think they may be doing something more correct than what you are doing, to that degree you are disintegrating your experience of your Self as the One that constitutes the Many. If you try to make comparisons or cross-references to attempt to validate or invalidate what is going on with you, you will lose your awareness of your cohesiveness.

Your gut-level feeling of frustration and anger is just a small taste of the suffering that will be in store for you, if you attempt to move back into a three-dimensional frame of reference.

It doesn't matter what day the announcement of Maitreya's return is made on. It doesn't matter by what means, or for what purpose, you and Susan are receiving an influx of inspiration and enlightenment — whether you're awake, asleep, in meditation, or flying a kite. The fact is that no matter what is going on anywhere else in the world, you are experiencing the inexorable unfolding of your Being as Conscious Being. You might as well accept it.

Now, tomorrow morning when you get up, take care of your everyday activities. But, before you do them, or have a conversation with me, I want you to get into that Place where you are being as Conscious Being, as Fourth-dimensional Man. Then, from that point, take care of the things that need to be taken care of. Then, when you have completed those, if you would like to converse with me, I will look forward to talking with you. In the meantime, for God's sake, let go of all this folderol and get back to the point of being the Door.

I can promise you this: So long as you are seeking position, power, prestige, by virtue of association with the Masters or Maitreya — no matter how subtly — They will not come near you with a ten-foot pole. The only reason that the three gentlemen were present at all was because at that point you were truly being the Presence of the Christ. Paul, "person," was nowhere to be found.

Learn this lesson well, and you will move forward with great ease. Continue in the frame of reference you are presently indulging in, and you will be sorry.

I know that you are not presently experiencing my presence with what you recognize as a feeling of Love. Nonetheless, Paul, it is time for your concept of Love to be broadened. It is time for you to realize that Love is "whatever it takes to bring forth the Reality, right where the belief insists on being." With that I will say good night for now, and I will look forward to speaking with you tomorrow.

PAUL   [Pause.]

RAJ   Say "good night," Paul.

PAUL   Good night, Raj. And thank you.

March 2, 1982
Monday

PAUL   [Period of meditation.]

Good evening, Raj.

RAJ   Good evening, Paul. I want you to realize that you are constantly living in the Light of your Being. It constitutes You. It constitutes the atmosphere you move and be in. It is never absent, and it is never out.

I am glad you did a meditation before beginning our conversation. I would like you to do this kind of meditation more often when we are not speaking together, just to provide yourself with the experience of moving into a deep meditation without losing contact with your world. You have found that you can be in a much deeper state of meditation while not losing any sensory awareness of the first three dimensions. I would like you to get more experience at this.

PAUL   I shall endeavor to do it, Raj.

RAJ   Paul, I want you to take a few more minutes to get even deeper.

PAUL   All right, Raj.

[Further meditation.]

[I then took a short break.]

Raj, as you are probably aware, we seem to be at a crossroads here. Demands are being made for payment or return

166

of the copy equipment. Specific steps need to be taken regarding Julie's schooling, since the setup with the tutor is not as desirable as it ought to be. I have been being consistent for the last three weeks in giving as much attention as possible to our conversations — to growing, being willing to let go of old concepts, and to expanding. I feel that a tremendous amount of expansion has occurred. I find that there seems to be very little change in terms of income, or supply, or in the schooling situation, et cetera, et cetera.

I even got over the hump of talking with my Supply, and have done it twice now. Both times it has indicated to me that the definitely needed $5,000 was on its way, and was a completed fact when I had the first conversation. Since that time, we have only received bills.

From a finite perspective, I have neglected my responsibility in favor of going within and being as Fourth-dimensional Man, as Conscious Being. And I believe that I have done it willingly and totally with all my heart. And yet, not even a small part of the $5,000 has come into view. The situation seems to be growing worse.

I am not saying that I am looking for a pat on the back or a reward for what I have been doing, since it has been most satisfying. I have felt that I was on the right track. But at the same time, it seems to me that if the One constitutes the Many, and if I have been being true to my Self, then there ought to be some practical evidence of it in terms of an improved living situation.

RAJ   Go ahead and state the rest of your question.

PAUL   I guess I'm wondering whether or not I need to lead sort of a double life. In other words, do I need to be living according to three-dimensional structures part of the time? Then, when I am with you and other times, continue in what we have been doing together in experiencing the unfolding of my Being as Conscious Being? Must they be kept separated?

Have I misunderstood or misinterpreted what has been unfolding, insofar as I felt that, if I devoted myself completely and totally to being the Door, that in so many words "all these things shall be added unto you?" Is there an even larger picture that I am unaware of that will become clear?

I definitely feel the need for clarification on these points.

RAJ   Paul, you have been faithful. You have been attentive. You have been cooperative, willing, and have, indeed, grown a lot during the last three weeks. You have listened to what I have said. It has made sense to you. You have believed it, and acted accordingly.

The need now is to be willing to go all the way. You were correct that there are innumerable structural safeguards against breaking through the three–dimensional frame of reference. You are running into them popping up in front of you — as in a fun house ride. They are calculated to scare you into backing off and not proceeding any further. You must be willing to stand with what is unifying to your conscious experience of being as Fourth–dimensional Man, rather than what is disintegrating or disunifying to you.

PAUL   Is it this difficult for everyone?

RAJ   In each one's way, it is. Yes, indeed.

PAUL   You are saying that, if necessary, I must be willing to let everything apparently collapse around me, and be unmoved?

RAJ   There is no other way. Mind you, the key word there is "willingness." The emphasis is not meant to be placed on the collapse of everything around you.

PAUL   Does this mean that the unfoldment cannot be harmonious?

RAJ   No, it does not. But, you are not going to see the harmony of it when your attention is focused on the appearance.

You see, Paul, all of you is always present, and all of you is always functioning. This means there is nothing that exists that can be added unto you. What you are doing is already done. What you are learning, you already Know. You are in the process of simply beginning to experience what has always been true of you and *as* You.

PAUL   But it seems like I am experiencing it only within.

RAJ   There is no other place to experience it.

PAUL   But why does there seem to be an inconsistency between what I am experiencing within, and what is manifest as visibility and tangibility in the three–dimensional frame of reference?

RAJ   This is perhaps one of the most difficult things to grasp, and I have reiterated it many times. Your Substance, or Supply, also brought it out to you, and that is: As long as you are bouncing back and forth, from inside to outside, to verify what is going on "out there" against what is going on "in here," you are losing the continuity of being as Conscious Being.

The necessity is to be willing to stand still *as* Conscious Being. It is similar to using a P.A. system which you have set up in your house, and from which you can speak through speakers which are in your front yard. If you stop speaking into the microphone to go out into the yard to see whether they are working, you will naturally find no sound coming out of them, because you have left the microphone and are not speaking into it.

You could easily come to the conclusion that the speakers were not functioning properly when, in fact, the only reason they were not broadcasting your voice is that you were not at your place at the microphone. There is no way to make it any clearer at this point.

In effect, I have shown you where the microphone is. I have shown you what it feels like to be there. I have shown you how to get there, and how to get back when you slip away. Believe it or not, I am working with you to help facilitate your ability to stand at and *as* that Place.

PAUL   Raj, something is blocking me from being able to be comfortable with what you are saying.

RAJ   I would think by now that "comfortable" and "uncomfortable" would no longer be valid guideposts for you, since those are three–dimensional points of view. You know that when you are in that Place, you are experiencing Absolute Comfort, undivided in any way. If you want to bounce back out onto the surface of your finite consciousness, you will, indeed, find comfort and discomfort, pain and pleasure, gain and loss.

I am afraid, Paul, that this is the one essential step which you must make yourself. I can encourage you to take it. I can explain to you why you can take it. But it has to come from within your Being. What is blocking it is simply fear. There is no actual opposition or roadblock.

PAUL   In the past, I have experienced healings without taking this radical step. I have experienced benefits of prayer and metaphysical work. I did not have to be under the gun, so to speak. Isn't unfoldment supposed to be natural?

RAJ   It doesn't really matter how it has been in the past, and it doesn't really matter how you think it ought to be. This is simply the way it is. These are the factors which you are given to deal with.

A radical stand is required, and you are not being given any alternative. The eye of the needle is unyielding, and you must pass through it on its terms.

Now, you can wait until your experience becomes so uncomfortable and unyeilding that you realize this is the only choice you have. Or, you can act on it now, when it is not really causing you to knuckle under and say "Uncle." You can't glide through this one on the surface.

If you feel that you are backed into a corner, the fact is that you are. The only way out of this one is to grow. And you have no choice about it.

PAUL   Raj, I need some time to let this sink in.

RAJ   I understand.

PAUL   I will get back with you.

RAJ   That's fine, Paul. I will be waiting, and I will be with you. Do not forget that. You are not doing this in a total void.

PAUL   I appreciate that. I will be back with you. Thank you.

March 3, 1982
Wednesday

PAUL   [Meditation.]

[This was a deep meditation, during which there was a subtle exchange of ideas. When that was over, Raj suggested that we resume in the morning. I agreed.]

March 4, 1982
Thursday
(Afternoon)

PAUL   Raj, I am really having difficulty getting into that place of Peace. I do feel that I am getting help, because I feel the sense of relaxation. I would just like to listen to whatever you might have to say at this time.

RAJ   Paul, you are being too serious about this in the sense of emphasis, intensity, and drive.

You are not faced with the end of the world. You are not faced with destruction of any kind. What you are faced with is a greater cohesiveness of the All One which You are. If all of you is always present, and all of you is always functioning, then the idea of "incompleteness" and "coming up short" is absolutely invalid. It is on the basis of your completeness — and on the Activity of that completeness — that you must let your feelings, your dependence, and your confidence lie.

If you try to deal with the way things appear, if you pay attention to what the five physical senses are telling you, you will scare yourself shitless.

On the other hand, if you are going to agree with the omnipresence and omniaction of your Being, you will find yourself at peace. And, *inevitably,* you will find that omnipresence being omniactive in concrete, tangible ways.

You are beginning to get the idea, and you do have what it takes to follow through all the way on this.

You must realize, Paul, that the only bluff operating here is that doing this will not work. There really is nothing else presenting itself to you as a valid reason for not continuing. You literally only have two choices — you either do it, or you act upon the basis of a bluff.

Now, let's be good and clear on this: Under what circumstances would you ever base your actions upon a bluff? Normally, you wouldn't. But, under a sense of pressure and fear, you could possibly be fooled into believing that there was no point in continuing further. That is why I am pointing out the simple, intelligent overview of the situation here.

You might as well go ahead and follow through, because the only other alternative you have is a big fat zero — don't do anything at all. I think that's clear to you.

Things are not going to collapse around you between now and Monday. So, for at least that period of time, I suggest you drop your concern and your worry, and devote yourself wholeheartedly and completely to getting into that Place most firmly, and to becoming more familiar with it. Feel what it feels like, and see what it looks like. Simply stay there, and stay there, and stay there. Be it, and be it, and be it.

Remember that the threats of destruction are not valid, but they do certainly attempt to stand in your way and turn you back from the one essential thing that needs to be done. You don't have to agree with them at all. You don't have to believe them at all. It's entirely up to you. They cannot validate themselves in any way, shape, or form. Only you can seem to validate them by responding to them, and carrying out their statements in your life as though they were true. But there is no requirement to do that.

Now, I know that it is time for you to go. I would like to talk to you later when you return, as soon as it's convenient.

Good afternoon, Paul.

PAUL   Good afternoon, Raj. Thank you.

March 4, 1982
Thursday
(Evening)

PAUL   Good evening, Raj.

RAJ   Good evening, Paul.

PAUL   First of all, I am curious: Are you still with me constantly all day long, every day?

RAJ   Yes, I am, Paul. I will be until further notice, and you do not need to doublecheck. I will specifically let you know when I will not be with you constantly any longer.

PAUL   Thank you, Raj. I have only fifteen or twenty minutes here to talk with you. As you undoubtedly know, I have some questions, but I am going to save them until later this evening.

Right now. I am going to be quiet and listen to anything you might have to say.

RAJ   Thank you, Paul. The reversal of any situation is accomplished by proclaiming the Fact at the point of being as Conscious Being.

You must realize that doing this does not actually reverse a thing, since what appears to need reversing is not a "presence" at any level. It is, instead, the apparent absence of one's awareness of his Omnipresent Being.

Proclaiming the Fact from the standpoint of being as Conscious Being opens the apparently closed door to the Actuality.

It is the method by which you practice or *be* what you *are* successfully.

We are going to go into the subject of Practice later on this evening, when we continue our conversation. But it is put quite neatly into a nutshell right there, for you to appreciate and employ as necessary between now and then.

I am aware that we have not covered the subject of Practice since we began our conversations, and this was for a very specific reason. I did not want you going out and dabbling, as it were, by practicing a little bit here and a little bit there. But the background has now been given, and the experience has been had. It is indeed time for you to begin to understand what we have been talking about from the standpoint of Practice. As I said, we will go into that later this evening.

I am aware that there has been some growth this afternoon, during your conversation with Susan. I also understand that although you have a glimpse of what your Being was unfolding then, you still feel unable to "connect" it up.

Paul, yes, do notice the apparent beginning of a headache that you are experiencing right now. You are aware it is not truly yours, nor is it truly a headache. Contemplate it for a moment, please.

PAUL   [A few moments of contemplation.]

RAJ   You are correct, Paul. It is a dinner bell only. It indicates the need to be alert to the thought processes which are going on in your home at the moment, and the need to not observe this evening from the standpoint of the cordialities and formalities of the appearances.

As you told Susan this afternoon, keep in mind the larger subjective view, and do not get caught up in the details of any particular thought processes. As Susan said, "you are the Observing," here — as is everyone else, actually.

For now, I will say good evening, and will look forward to a conversation later on.

Good night, Paul.

PAUL   Good night, Raj.

March 5, 1982
Friday
(Afternoon)

PAUL   Good afternoon, Raj.

RAJ   Good afternoon, Paul.

PAUL   Yesterday, you indicated that you were going to spend some time talking about Practice. I won't hold you to that. I do understand that what is seen, heard, and felt is the visibility and tangibility of Conscious Being. What I don't understand is, why do we not have the evidence of orderliness, constructive action, and good employment, especially since I have, to paraphrase Mrs. Eddy's words, left the mortal basis of belief and united with the one Mind?

RAJ   Paul, we will get into this subject.

You are the masculine figure, the point at which Life emerges into manifestation. You are also the feminine figure, that out of which the form is formed. You are the Life, and you are the Substance by means of which Life is Self-expressed. It is a total and complete Life process. Your Being is the Father/Mother God referred to in one of your prayers. As I said, all of you is always present.

Now, it is important for you to understand that everything which is manifest, or appears, has its basis in the creative flow of Mind. You are not the creator in the sense that you, as a point in the universe, have a creative thought and put it forward into manifestation. Rather, you are the Totality, you are the One that constitutes the Many. And, it is on the basis of this Totality that this creativity is expressed.

Every creative action by which Being unfolds Itself is in total harmony with the whole of Its Self. Therefore, it becomes clear that the creative process is the harmonious unfolding of the Totality of Being which brings forth Its individual, creative ideas — and not of a single point in that Totality.

This means that creativity does not occur from the standpoint of a three–dimensional consciousness called a "person" or "personality." This means that your experience of being Creative will not feel the same. The experience of *being* it will be different from the experience of *having* it, which you had from a three–dimensional frame of reference. You could say that Creativity is a *Universal Action* which is experienced *specifically*. It is not a *specific* action which is experienced *universally*.

This is why you might as well not waste any time in attempting to solve the needs or problems confronting you from your old standpoint. As you have found, it no longer works. This is why we are spending so much time in meditation, and in becoming familiar with what it feels like to be out from the Universal Actuality of your Being — as opposed to the shallow, surface, finite, three–dimensional thought processes to which you are accustomed.

Until you become satisfactorily accustomed to what the experience is as Fourth–dimensional Man — which means Universal Being — you will not be in a cohesive, substantial position from which to be the Creative Process which will be experienced specifically as the resolution of the financial, school, and living problems that you seem to be faced with.

You see, Paul, Practice is that Creative Process which spontaneously occurs when one is being out from Mind *as* Mind. Right now, it is not possible for you to practice it, because you are not sufficiently familiar with that Place where you are being out from Mind. In effect, it would be like trying to begin swimming before you have gotten in the water.

Once again, I have asked you to be patient. I am fully aware of the apparent demands on you from your world standpoint. If you will follow through all the way, you will not suffer for your apparent lack of responsible three–dimensional reaction in a three–dimensional frame of reference.

As I said yesterday, your world of appearances is not going to collapse around you between now and Monday. If you will stick with the job at hand, you will, indeed, have your goal or direction set properly. You will not suffer.

I know you wish to spend as much time as possible over this coming weekend working with me. This will, indeed, be well worth your while. You are, relatively speaking, very close to making the "connection," as you put it. You do not need to be frightened that it will be difficult, insurmountable, or even impossible to do within the orderliness of things.

PAUL   Thank you, Raj. If I may, I would like to have a chance to review what you have just said, and get back with you very shortly.

RAJ   That will be perfectly all right, Paul. I will talk with you in a while.

PAUL   Thank you. Good-bye.

March 5, 1982
Friday
(Evening)

PAUL   Good evening, Raj, I'm back.

RAJ   Welcome back, Paul. As I was saying before you realized the tape recorder was not recording, you don't need to go through the process of encircling yourself with white light. Nor do you need to visualize a pyramid of light over you. Nor do you need to do anything else in order to speak with me. It should be becoming clear to you that, since there is no evil power, presence, or force, you do not need to protect yourself from it under any circumstances. Certainly not in order to speak with me.

The more you become comfortable with the fact that I am available to you under any and all circumstances — on the spur of the moment or whatever — you are going to begin to be able to grasp exactly how easily all of Your Self is available to you. It does not require ritual, or deep purpose, or great preparation in order to have it all available to you instantaneously.

You see, Paul, Being is not complex, hard to get at, or hard to understand. Half of the problem we have is our belief that it is not easy. We believe that it is bound up in complex religious or occult rituals or mental structures which we must pass through, like mazes, in order to prove our worthiness. It is not true.

Paul, we do not have to do *anything* in order to deserve to be in immediate and total contact with the infinitude of our Being. The main, essential step to making such contact is to realize that everything we see "out there" — universally — is, indeed, our Being. What separates us from our Good is the belief that our Good is not our Self — nothing more!

As you found, all you had to do in order to contact that part of your infinite Being called "Raj," was to simply acknowledge my existence. Even though you had no idea who I was, you reached out with a simple, heartfelt acceptance of the possibility of my responding to you; and I was there. So is every other aspect of your Being. *It's all present. It's all active. It's all You.*

However, as long as you are blinded by the belief that it is not You, and that it is "out there" — separate, apart, and existing on its own — it is not available to you for you to experience as your Self. This is a key point in the unfoldment of one's conscious experience of being *as* Conscious Being or Fourth-dimensional Man.

PAUL   [Nothing perceived.]

Raj, I am not hearing you at the moment.

RAJ   I know you are not, Paul, and it is because you let your attention drift to the conversation going on outside your door. I decided to wait until you approached me again.

Now, before we continue discussing the subject of Practice, I want to take a moment to discuss Law.

Law, from a Universal standpoint, is constituted of Intelligence. It is the Mindful orderliness, the constituting Harmony, of every aspect and activity of Being. It is not a means of enforcement, but is, instead, the spontaneous but Absolute Principle according to which the functioning of Being occurs. Law is not a tool to use, but is the predisposing Nature of Intelligence to be inherently Principled.

Now, what does this have to do with you? It is that which constitutes your Being. What it is and how it works as the inherent Nature of your Being is essential to understanding how to Practice what You Are. You see, you cannot put these Laws into practice, you cannot set them into motion, because they are already functioning totally before you can even make the mistake of thinking that you are a finite mentality — a three-dimensional awareness — which could use them to bring about your good ends.

Practice is truly a matter of not doing anything from a manipulative standpoint. It is truly a matter of relinquishing that finite concept of self, and going willingly within to that point where your Being is being consciously perceived as your *Conscious* Being.

Immediately upon such willing relinquishment of the false sense of identity, the Intelligence of your Being, which constitutes the Law of Your Being, may be recognized as already functioning. This will further relieve any false sense of responsibility, and inhibit any sense of attempting to bring along the finite concept of "putting these Laws into action."

Practice does not involve manipulation in any way, since the very experience of being conscious is a statement of the fact that Law is already functioning totally.

The word "Practice," in itself, is a very poor word to use. However, it is a prominent word in your experience in terms of medical practice, Christian Science practice, the practice of law, and so on and so forth. We can use it as a bridge to get to the Reality, wherein you may comfortably put the concept of Practice down in favor of the Actuality of *being* the Law.

Now we are going to talk for a bit about the idea of what it is that you are going to practice on. As your entire Being is becoming consciously integrated as your conscious experience of your Self, it will appear as though the Reality of your Being — to whatever degree you are aware of it — will be brought to bear upon that disowned portion of your experience which it is not clear to you *is* your own Being. It will appear as though that aspect will be "healed," "improved," "changed," or "reversed." But, the actuality of such appearances is one of the revealing of its true nature as your Being.

Every time you have a healing session with anyone, do not believe for a moment that, through your inner growth and development, you are being able to do something wonderful for "them." It is your *Self* that you are experiencing, working with, and handling. Figuratively speaking, it amounts to nothing less than your discovery that that piece of the puzzle — which is difficult to identify on its own — is actually some part of the universal portrait of your Self. The Bible quotes Jesus the Christ as saying, "I have overcome the world." This means that He had come over into the Christ-consciousness of His world, and no longer disowned any part of it as being separate or other than His Being.

These points are all important points in "connecting" things up for you, Paul. And, over this weekend, we may well take short bits and pieces at a time in order to move solidly and securely to the point where there is no doubt, whatsoever, in your mind as to what is going on. So, I am going to stop for the moment, and ask that you type up what we have considered so far. Then we will continue.

PAUL   Thank you very much, Raj. I shall be back.

March 6, 1982
Saturday
(Morning)

PAUL   Good morning, Raj.

RAJ   Good morning, Paul.

PAUL   I believe that the way is cleared for us to spend the majority of this weekend working together, and I am looking forward to it.

RAJ   I am, too, Paul.

PAUL   Raj, unless some particular questions come to mind, I am going to let you lead the way this weekend.

RAJ   Thank you, Paul. I want to begin right now with what you are going to be faced with. We are going to cover a number of things which will all deal with the appearing of the Christ in your consciousness *as* your Consciousness of Being. This will be essential in order for you to function cohesively as the All One that you are.

You see, the Christ–consciousness is that consciousness of things which embraces the Totality of Being as It Actually Is, *consciously.* It is that which sees and experiences the Reality of all appearances, because It does not have Its attention focused on them — but rather on that Awareness which is Mind being Aware of Itself. Mind sees from the inside, as it were.

Right now, you are seeing from the inside. Although you do

183

not see me with your eyes, and do not hear me with your ears, you are, indeed, perceiving me and the ideas which I am expressing. You are perceiving the meanings which my Being is expressing at that point of my infinitude which is called "Paul." The five physical senses play no part in this exchange or process, and yet the process is Actual and experienced.

As I said yesterday, observe the process of communication that we are enjoying. As you do, you will begin to grasp the process by which you may communicate with and understand the meaning of any and all parts of the infinitude of your Being, whether it is visible or invisible to the five physical senses. Everything about this process of communication illustrates and includes lessons to be learned and understood.

Paul, the three–dimensional frame of reference is very much like the image on a motion picture screen. Where it appears to be full of meaning it, nevertheless, remains an image no more than a fraction of a millimeter thick on the surface of the screen. The meaning is not in the image at all, but is supplied within the awareness of the observer.

If the observer dislikes something appearing on the screen, it is foolish for him to attempt to change the image in any way, because the meanings which he would like to alter are within him.

What is faulty with that illustration is that, in a theatre, there is a projector — separate from the screen and the observer — which is projecting the picture on the screen. In Reality, there is not a third aspect called a "projector," which places the image on another aspect called a "screen." In Reality, all three aspects are constituted of the one conscious experience of Being.

Stop trying to figure it out, Paul.

The process of "observing" is the Conscious Function of Mind. That which is being "observed" is Mind's Universal Function of *being* Conscious Being. In other words, Being — Mind — by *being,* projects or manifests Itself, and is the Observing of the Process. It is the projector, the image, and the observing of it.

The more you learn to be out from Mind — rather than believing that you are some part of the image on the screen — the more you will become aware of the total harmony of the total process or function that constitutes your Being. What you apparently do, and what apparently is done to you, will become apparent as being totally harmonious. There will be no sense or experience of separation, lack, division, or opposition.

The conscious experience of Being is all that is going on. The details, the drama, the story line, et cetera, are incidental to the whole Process.

When observing them from the position of the image, we seem to be trapped into the story line. But, as we leave that position for the standpoint of being as Conscious Being, we apparently gain perspective. The story line appears to change and identify the Universal Harmonies of Being, which we could not see when we thought that we were one of the characters on the screen. It is in this process of leaving the basis of the image and uniting with and as the One Mind that the Reality of things begins to appear. This is why we have taken the last four weeks to effect this change of view. It is time for you to stop operating from the dimension of the image, and to begin functioning *as* Fourth-dimensional Man, being out from Mind.

Until you thoroughly understand that nothing occurs at the point of the "image" — the three-dimensional frame of reference — until you realize that Cause does not reside at that point, out of habit you will be inclined to continue to try to rearrange things on the screen, to try to improve them, to try to make them more comfortable. And this will be a waste of time.

As I said, Paul, we will take this in short steps this weekend. I would like for you to stop and transcribe what we have said so far, and then let us continue without your taking a break to share this with Susan.

I shall be talking with you shortly.

PAUL   Yes, Raj. Thank you very much.

March 6, 1982
Saturday
(Early Afternoon)

PAUL   All right, Raj, I am back.

RAJ   Good. Although we are going to be conversing more continuously today and tomorrow than we have in the past, it need not involve any sense of urgency or rush. Let it flow at its own rate, and you float with the current. The river will get to its destination.

The river, of course, is the flow of your own Being unfolding Itself as Itself, and constituting your conscious experience of Being.

Remember that your Being is unfolding Itself in Its Totality, and therefore the events going on "out there," three-dimensionally, are all part of this Totality. You cannot get out of sync. You have not taken any time out from anything, not now nor during the past four weeks.

You could say that when you have been actively engaged in living out your life from the position of the "screen" or the three-dimensional frame of reference, at that point you were taking time out from your Being, and that was where you were in error.

Right now you have yourself placed properly. Your attention is where it should be, because it is at that Place where Being is occurring. Do not feel that you are taking time out from life, or from your responsibilities, in order to do this necessary work or growth. Right "here" is where you should have been all along, but did not know how to be.

Paul, has it ever occurred to you that Being is. . .

PAUL   [Nothing perceived.]

RAJ   I want you to observe that you are still not positive that these communications are not just a figment of your imagination. When I begin to say something new, you immediately begin to race your mental engines to see what it is you can come up with that's new, instead of relaxing and continuing to listen to what it is I am saying.

You have found that sometimes I am not even going to say something new, in the sense of something radically different from what you are able to understand. Observe, Paul, that it effectively cuts off communication when you begin to try to think for yourself and figure this out.

Let's try it again. Has it ever occurred to you, Paul, that Being is more than the flow of conscious ideas? It is, indeed, far more than the streaming of thoughts through consciousness within an individual living on a planet in the middle of a solar system which, in turn, is located somewhere in the millions of galaxies in the universe.

Conscious Being, or the Function of being conscious, is actually the Thing, Itself, which is manifest as All — as this Universe full of galaxies, planets, individualities, and thoughts. This Function of Conscious Being is not only what you have called God, but God is what you are to experience as your conscious experience of Being.

Mrs. Eddy said, "All consciousness is Mind; and Mind is God—an infinite and not a finite consciousness."[1] Now, if there is no other might nor Mind but God, then there is no other consciousness of things to be experienced than that one conscious experience of Being, which is God's.

Paul, the shift which you have been experiencing for the past four weeks is, indeed, a shift from a personal, finite, limited sense of universal facts to that Awareness which is Mind's experience of Itself as All. This is why there is great need for trust, for willingness, and for letting go.

Your experiences during the past four weeks, when you have been unable to hear what I am saying, have proven to you that it is the belief of what you cannot do and cannot understand that keeps you from moving beyond your limited frame of reference. This belief keeps you from understanding things which you *are* quite capable of hearing and understanding. That which lies beyond your sense of limitation is not beyond your capacity to understand and comprehend. Please underline that sentence, and remember it.

The Fourth–dimensional view of infinity is far more expansive than anything you have conceived so far, but it is not beyond your capacity to understand.

When it comes to dealing with the financial, living, and school situations which are confronting you in your daily experience, you are blocking yourself off from the answer by believing that it is going to require you to do something which you have neither the resources nor the capability to do. The whole emphasis of your approach is totally three–dimensional — doing, becoming, getting, overcoming, et cetera.

Now, I want you to stop recording. I want you to do a meditation, but I do not want you to lose sensory contact with your environment. During this meditation I want you to move, as you understand the term, to that Place where you may consider these three aspects — the financial, the living, and the school situations — and contemplate them. When you feel that you are through, then I want you to transcribe this portion of our conversation and get back with me.

PAUL   Okay, Raj. Thank you.

[Long meditation.]

---

1   Mary Baker Eddy, *Unity of Good*, 24:12.

March 6, 1982
Saturday
(Late Afternoon)

PAUL   Raj, I am back. I just finished the meditation. I am afraid I was not able to stay at that fine line and, instead, went past it a number of times. As a result, I cannot say that I was able to remain in a position of observing the unfolding regarding what I was to contemplate.

RAJ   Paul, do not be concerned. It was, nevertheless, of benefit to you. We conversed, and you were active during the periods when you were not in sensory contact with your environment.

I want you to consider for a moment that you are very structural regarding what is and what is not right, and what is and what is not done properly when it comes to yourself. It takes very little for you to feel that you have not done well enough — or that you have not measured up to the mark — and therefore, you are deserving of those negative feelings which are appropriate for such a person.

This is unfortunate, because each successive, little dig you have made at yourself — by pointing out to yourself those ways in which you have not measured up — has developed into a rather strong subjective "put down" of yourself. This subjective "put down" is part of what tells you that you can't move beyond where you are, or you can't see this, or you don't know what the answer is to that, et cetera.

You must learn to flow. You must learn that you are not self-directed in the sense of being a puppet with no strings attached, three-dimensionally speaking. From this standpoint, you will always seem to be a puppet with strings attached, and you will not have hold of the controls. From the standpoint of being as Conscious Being, as Fourth–dimensional Man, the concept of strings and controls is irrelevant.

I point this out because, after having a wonderful, productive period of meditation, you spontaneously, immediately, and without questioning, were criticizing yourself because you did not do exactly what I had told you to do. The fact is that there is no justifiable reason to be found for self–criticism.

Watch for this in your experience, and don't continue in this habit.

PAUL   Very well, Raj. I will certainly do my best.

RAJ   Now, Paul, I want you to take a break. Get the lay of the land in your home, and then we will continue.

PAUL   Very well, Raj. Thank you.

March 6, 1982
Saturday
(Early Evening)

PAUL   Good evening, Raj. I have had a break, I have had some dinner, and I am ready to go.

RAJ   Paul, you find yourself feeling uneasy, and actually experiencing two sets of feelings — one of which is being ready to go, and the other is being ready to stop. The reason you are ready to stop is that you are afraid that what you are doing will not do any good.

Paul, I want you to rely very heavily on the Actuality of our conversations. You are well aware that these communications are not common among your friends. You know that you most certainly are not communicating with anyone in a "normal" way when you are speaking with me. You have no idea where I am, but you know that the process is one which you call telepathy. You also know that the communications are not nebulous, but very definite. You know that they happen with ease. You know that they occur no matter whether you are upset, depressed, happy, or quiet. If you have nothing other than our conversations to lean on in terms of your seeing beyond what the five physical senses perceive, then lean on them heavily as verification that you can get beyond and through the apparent limitations which confront you.

Now, let's move on. I want to correct a misconception on your part — a spatial misconception. You are feeling that you are moving forward along a path, building upon a foundation of knowledge and ability to reason, which you have developed and exercised in the past. This is not the case.

The fact is that you are moving backwards on the path which you have come. This is because, to a large degree, your path took you away from your Being and into a three–dimensional frame of reference. You are, so to speak, relaxing back out of that thinking process — that finite, reasoning, intellectual structure which you felt was getting you somewhere in a progressive sense.

Our conversation right now is not the result of a thinking process at all. When you stand at the Door *as* the Door, the Wisdom, the Truth, the Knowledge that flows through and *as* your conscious experience of Being, is not the result of thought processes, nor of reasoning. Because It continues to flow on past you, It truly does not become a stored body of knowledge from which you may draw in the future. Standing as the Door means that, in this so–called "future," whatever Knowledge and Understanding is applicable to the unfolding at that time will be there in exactly the same manner that It is here right now.

You see, Paul, we are beginning to redefine what constitutes your conscious experience of Being.

Go ahead and take care of the need in your home at the moment, and we will continue when you get back.

PAUL   Thank you, Raj. I will be back in a minute.

      [Short break taken.]

I am back, Raj.

RAJ   Very well, Paul. We will continue. Susan has grasped the essential point. I see that you are feeling it and relaxing with it, and that is good.

I am going to ask that you do a meditation right now with the microphone in your hand. And, once again, I want you to remain sensorily aware of your surroundings.

PAUL   Okay, Raj.

      [Short meditation.]

Raj, I always want to be at this point of experiencing my being as Conscious Being. It is heaven.

RAJ   I understand completely, Paul. This is when you are experiencing the cohesiveness, the Oneness, of your Being. Your conscious experience should constantly be experienced from this Place. Go ahead and feel it and be consciously there.

Notice that although you are relaxed, you are totally aware, and you are totally capable of movement and activity. But, you are quite aware that you are not *in* it and you are not investing your Self into any single experience. This is important.

PAUL [Short period of contemplation.]

RAJ Paul, do not sit there and attempt to figure out what we are supposed to accomplish this weekend. We are not going to accomplish a thing in the sense that you are thinking of it. We are going to stop "accomplishing" altogether. We are going to begin to simply *be.* Let go of all this attempting to figure out, reason, and come to enlightened conclusions.

The conclusion to processes of reasoning and thinking has never, ever been Enlightenment. No matter who it has been, the enlightenment they have experienced has occurred only when their three–dimensional consciousness has been totally silent, or it has broken through in spite of their thinking. Thus, it has illustrated that the thinking process is never responsible for growth.

It is absolutely foolish for you to think that you can peg this weekend, when not even I can do that. You are the Door, and your function as the Door is not to peg anything. Being can never be pegged. If it could, it would become one of the "butterflies" in the collection of a colossal, larger–than–Universal giant. That is ridiculous.

Being is the Universal unfolding of It's Self–perpetuating Action. Give up your attempts to grasp it, hold it, turn it over, and understand it by means of such examination. You must be willing to understand by virtue of *Its* Self-explanation. You must let go.

Now, I am going to give you an assignment, but remember, you are not going to be graded. You had better not grade yourself.

The assignment is this: We are going to break, and I want you to transcribe this. I want you, as well, to go out of your room and spend ten or fifteen minutes with your family. I want you to do your best to do that from this Place, without becoming uncentered.

When you are through, let us have another conversation.

PAUL   Okay, Raj. I will. Thank you very much for everything so far today. I appreciate it immeasurably.

RAJ   Good–bye, Paul.

PAUL   Good–bye.

March 6, 1982
Saturday
(Late Evening)

PAUL   Okay, Raj. I'm back. I feel that I did a fairly decent job of remaining in that Place, although it is not as strong a feeling of being there as when we finished our conversation.

RAJ   That is all right, Paul. You did very well.

PAUL   Raj, can you explain to me what or why there is a feeling like I wish this would be over with? I am realizing that this feeling comes to me quite often in many various disguises. I would like to understand it, so that I know what it is I'm disagreeing with, or putting down, or ignoring.

RAJ   It is a feeling of jitteriness, of being ill at ease.

PAUL   It seems to be a feeling which would be appropriate if I were to discontinue the conversations today and go do something else. But, instead, it makes me feel like stopping the conversation and doing something else so that I could relax. And, the fact is that what's going on is not, at least it doesn't seem like it is, uncomfortable in any way.

RAJ   It is causing you discomfort and uneasiness, because what we are discussing is flying right in the face of many well–established concepts which you have entertained and employed in your lifetime. This feeling may well be the last whimpers of your inclination to utilize them. I would allow them, if I were you, to simply do their whimpering, since they

195

will spontaneously fade out. Do not give them credit, and do not act upon them.

PAUL   Very well, Raj.

       [Short period of meditation.]

RAJ   Paul, I am going to interrupt your meditation because you are doing it for a reason that has no basis. You think you cannot hear me and need to relax. It is obvious, by virtue of what I'm saying right now, that you *can* hear me and do not need to do a meditation.

I want you to consider that in everything we are doing, we are harmonizing and flowing with the divine energies — with the outpouring of the river of Life, right at Its source. This river of Life flows freely and totally through and as your conscious experience of Being. It is always doing this, whether or not you have placed yourself properly in that Place. This is important to understand, since it makes clear that the only thing we need to do in order to find the resolution to whatever situation we are faced with, is simply go to the Source as the Door.

Now, I realize that you have spent almost eight solid hours conversing with me, together with transcribing our discussions. So, I am going to suggest that, having put in a good day's work, you retire for the evening and enjoy whatever you care to do.

If possible, I would like to begin earlier tomorrow morning than we did today, and I will look forward to speaking with you then.

Good night, Paul.

PAUL   Good night, Raj, and many thanks, again.

March 8, 1982
Monday

PAUL Good morning, Raj.

RAJ Good morning, Paul.

PAUL Well, I don't know if my faith is being tested, or what. But I am feeling weak and thrown for a loop this morning. To be blunt about it, I don't know what I'm going to do, or what I'm supposed to do. The demands are overwhelming and they are not going away.

RAJ Paul, this is excellent!

PAUL Am I understanding you correctly?

RAJ Yes, Paul, you are. This is excellent news.

PAUL Raj, sometimes you blow my mind. In what way can this be excellent?

RAJ It is excellent because it is proving to you that what you *think* you have to do is coming face to face with what you *have* to do.

PAUL I don't understand. I understand the words, but I don't understand how they apply or how it could be excellent.

RAJ Paul, it is not hard.

PAUL   Please continue.

RAJ   You see, Life — your Being — is preparing a feast for you, but not in the direction in which your vision is directed at the moment.

PAUL   Obviously, then, the next question is: In what direction should I have my gaze directed?

RAJ   In the direction which we have been working on, and which you have been experiencing for the last four weeks.

PAUL   But Raj, it hasn't been doing any good!

RAJ   You are incorrect, Paul. You are not able to see the good it has done, because you insist on looking in the wrong place. You insist on looking "out there," rather than remaining solidly, steadfastly, and faithfully at that within point which you call the Place.

PAUL   This feast that is being prepared — do you mean that it is actually being prepared in the sense of not yet being completed? Or do you mean it in the sense that it is already completed and is there for me to discern?

RAJ   Paul, I mean it both ways. All of you is always present. Yet, in that omnipresent Action of your Being, there are cycles — cycles of time and cycles of growth. This is why I referred to the "fitness of time" the other day. I indicated that you must wait until the fitness of time in order to discern and understand what is happening here.

PAUL   Raj, I am having trouble with that, since in Infinity and Eternity there is no such thing as "time" as I perceive it three-dimensionally. It is all the Eternal Now.

RAJ   You are correct, Paul. All of you is always present, and all of you is always functioning in the Omnipresent Now. There is no such thing as progress on a time line, in the sense of moving from a point in the present to another point in the future. Nevertheless, there is the nonspatial Omnipresent Unfolding of Being.

    If you will stop resisting this idea, you will be able to hear and understand what I have to say with greater ease, and I would suggest that you relax on that subject.

PAUL   [Telephone interruption.]

Raj, that was a call from someone who wants past due monies for a violin we are renting for our daughter. I told her I would return her call later this afternoon, after I had had a chance to look at my books. I was stalling for time in hopes that during our conversation, we would come to some understanding that would allow me to deal with these calls that I am faced with.

Raj, I am going to ask a straightforward question. I need an answer on it. It was mentioned to me by someone who is in contact with her Guide that it has been a long time since he was living here on earth. Consequently, the Guide is somewhat out of touch with the way things are here at this time. He sometimes does not grasp the things that are necessary for us to deal with here and, therefore, is not able to be realistic about what needs to be done from day to day.

RAJ Paul, in the first place, I am not viewing you, or experiencing you, by remote control through the vast outreaches of space. I am, as you have been aware, present within your conscious experience of things. I see what you see. I know first-hand what you think and feel about what you see. And, I am aware of the total picture. As I said in the beginning: I know how things *appear* to you, and I know how things actually *are.* This is why I can tell you to sit still, and be patient, and not be worried that you will come to some harm as a result of that instruction.

I am not some individuality hanging around the earth realm in an attempt to find somebody to help so that I can feel my existence is worthwhile. Other than that, I will make no further comment in response to your friend's understanding of how things are.

I know you have things that need to be taken care of today. Make the car payment. Make the calls that you need to make at this point — the ones you have already planned on making. Do it without investing your Self in any single action that you appear to be doing.

Before you do that, please type up this conversation and review it. Finish those things which you know you need to do and have the money for. Make the necessary phone calls. Then, before you attempt to tackle dealing with the things you are not able to pay for, I want you to get back with me.

I want you to be aware that between now and the time you get back with me, you will be receiving considerable help from my end. I want you to leave your thought wide open for fresh thoughts and insight.

I reiterate that you are not faced with the end of the world, and this is not the final exam. It is, you might say, a quiz, but it is one that you are well prepared for. You do not need to be concerned.

PAUL All right, Raj. I will do that.

RAJ Thank you. You will not regret it.

March 9, 1982
Tuesday

PAUL   Good morning, Raj.

RAJ   Good morning, Paul. I know you have had a rough time since we talked yesterday, and it is not my intent or purpose for you to be uncomfortable or suffering. It does not fulfill any purpose for you to be suffering. You were incorrect yesterday when it occurred to you that the only way you can tell you are growing is if you are feeling some discomfort. Discomfort can be an indication of growth, but it is not the only indication of growth.

We are entering a new phase of these conversations, and in this phase we are going to be dealing with the Light energy that constitutes your Being.

Before we get into the questions that you have, I would appreciate it if you would bear with me and listen to what I have to say.

PAUL   Very well, Raj.

RAJ   Paul, all energy is Light, and Light is the omnipresent energy that constitutes all life forms, all ideas, and all of every aspect of Conscious Being. It is the pure Light that is Love. It is the pure Light that constitutes Substance. It is the pure Light which differentiates Itself according to Intelligence as all that appears and all that is.

PAUL   [Whereupon I experienced a number of visual images which Raj said to ignore.]

RAJ   The delight of Life is the signal which indicates the successful completion or Awakening in individual thought. This is because it indicates the amalgamation or connection of the Alpha and Omega — the inside and the outside — the spiritual and material — the Fourth Dimension with the first three as Conscious Experience.

I know that this is very difficult for you to put up with, because you feel there are more pressing needs, but if you will bear with me a little longer, it will be worth your while.

PAUL   Very well, Raj.

RAJ   This Light energy, which is constituted of the Christ-consciousness — God's view of Himself — is what constitutes your consciousness and your experience, Totally and Completely. You must understand that there is nothing else going on — no other Presence but this Light. It is the Light of Living Love.

Paul, it is impossible for your world to become integrated if you do not understand what the Substance of that Totality is. This is why we are discussing this point this morning. The only Substance there is throughout the Universe — and throughout all dimensions — is Light. This Light, in Its various aspects, is Life, Truth, Principle, Mind, Soul, and Spirit. It is also Intelligence and Substance.

In everything you do, I want you to begin to be conscious of the idea that all there is to you — and all there is to everything — is this Light of Living Love. There are not two things going on. This Light is eternally living Itself as the intelligent expression of Conscious Experience, universally and specifically.

Now, I want to correct a misconception on your part. Your ability to reason and think is not the equivalent of the three-dimensional frame of reference. Your thought processes and reasoning processes are not to be ignored. We would not be communicating at this very moment if you did not have the means to translate the meanings I am communicating into words and phrases. It is only by virtue of the fact that you have imagination, reason, perspicacity — all of the various capacities and functions of Consciousness — that you are able to correctly translate that which unfolds to you. This is true whether it is coming from me, or from that Place wherein you directly experience the Reality of Being.

We run into trouble when we stand away from the Door, and begin our thinking or thought processes from their standpoint, and then extrapolate and come to conclusions without going within and being as Conscious Being.

You see, Being unfolds Itself as *meaning,* not as language. It is through the function of Reason and Imagination that language is brought into play, for the purpose of verbalizing these infinite meanings which Being is unfolding.

You do have a right to answers which will identify the Absolute Oneness of Being throughout your entire experience of Being.

Now, I am going to suggest that you transcribe what we have considered so far. Then, I am going to suggest that you sit down and go into that Place and consider each question that you were going to bring to me. Be open and receptive to the meanings which will unfold, and let your conscious ability to reason, extrapolate, and verbalize come into play. After you are through, I would like to speak with you.

Good morning, Paul.

PAUL   Good morning, Raj.

March 10, 1982
Wednesday
(Midnight)

PAUL Tonight I am frustrated, and I am also a little depressed...

RAJ Go ahead, Paul.

PAUL ...and I realize that lately it seems like all I'm doing is complaining, or saying I don't understand, or being concerned because nothing is working. I hate to lay that all in your lap all the time. When these conversations first began, I thought that I was going to begin to understand something that I didn't understand —something which would help me see my experience begin to be constructive, forward–moving, and harmonious. This has not happened. And I guess I have a whole lot of different feelings: angry, hopeless, hopeful, discouraged, and so on.

It seems a little incredible to me that these conversations can occur — which is really far out — but that something as simple as being able to pay my bills doesn't seem to be possible. It's sort of like being able to send man to the moon but not be able to feed everybody right here on earth, you know. At the risk of being disrespectful, "Big deal!"

RAJ I understand what you're saying, Paul.

PAUL Raj, can you tell me why it would be indicative of the omnipresence and omniaction of my Being for us to have to declare bankruptcy, and for the people to whom we owe money to be out that money that is rightfully theirs?

RAJ   No, I cannot, Paul. You see, Paul, we are not working conceptually at all, here.

PAUL   You've lost me, Raj. What do you mean we're not working conceptually at all? What relevance does that have to the fact that I have about $400 to my name, and at least four times that much that needs to go out just to pay the current month's bills? People are not willing to wait much longer for it.

RAJ   It has a direct bearing, an exact bearing, on it. You are trying to make everything fit into your concept of what is right, instead of simply flowing with What Is. You are so busy reacting to your own thought structures and concepts, and how things look to you, that you are not able to perceive what is really taking place. It is not destructive or unprincipled in any way.

PAUL   Raj, is there any way, while I am sleeping tonight, for me to get some help on this — some background information, or something which will help me to understand this point — when I am not in a conscious position to resist it or block it with my fears and conceptual thinking?

RAJ   I will, indeed, work with you tonight to clear debris and unnecessary garbage which stands in the way.

PAUL   I will truly appreciate that very much. To tell you the truth, I can see that I am beginning to panic somewhat here, and I don't like that feeling.

RAJ   Paul, do not resist that feeling, but simply do not invest too much attention in it. You can move away from it, where you will not be reached by the apparent dynamics of its meaning. Even if it does not appear to resolve anything from your present point of view, you will, nevertheless, be in the best position possible to have the answer be revealed as your conscious experience. I will ask you to do that this evening before you go to sleep, in preparation for the work we will do while you are sleeping.

PAUL   Very well. I will do that, Raj.

I will say good night for now, and speak with you in the morning.

RAJ Very well, Paul. Good night, and be aware that I will be working together with you all night tonight.

PAUL Thank you very much, Raj. Good night.

RAJ Good night, Paul.

March 10, 1982
Wednesday
(Morning)

PAUL   Thank you for your help last night. I feel in a much better frame of mind this morning, although I am not out of the woods yet.

RAJ   Paul, you must realize that you are not "in the woods" in the first place. The "woods" are in you. You are that omnipresent conscious experience of Being which constitutes Fourth–dimensional Man. You will always feel trapped when you are seeing yourself as being inside that Omnipresence which constitutes your Being. You will always feel uncomfortable because you are believing something which is not true.

    I see that you have gotten the point that you can utilize your ability to think and reason when it is based upon what you have learned when you have been experiencing your being as Conscious Being.

PAUL   I am listening, Raj.

RAJ   I know you are, Paul. You must realize that we are not going to be doing anything spectacular here. We are simply going to be bringing out the uncomplicated Facts of Being. You are not faced with anything which requires an astounding understanding. You must trust that this is so. No matter how big the problem claims to be, keep it simple.

PAUL   I will do my best, Raj.

RAJ   I know you have to get to this job which you have at hand. Keep yourself centered in that Place to the very best of your ability. I will be helping.

Remember not to get into the picture. Do not see yourself the way the three-dimensional frame of reference sees you and wants to convince you of. Remember that Being is Eternal. No single event in the Eternality of your conscious experience of Being takes precedence over that which is *aware* of it. You are not *in* it. It is not larger than you, and it is not controlling your Being.

Take care of the necessary things that you are able to take care of. Recognize the Facts about what you seem not to be able to take care of, and *leave it at that!*

I will let you go ahead with what you need to do. I would like you to keep in mind what I have just shared with you while you are doing what you need to do. If you have any questions, do not hesitate to ask.

PAUL   Thank you very much, Raj. I appreciate your utter patience with me, and I will be back with you. Thank you very much.

Good-bye.

March 10, 1982
Wednesday
(Evening)

PAUL   Raj, I'm back with the same old question.

RAJ   I know you are, Paul.

PAUL   What I guess it boils down to is this: If all of me is always present and always functioning, then it seems as though we have a right to either see the fulfillment of that fact as actual, concrete evidence in our experience, or at least we should be able to know what it is we are going to be faced with. In this way, we won't just walk up to the edge of the cliff and be forced to jump off, as it looks like we are presently doing.

Each time I have asked this question I have gotten an answer which neither Susan nor I understand. And I could go into all the rest of my thoughts on this, but you are undoubtedly aware of them. So, I would like to know what you have to share on this subject.

RAJ   Paul, we are arriving at a time in which the answer is going to be made clear.

PAUL   When are we going to arrive at that time? For how much longer do we have to wonder?

RAJ   Paul, I know you are upset. The fact is that I cannot give you the specific answer.

PAUL   Is there some other source that I can go to for the answer?

RAJ   No, there is not.

PAUL   Then it sounds like you are saying that although all of me is always present and always functioning, all of me is *not* always available to me to perceive and understand. Is that correct?

RAJ   No, it is not.

PAUL   Will you please amplify then, because that doesn't make sense. Why am I not able to have the information if it is available to me as the Completeness of my Being?

RAJ   The simple fact is that You are the Answer, and this is why I cannot give it to you. This is why you cannot get it.

PAUL   Raj, when we first began speaking, you were very direct with me. It seems, as we have gone along, that you have begun turning things into riddles.

RAJ   This is not a riddle.

PAUL   It also is not an answer. At least, it is not an answer that I understand. I want you to tell me why you cannot answer the question straight out, direct, so that I may understand it.

RAJ   Because, for you to know the answer would create an imbalance in a rather delicately balanced system of events which are at work at this very moment.

PAUL   May I bring Susan in here, and may we both speak with you?

RAJ   You most certainly can. I will appreciate having the opportunity to speak with both of you together.

PAUL   Thank you, Raj.

      [Susan came in.]

    Are you saying that I need to sit here without raising a finger in response to anything that is going on, and let the axes fall as they appear to be going to?

RAJ   That is exactly what I am saying.

PAUL   Did I get that correctly?

RAJ   Yes, you did.

PAUL   And you are saying that you cannot tell me why I should do such an extreme thing?

RAJ   That is correct.

PAUL   You understood when I said "axes falling" that I was referring to the possibility of being kicked out of our house because we can't pay the rent, being sued by IFG Leasing Co. because we can't come up with $12,000 in ten days, and so on?

RAJ   I understood exactly, Paul.

PAUL   And your answer remains the same?

RAJ   It remains the same.

PAUL   Do these subtly balanced events have to do with me, within myself, or do they refer to events on a larger scale, out of the range of my immediate personal experience?

RAJ   Paul, your development and growth has nothing to do with these events. Although you are on rough ground right now and are noticing the bumps, you are, nevertheless, moving across this territory quite steadily, and your fears and doubts are not hindering your progress at all.

PAUL   Raj, you know I could be doing this growing in jail. Being in jail would not keep me from doing this growing at all, but I don't particularly care to do it there.

RAJ   You will not end up doing it there. I told you early on that what was unfolding here would not cause the breakup of your family nor your life, and that remains the fact.

PAUL   Raj, Susan wants to know if she's just supposed to get up and do the sewing and cooking, as though nothing is going on.

RAJ   [Addressing Susan.] Susan, nothing *is* going on of the sort you are looking at and reacting to. I cannot tell you what is going on. But, I have told Paul that what is going on Actually in your experience is not destructive and will not be experienced that way. You are both caught up in your past conceptualizations and *what has worked*. But, what governed those appearances is no longer in force. They are not in force for *anyone* any longer.

You and Paul are being led through this change. In a way, you both have an advantage, in that Paul chose to speak to his Guide just prior to this occurring. So, you are getting information that most do not have. This is simply because they were not listening, and did not ask to speak with someone who could do what I am doing with you. If others are not aware of this change having occurred yet, they will soon. And you have an opportunity to be grateful for the information that you have at this point. I undersatnd that it is not easy to believe this because, based upon your prior concepts, the whole process by which you are becoming aware of it is not "usual" or "normal" as you understand it. It is, nevertheless, true.

Paul is being guided and pressured to move along a new path because he desires it and asked for it. You, Susan, are at the point where you are capable of understanding exactly what is going on. But both of you are hanging onto patterns which are no longer in force, and trying to make these appearances fit in.

I can do no more than advise you of these facts, and guide you as long as you are looking for help in understanding what is available to you to understand.

PAUL   Raj, there are those who believe that the lining up of the planets today is of some significance. They think it is going to allow Maitreya to identify Himself to at least the group with which He is working at the present time. Can you expand on this, or can you share with me how things stand in terms of Maitreya's announcement of His presence?

RAJ   Paul, there is significance in the lining up of the planets, but . . .

    [Pause.]

PAUL   Are you speaking with someone else right now?

RAJ   Yes, I am. Excuse me just a moment.

    [Pause.]

PAUL   Raj, if, as you said in one of our first talks, you are able to slot your answers into my time frame, why are you asking me to wait a moment?

RAJ   Because, Paul, we are talking in *real* time right now, and I am not at a great distance from you. Please excuse me for a moment.

    [Pause.]

Paul, to answer your unspoken question: Yes, I am on planet Earth at this moment. Please be patient, and I will be back with you in just a moment.

    [Pause.]

PAUL   [At this point I experienced a number of mental images.]

Raj, are you still there?

RAJ   Yes, Paul, I am.

PAUL   I am sorry to interrupt you.

RAJ   That's perfectly all right, Paul.

PAUL   [Nothing perceived.]

Are you saying anything to me at the moment?

RAJ   No, I am not.

PAUL   Are any of the things which I saw — the large red and white room from which an announcement would be made, which looked out through a Greek porch onto Saturn, very large in the sky, plus my sensing that you are in a place that is bustling with activity — are any of these things of significance? Am I perceiving any of them accurately?

RAJ   Paul, you are correct that I am in a place that is bustling with activity, yes. The other things you will simply have to wait for verification on.

PAUL   During the wait, one of the thoughts that went through my mind was to be sure to watch TV at 8:00 o'clock this evening.

RAJ   All I can say is to follow your intuitive perceptions. Then I would like to speak with you later this evening before you retire. I cannot say any more at the present time, and I will look forward to speaking with you this evening.

PAUL   Very well, Raj. Thank you very much.

March 11, 1982
Thursday

PAUL   I am feeling really frustrated this morning. I appreciate the help you gave last night. I appreciate the fact that I am getting the same message from a number of different points — that being that I am the Answer. However, I don't understand in what way I am the Answer. At least, I don't understand in what way *being* the Answer has any connection with my experience of not being able to pay my bills. I am not going to say anything more than that. I am just going to be quiet as best I can at the moment, and listen to what you may have to say.

RAJ   Paul, do not despair. You are going to find the answer unfolding within and as your conscious experience of Being as being already completed.

PAUL   That is nice to hear, but it is not making me any more comfortable.

RAJ   Paul, you are suffering from your "should" system. You are experiencing how difficult it is to lay down conceptualized processes and theories. I will not leave my position that this conceptual thinking relates in no way to what is Actually going on — which is the infinitude of your Being unfolding Itself perfectly, properly, and nondestructively — except, of course, in terms of these concepts which are binding you. They will be destroyed. They no longer serve to move you to a new base. As you are discovering, the concepts are actually impeding your growth. You must lay them down.

The growth will occur. The growth is occurring. This is why you feel shoved into the corner right along with the concepts. Figuratively speaking, this is why you feel that you are going to be blown up in the blowing up of your concepts.

There is no reason for you to feel that you must be able to understand the new view before you see it. There is no way for Revelation to mean the revealing of what you already know, except in the Absolute sense. Your Being has always moved beyond your present concepts of Reality, and you have always recognized it as a sudden influx of inspiration and understanding which went beyond what you had previously been aware of.

You have simply never been aware of the *process* before, only the *result*. This time you are aware of the process — of the breakdown of the old concepts and the appearing of the Revelation. In actuality, the whole process of breakdown and the new view is the One, Total Function of Being called Revelation. It is happening in slow motion, so to speak, and you are having the opportunity to observe the process.

You are, indeed, the Answer. I would stick with this Fact as constantly as you are able, even if it appears not to be so, and not to be evident. You are going to stick with something, and it might as well be the Fact.

PAUL   I feel like I'm going crazy.

RAJ   I know you do. But remember, Paul, that is just an idea, just one of an infinitude of ideas, and it therefore holds no position of authority or dominance in your experience. Do not credit it with any value, for it has no more value than any other spurious thought which states an absurd impossibility. Do not attempt to handle it, but simply pass on by.

I will be with you all day, as I have said before. If you have any questions, please do not hesitate to ask.

PAUL   I don't care how strong the measures are, but may I ask for you to continue to do what you can to help me see what needs to be seen as easily, as quickly, as possible? And, can you do it while I am doing the other things that need to be done?

RAJ   I will do what I am able.

PAUL   Thank you, Raj. I will talk with you later.

RAJ   You are welcome, Paul. I will look forward to it.

PAUL   Good–bye.

March 13, 1982
Saturday

PAUL   Good afternoon, Raj.

RAJ   Good afternoon, Paul.

PAUL   Raj, I don't know what I want to say, so I am going to be quiet and listen to what you have to say.

RAJ   Thank you, Paul. You have been very patient and cooperative. Everything that we have done has been absolutely necessary. It has caused you and your family to grow beyond what they would have otherwise.

Just as you feel you are coming to the end of your rope, likewise a cycle is coming to the end of its rope. There will be major changes. You have been faithful, and you will not be sorry.

As you already know, the road will not be immediately smooth. But, the overall burdens caused by misconceived theories and concepts will immediately begin to melt away upon Maitreya's announcement. Mankind will begin to be able to rally around a central idea, a central purpose. It will not take long for man to put his energies behind that focal point and begin to move out of the dream of suffering, lack, starvation, and poverty.

There is going to be a lot to do. It is going to take the kind of strength that comes from inner Knowing, as well as inner Faith. What we have been doing over the past five weeks is simply giving that inner Faith and Knowing some practice, so as to allow you to come to a point wherein you could feel that strength from an experiential standpoint.

I am well aware that, at this moment, you do not feel strong. But the fact is, that in spite of your thinking mind, in spite of your finite concepts, you have continued invisibly to grow and become strong with the kind of strength I am speaking of.

Your faith has been almost immaculate. I know you are almost totally convinced that it has been foolish, and that you have been gullible to the point of insanity. But, the fact is that you are here, once again communicating with me and believing, still, that these conversations are valid.

Paul, you could not have the strength to continue to this point if it were not for an inner, nonconceptual Knowing of the events which are about to take place, although the details are not consciously available to you. Do not worry. You will not appear to be a fool in any way.

PAUL   Do you still say that Maitreya is going to announce His presence tomorrow to the world?

RAJ   I still say that He is going to announce His Presence as who He really is tomorrow, yes.

PAUL   And do you still say that between now and that time we will be visited or contacted by someone in the flesh regarding these events, together with the clarification of what I and my family will be doing from now on?[1] Also, will the financial means by which we are going to proceed be explained to us?

RAJ   Yes, Paul, you will find my words taking place in your experience exactly as I have said.

PAUL   Are you still here on the earth?

RAJ   Yes, I am.

PAUL   Will you be leaving shortly, or will you be staying for an indefinite period of time?

RAJ   That will remain to be seen. It all depends on what the need is.

PAUL I feel that during the last week or two, when our family's financial position has become more dynamic, that I have not grown nor have I learned much, if anything — at least not compared to the first few weeks in which we were conversing. I apologize for being frightened, but I have not been able to deal with the apparent demands in an uninvolved way, and I am concerned that this has gotten in the way of what truly needed to be dealt with.

RAJ Paul, you are who you are, what you are, and where you are at this very moment. You cannot do more than you can do. Do not waste your time in self-criticism or self-doubt. As you shall see, it is totally unnecessary. There has been no requirement for you to be something that you are not able to be. What you have needed to learn in order to fulfill your place has been accomplished. You have done well.

As I have said before, at present, you do not have enough information in order to make a correct judgment about what is occurring. But this will be clarified by the end of tomorrow.

PAUL What is the necessary thing for me to do between now and the time of this contact?

RAJ First of all, remain as calm as you can. If you need to meditate to do that, then do so. But it is not necessary for you to remain constantly in meditation, as though that will facilitate the events which will occur. You are already solidly locked into this unfoldment.

PAUL [A few minutes of meditation.]

Is there anything further you want to say at this point?

RAJ There are lots of things I want to say, but none at this time.

PAUL How will I know that this individual who will contact us will be the person you are referring to?

RAJ He will tell you that Raj has sent him.

PAUL Do you still maintain that no suffering, loss, or destruction will be experienced by any member of my family as a result of this, but rather will result in the perception of new and more expanded freedom and experience?

RAJ   You will find out that that is exactly correct.

PAUL   And I will find this out tomorrow?

RAJ   You will find it out tomorrow.

But, between now and then I want you to attempt, as best you can, to have an attitude of expectation, an open heart, and an open mind, both to the contact which will be made with you, and to the announcement by Maitreya.

PAUL   I will do my very best. May we talk later if I feel like it?

RAJ   Of course, Paul. Nothing has changed in that respect.

PAUL   Thank you very much. I very likely will speak with you later on. Good night.

RAJ   Good night, Paul. I am with you one hundred percent.

PAUL   Thank you.

---

[1] Raj had shared with me, in a brief exchange that wasn't recorded, that a gentleman would come to our house, identify himself as being sent by Raj, and discuss the things mentioned.

March 15, 1982
Monday

PAUL Good morning, Raj.

RAJ Good morning, Paul. I am glad to hear from you this morning. I know yesterday was a rugged day for you, as it also was for Susan.[1]

PAUL I do not understand why it was necessary. However, I do not want to dwell on that level or in those feelings.

RAJ It will be well if you don't, Paul. You see, you have not been flowing with What Is. Instead, you have become increasingly aggressive in your attempt to make things fit within your present concepts, even though those concepts are moral, righteous, and upright. You are assuming that if you let go of this control, what will happen will not be moral, just, and upright.

Paul, there is only one thing going on. That one thing is the Life Principle Itself, which constitutes Your Being. It is not necessary for you, as a person, to duplicate what your Being is already *being*. I know you are having difficulty relating that to your experience, since it appears that everyone is demanding that you, as a mortal, respond to and fulfill these demands.

The fact remains that as you let go in those other areas, just as you are doing right now while talking with me, the fullness will flow and be recognized by you —the fullness of your Being, that is.

It is not your prerogative to decide how someone else's fulfillment will apparently manifest itself. Your responsibility is entirely to being in that Place where your Being may fulfill Itself without Paul, person, duplicating or manipulating or meddling in the picture.

You don't have control, and have never had control as a person — as a thinking mind — whereas your Being has always had complete Control in Its Self-expression. It will forever continue to do so.

Nothing has ever happened as a result of your thought. You must get used to the idea that your thinking mind is there to give words to the unfolding meanings which your Being is manifesting as Its infinite identification. It is not something which can be used to *cause* that infinite manifestation of Its identification.

You are having difficulty because you are trying to bring your "thought processes," which you have mistakenly identified as "your self," into that Place where your Self is already *being* Itself infinitely and perfectly. In this Place, there is no thought process whatsoever.

The need here is to let go of the thought process, which you are already rather proficient at, as well as the misidentification of your self *as* that thought process. You are that Mind which functions perfectly and infinitely without thinking a thought in order to do so. This Mind has, as one of Its capacities, the ability to formulate verbalizations of Its infinite Self-action. Yet, It is never *in* Its verbalizations, and never mistakes Itself as being the "thought process" by which means the verbalizations are developed.

Verbalizations are finite means of describing That Which Is — and Is infinitely — and, therefore, cannot be in any way circumscribed by the verbalizations.

Do not fret yourself. That action is a thought-process action based on a sense of limitation, and, therefore, a finite reaction to a finite process can only compound this sense. Again, do not attempt to do anything to that finite experience. Also, do not invest yourself in that experience. Rather, pass by or sink out of that particular experience or thought.

You think that because I am not talking to you about "money" or "actions in the three-dimensional frame of reference," that I am not responding to your need. You think that you are not receiving help for the very situation which prompted you to contact me in the first place. But the fact is that the realization of what I am sharing with you is the *only* Answer to the need.

If you feel that you must respond to the need as though it were Actual, I certainly cannot stop you. Whatever you do can only serve to verify that, ultimately, you will have to come to the Answer in order to be relieved of the continuing illusion of lack.

Whatever you do, lean to the best of your ability on your Intuition. I know you feel rather shaken at the moment, but this will pass.

PAUL   Thank you, Raj.

RAJ   You are welcome, Paul. Do not try to avoid anything at this point. Everything that seems to be going on is fitting perfectly into its place in serving to move, guide, and illustrate to you experientially the Eternal Facts of Your Being. If you will listen for their meanings as Self meanings, you will begin to enjoy a fruition of understanding, as well as abundance, that exceeds anything you have imagined.

I continue to be with you constantly. My purpose has not changed in any way, and you have my full support.

PAUL   Thank you, Raj. I will continue.

---

[1]   The 14th came and went — no announcement, no gentleman at our door, nothing. We were greatly disappointed and frustrated. I did not bring the subject up again.

Sometime in May or June, Raj brought it up and explained that it was an object lesson; that it was the most effective means of getting me to stop looking outside my Self for either the Christ (Maitreya) or my answer. He explained that as long as I was looking "out there" for my Good, I would stand waiting, unfulfilled, as we had on the 14th.

I got the message!

March 19, 1982
Friday

PAUL Before we begin, Raj, I sincerely apologize for cursing you out this afternoon.

RAJ I understand, Paul, and although it was not necessary, I accept your apology.

PAUL Raj, as you know, nothing has apparently changed since the first conversation we had — objectively, at least — although subjectively speaking, I feel a lot has occurred. As we have progressed into the last few weeks, I have become more and more concerned about the dire straits I find myself in, objectively speaking. It has been very difficult for me to relax and to have faith in the validity of what you have been telling me.

Nevertheless, something keeps me coming back, and here I am again. I will do my best this evening to be still and attentive and receptive. I will listen to what you have to say, and not busy myself with arguments and questions and doubts and fears.

RAJ That will be a good idea, Paul. The wheel of history repeats itself, but Being never repeats Itself. It is forever making Itself new. The dilemma in which you seem to find yourself is just such an example of Being making Itself new. This Being which is making Itself new is *your* Being. You are having difficulty because there seems to be a gap between what your Being is *being,* and what you are conscious of your Being as *being.* This is because you are, so to speak, riding bareback on the surface of your three–dimensional, or objective,

225

sense of being conscious. You find yourself involved in the drama, and experiencing the need of responding to demands which, apparently, are coming from outside yourself.

These demands are your Self declaring the presence of that which appears to be absent when viewed from the standpoint of the apparent drama. It will not appear truly as your conscious experience of being until you are viewing from the point of your Being *as* Conscious Being — not that of finite man.

That which makes abundance appear to be lack is entirely in the standpoint. It depends entirely on which end of the binoculars you are looking through. As I have said before, you have a habit of switching ends quite frequently. This is what is frustrating you.

When you receive a telephone call, or a statement in the mail, which claims that your Supply is not omnipresent — some part of your universe is coming up short — you must recognize this as being totally false. Your Being is omnipresently present and active. Since that is the Fact, then it would be foolish for you to go out and attempt to correct that illusion on the basis of the phone call or statement. The attempt is made on the basis of a false assumption.

You must be alert at the inception. Then you will not waste your time attempting to do something which is already done by virtue of the immovable completeness of your Being.

Indeed, your Being will be identified completely, and *is* identified completely — and that means manifest completely. Otherwise, the omnipresence of your Being would be only partial, which is an impossibility.

You must be willing to face the suggestion of lack, and meet it head on, with the recognition that such a suggestion is an exact opposite of the Fact. If you will reverse the suggestion and be conscious of the specific truth which you will discover in that Place where you are right now, and abide with that truth, then you will be able to respond appropriately. Everything you do will identify the Fact.

It is not enough to know what the Fact is. You must also include consciously in your awareness of the Fact that It is not omnipresent if It is not present as that which identifies your completeness. This must be done from that Place wherein you are experiencing the omnipresence of your Being as Conscious Being. It is essential that you keep this is mind.

Please think about this for awhile and then get back with me again later.

PAUL   I will, Raj. Thank you very much.

March 29, 1982
Monday

PAUL   Good afternoon, Raj.

RAJ   Good afternoon, Paul.

PAUL   Well, it's been a long time since we've had a recorded conversation, and you're well aware of what has occurred in the meantime.

I would like to listen to whatever you might have to say today, and afterwards I might have a few questions.

RAJ   Very well, Paul.

Today we need to deeply consider the orderliness of things — the orderliness of Life in Its infinite manifestations. We need to remember that all of Life, infinitely speaking, is unfolding Itself at every moment, and not just an isolated part of that infinity. It is essential for you to realize that your thinking processes do not in any way have any effect, whatsoever, on this infinitely detailed, yet harmonious unfolding of Being. This does not mean you have nothing to do with it, but it simply means that you have no three-dimensional control over it.

You must come to the realization that it is your Being which is unfolding Itself infinitely on the basis of Its Nature as Intelligence, as Life, and as Mind. Therefore, It is — before you think a single thought about it — unfolding Itself (your Self) with all the precision, Intelligence, and Principle which constitutes Itself.

It is this infinite unfolding of your Self that you must learn to bring your thought in line with. You cannot use your thoughts to bring your Being into line with them. This is a part of the letting go which is necessary for you in order for you to experience the unfolding of your Being as complete Harmony.

Until you are willing to let go of this concept — that you must in some way be able to control your environment and your life experience with your thought — you will seem to suffer from the unfoldment of your Being.

You see, Paul, the flaw in the Power of Positive Thinking lies in the fact that it assumes that, if one does not engage in positive thinking, the Universe will not unfold Itself in a positive manner. So, this theory and practice creates a fundamental distrust of the Universe Itself, of Being Itself. This, of course, puts one at odds with his Self, with his Being, since any distrust in the basic Nature of the Universe is a basic distrust in one's own Nature and Being. This is basically why you are having trouble letting go and simply *being*.

The world literally is not going on "out there" at all, but within You, *as* your Being. More correctly, your Being is unfolding Itself and is seen and experienced by Itself (your Self) as conscious experience. As I have said before, the difficulty you are having is because you flip–flop back and forth, in and out.

It has been a habit of yours to attempt to live your universe from the standpoint of your conscious thought, rather than from the point of your subjective Being. This is why I continue to say that, as you are willing to be *in* and to *be* that Place where you experience your Being as Conscious Being, then you will find that your Being is the Answer which has already answered Itself by *being* Its own fullness and completeness with total success. You must be willing to stay at that point, no matter what activity you may appear to be involved in, and to not attempt to exercise any control, whatsoever, over what your Being is *being*.

I recognize fully from my own experience that this is not an easy step to make, because it is not a head trip. Rather, it is a matter of being willing to be —without conscious thought processes being used for any purpose other than relating or describing what your Being is *being*.

Fundamental to your being able to let go is going to be your willingness to trust what you already theoretically know: That the entire Nature of your Being is absolutely and totally constructive — that It is actually fulfilling Itself at this very moment in all Its completeness with absolute perfection.

If you are able to trust that Fact, even though it may require some imagination, rather than some believing, you will find it easier to let go of any vestige of control that you think you ought to be able to exercise. As soon as you are able to do this, you will find the picture change, as we have talked about before. In effect, you will be seeing from the Center of your Being, rather than from the surface of your concepts.

Seeing out from Being is that perfect Awareness which Mind experiences of its own infinite Self-expression. All that actually happens is that the illusion, or misunderstanding, caused by conceptual thinking simply evaporates. One is left with a clear view of the Actuality of one's own Being and the Harmony of it as one's own experience.

As you can see, Paul, in spite of the fact that we have not had regular communications over the last two weeks, there has, nevertheless, been a continued improvement or facility in your fluency at relating our conversations. This should be encouraging to you, in that it is evidence that there has been no loss of your ability to communicate.

Further, even though you have been highly distressed at times during these past two weeks, it has in no way retarded the work that we are doing together. This also should allow you to relax somewhat, because it is evidence — you might say "objective evidence" — of the fact that there is something real occurring here. It is not simply a figment of your imagination. You will know soon enough for an actual fact, that these communications are not fictitious, but that must wait in order for fulfillment of purpose to be accomplished.

Things are progressing well in regard to Maitreya's announcement. Although you are still curious to have me share with you a date for that announcement, and although you have some idea when it might occur, I will continue at this time to refrain from giving you that information. I will say that things are progressing very well. The event will occur as planned, and it is relatively imminent.

In spite of your feeling that your preoccupation with the circumstances you are faced with in your daily life has gotten in the way of our work together, it has not. Let me also affirm to you that it is not necessary for you to advise me nightly that you have given me full authority to exercise any control within my power to aid you in your Awakening. I know that is your desire. Until you retract that authority from me, I will continue to work on your behalf, as will Almee and the others. I appreciate the trust which you have displayed. This has occurred even in the midst of very serious doubts on your part, and right in the face of great discouragement which you have experienced over the past few weeks.

Rest assured that things are moving forward as they should. You are not failing in any area, and this includes every aspect of your daily experience at the present time.

Both you and Susan continue as you have been in listening for the direction in which you need to move. I do not want you to throw the responsibility for figuring everything out in my lap. You must continue to be aware that you are yourself, and I am myself. I am doing what I need to do, and you must do what you need to do. Do not give away any responsibility to another at all.

As I have said before, I cannot help you with things that will deprive you of your own growth. I am here to help, nevertheless.

PAUL   You have indicated that it is not appropriate for us to consider moving to California, and that we should stay in the state of Washington, although it does not matter where.

RAJ   That is correct.

PAUL   Susan senses that the west coast of the state of Washington is an unstable mass which will be subject, in the next few years, to earthquakes and greater volcanic eruption. This is something I am not sensing, but I am not discounting what she is becoming aware of.

Because of this, I am wondering if it would be wise for us not to act upon anything that might unfold in terms of staying on the west coast of Washington.

RAJ   Here is a perfect example of the thought processes you must be willing to let go of. In other words, if your Being unfolds the necessity of living in or moving to a particular area on the west coast of the state of Washington, then you must act upon that unfolding of your Being — regardless of Susan's "knowledge" of the unsettled land mass.

Since Being is unfolding Itself with absolute Intelligence and Principle, then It will not unfold *as* your conscious experience of Being in any way which is destructive or detrimental to your continued experience of Being. Therefore, you may trust that if you are led to be located in an area on the west coast of the state of Washington, it will not involve any destructive element, whatsoever, for you.

Certainly, if you had known in advance that Mt. St. Helens would erupt, you would have felt that it would be wiser to stay in the city of Spokane. However, not knowing any of this, you moved to Seattle. You did not receive any more than a very, very light film of dust, while Spokane was inundated.

Now, the simple fact is that if your Being, through the obvious, as I mentioned yesterday, leads you to make a move to someplace on the west coast of the state of Washington, then by all means you had best follow Its leadings. After all, it is going to be what will be, no matter what you think — as you are currently finding out. Once there, you must continue to be led by the "obvious." If at a later point you are led to move elsewhere, then you would be wise to do so.

The point is to always remain currently obedient to what your Being is unfolding. If possible, do it unthinkingly, willingly, and with a confidence in the absolutely cohesive manner in which It is unfolding Itself — with no sense of It being actually destructive in any way, shape, or form.

It is true that the west coast of the state of Washington is an unstable land mass. This simply means that it has a flexibility which is extremely constructive in terms of the natural release of energy. In fact, its flexibility is what will mean the difference between great destruction and the more subtle release of energy.

Energy which is released in an extremely stable land mass results in great violence and great shifting of plates. It is what has resulted in what you recognize as great mountain chains which, when they were formed, were cataclysmic in terms of released energy and violent shifts of land. I promise you that you would not want to be on an extremely stable land mass, if that were to be the point of the release of great amounts of energy.

I would suggest that you not become bound to concepts which are formed spontaneously as a result of insight such as Susan is aware of. Remember, it is simply information. It is not there to tell you what action to take. The only thing which you can afford to listen to with any confidence, is what your Being is obviously unfolding to you at any given moment. Then continue to be listening at that Place wherein your Being unfolds Itself *as* your conscious experience.

As I said to you on the way back from Spokane, the necessity here is for you to learn to flow. The only thing for you to flow with is your Being as It unfolds Itself universally and specifically. As I said earlier, you will be more willing and able to do this as you begin to trust the absolutely constructive, loving, perfect, principled, and cohesive manner in which your Being unfolds Itself. Its very Nature is infinite Intelligence, Mind, Consciousness, Life, Principle, et cetera.

This is the demand of the moment, no matter what steps come to you to take physically or objectively. Just remember that no matter what objective steps you take, be sure they are being done from a subjective standpoint wherein you are being at and *as* that Place where your Being is flowing through and *as* your conscious experience of Being. This is, you might say, the big secret.

I will discontinue our conversation at this point and will look forward to speaking with you again, unless you have any other questions.

PAUL   No, Raj, I don't at the moment.

RAJ   Very well, then, until I speak with you again I will say good-bye for now.

PAUL   Good-bye, Raj. Thank you very much.

March 30, 1982
Through
April 26, 1982

[During this period we relocated from Seattle to Spokane, Washington and I had no formal conversations with Raj. Although I continued to rely on him for guidance regarding the move, the questions were asked on the run, and no notes or recordings were made.]

April 27, 1982
Tuesday

PAUL   Good evening, Raj.

RAJ   Good evening, Paul.

PAUL   Tonight I need to hear whatever you have to share with me, and I will not ask any questions.

RAJ   Very well, Paul. Tonight it is very necessary for you to once again begin to relax out of the personal, three-dimensional sense of responsibility. I realize it has been difficult to take care of the necessities which have required your attention, and yet remain uninvolved and free of believing that you must respond as a three-dimensional man to three-dimensional demands. Nevertheless, you need to do so. I sense that you are more than ready, since it is, indeed, very tiring to believe that you are making the world go round.

PAUL   Raj, may I interject here my appreciation for the time you spent with both Susan and me this morning between 6:00 and 7:00. May I also thank you for being with me every day, even though there have been many days in which I did not even acknowledge your presence.

RAJ   I appreciate your gratitude, but it is not necessary. I am glad you have had this period of time during which we have not conversed. In spite of your feeling that you have lost ground by virtue of not taking time to have these conversations, the fact is that your growth has continued unhindered.

You must get over this idea that your life is actually occurring in the way you see and experience it from a three-dimensional standpoint. You must realize that whether you are consciously aware of it or not, your Being is infinitely unfolding Itself at all times, and is doing so in all of Its perfection. Infinitely speaking, you never become more nor less than You Are. Whether you choose to focus in on any particular *detail* of your Infinity or not, your Being continues to unfold Itself on the basis of Its Infinity, and not on the basis of what you choose to narrow your attention down to.

I want to remind you that your Being is constituted of infinite Love. That Love constitutes the Substance of your total experience. I want to remind you of that, because the apparently external demands which you have been faced with have caused you to withdraw your attention from your awareness of that fact. As a result, you have not been feeling the lovingkindness and the totally constructive and harmonious Nature of your Being as It is unfolding Itself as your conscious experience. Objectively speaking, Love is all around you, because Love is what constitutes your subjective Being. Whether or not you are temporarily caught up in the three-dimensional appearance of things, you are never removed from the ability to perceive the omnipresence of Love, because It is the warp and woof of all four dimensions.

I want you to consciously and conscientiously open yourself up to the perception and the experience of the Love that constitutes your infinite Being, no matter from what apparent point or dimension you seem to be experiencing that infinitude.

You will never be able to experience the infinitude of your Being clearly if you think that there are nooks or crannies — or "levels of belief" — in which the omnipresent Love which constitutes your Being is somehow not present. You must come to the realization that all of you truly is always available to you, no matter how things seem to be. Right now, I am aware that you are feeling as though you are somehow beyond the range of the direct perception and experience of the Reality of your Being as Love. It simply is not true.

You have kept yourself quite busy, and constructively so for the most part. But you are beginning to realize that you cannot operate successfully "out there," in the three-dimensional frame of reference, without, in so many words, shriveling up and feeling barren and dry. You need to take some time each day to specifically be out from Mind and ignore the demands which seem to be coming from "out there."

There is no requirement for you to labor through the desert of human experience without draughts of inspiration and the direct experience of the divinity of your Being. No matter what your situation claims, you are not required to exist that way. In fact, it is only the lack of taking the time to stand as the Door that makes your experience seem to be a desert.

Both you and Susan have done well in making the move, and although you cannot see its purpose, it will unfold in your thought and become clear to you. In case you were not sure, the move progressed very well and you are exactly where you are needed — both from the standpoint of your own individual growth, as well as in a more universal sense.

Do not be discouraged. As Susan suggested, by all means begin to set aside a time each day for at least one conversation with me. As you begin to do this, I want you to examine and be consciously aware of the differences between your experiences of life during our prior regular conversations, this period wherein we have not had regular conversations, and now, as we begin again. This will serve to help you understand and feel just exactly what benefit you experience from these conversations. It will also help you to give priorities based on the perspective you have gained.

Paul, this has not been a period barren of unfoldment and growth. This will become apparent to you as we continue.

PAUL   Thank you, Raj.

RAJ   I want to reaffirm to both you and Susan that I am with you every day, twenty–four hours a day. You are being constantly supported and loved. While you have been taking care of daily necessities, you have not been left alone to deal with them.

For the time being, I want you to begin your day with a meditation, and I would like to have us converse at the end of the day. I want you to get your attention focused again in the direction of being in the Place wherein you experience your Being as Conscious Being.

I will tell you this: No matter what demands are made upon you, they do not require you to give them precedence over your need to stand as the Door. Do not give them that much credit.

PAUL   Thank you, Raj.

RAJ   You are welcome. I shall let you go for now and will look forward to speaking with you tomorrow evening. Tell Susan that I am also available to her twenty-four hours a day if she wishes to speak with me.

PAUL   Thank you, Raj, I will. Good night.

RAJ   Good night.

April 28, 1982
Wednesday

PAUL Good evening, Raj.

RAJ Good evening, Paul. It *seems* to you as though you have had a strenuous and purposeless day today. However, these are the idiotic ravings of ignorance, which would fool you into believing the exact opposite of what *is* unfolding in and as your experience as purposeful, dynamic, fulfilling and intelligent manifestations of your Being.

As I have said before, you must learn to recognize that your Being is unfolding Itself at all times in perfect harmony with Its Nature. You must begin to accept *this* as the Fact, rather than what your imagination can come up with based upon what it sees, hears, tastes, smells, and feels. The Absolute Facts of your Being have never for an instant ceased operating, and never will. Therefore, anything other than this Fact is pure fiction, and you should not waste one moment on it.

The only reason you don't see it is because you are looking through your preconceptions about what is right for you. Then, when your Being unfolds Itself in a direction in which you are not consciously looking, it *seems* as though unfoldment has ceased altogether.

PAUL Continue, Raj. I have no questions at this point.

RAJ Thank you. I am pleased to tell you that you are, indeed, near the end of the apparent dilemma which has been confronting you for some time now regarding your finances and your purpose or goal.[1]

As you are already well aware, the schooling situation has been remedied, even though there are minor adjustments still to be made on the part of the children. They will make these adjustments with relative smoothness.

Wendy will find it somewhat more rugged as she learns to relax back into the natural state of her Being, and learns that everything that counts comes *through* her, not from *outside* her Self. Her Value can only come from within herself as she is willing to stand as the Door, allowing the Universal Value of her Being to flow easily, with no self-criticism or shyness because of Its originality.

This process will not be overwhelming to her, but it will demand of her what will seem to be strenuous effort. You can let her know, however, that it will be worth every labor that may be involved. Paul and Susan, you can rest assured that the move has been most constructive for all three of the children, just as you will find it will be for yourselves.

Paul, there is an element of distrust and cynicism which has grown in your thought. This is due both to the experiences which have occurred over the last few months, as well as to your inability to relate what we have been discussing to your daily experience.

Whenever you find yourself ready to express doubt and cynicism, I want you to recognize that you are doing so. Replace the specific doubt or cynicism with its specific opposite, and dwell with that opposite meaning *as the fact* until you are free of the negative imposition.

You are never bound to agree with your thoughts, but you are constantly required to agree with your Being.

As I said yesterday, your Being is unfolding Itself infinitely in all Its perfection. This is the Fact which underlies everything that Is, *as well as everything that seems to be.* Do not get hung up on what *seems* to be the case. Your Being is capable of manifesting Itself as your conscious experience of being, and has never stopped doing so. It is this ongoing, eternal, abiding Fact which needs to become an integral part of your conscious experience. Cultivate It and you will not be sorry.

PAUL   I would like to try to have two conversations with you each day for the time being — one in the morning and one in the evening, if you have no objection.

RAJ   I have no objection, whatsoever. That is fine with me.

PAUL   I feel as though I am getting back on the right track, and certainly appreciate the continuousness of your availability. It is much appreciated.

Good night, Raj.

RAJ   Thank you, and good night. I will look forward to speaking with you in the morning.

---

[1] The $5,000 I had asked my Supply for came as an unsolicited forgiveness of a $3,000 debt on a piece of office equipment, and various smaller amounts of cash amounting to $2,000, which were above and beyond my "normal" channels of income.

April 29, 1982
Thursday

PAUL   I don't know how much time we'll have before the family returns, but in the meantime, I would like to hear anything you might have to say at the present time.

RAJ   Thank you, Paul. You have had some interesting unfoldments today which are bringing you fresh energy and the actual experience of the omnipresence of your Being. This is a great improvement over yesterday.

It is very important to realize that Identity is something far different from ego. Identity is what exists before ego can seem to be formed. Yet, once ego develops, Identity becomes practically invisible. This is because ego supplies one with a "high," a thrill, an excitement which Identity does not.

Ego behaves exactly like a drug. As one gets used to it, it requires a bigger "fix" in order to get the thrill. It also engages one in a quest which had no foundation to begin with. Each additional "fix" requires the further development of a personality and an intellectual originality which can then become identified in a "thrilling" way, so that a higher "high" can be achieved.

Since ego has no basis in Actuality, this superstructure of "fixes" has not the strength to support itself. Therefore, the so-called ego is met with interminable collapses of one sort or another. Its "importance," its "skill," its "ability" are fabulous in nature — substanceless, incapable of providing a sustained high.

On the other hand, Identity, when It is perceived to be the expression of the Universal, omnipresent divine Mind or Intelligence, *is* capable of expressing Itself on a sustained basis — so sustained that the word "eternal" is the only word that describes It. It is so substantial by virtue of Its Nature as Intelligence, that It is called Omnipotent.

There is only one infinite Life/Principle, one infinite Identity, infinitely expressed and seen as all that exists. It is what constitutes the center and circumference of Being — Your Self as you experience It, Susan's Self as she experiences It, my Self as I experience It. Its omnipotence or strength is constituted of Its absolute omnipresent Integrity, which is Its Intelligent Nature. It is not thrilling or exciting when contemplated from an egotistical standpoint. But It is satisfying in ways that are so meaningful that they cannot compare to the "thrills" of the ego. It also has this benefit: The satisfaction is eternal and unchanging.

As one makes the shift from the three–dimensional frame of reference to the *being* of Fourth–dimensional Man, it seems as though one must give up his individuality and allow something which he does not recognize as himself to take over and speak through him. But,the fact is that that which is speaking through him is his original and unchanging Identity. It is only the false sense of individuality called "personality" which is being given up.

Paul, now that you have become aware of this, you have also realized that the false sense of individuality must give itself up on purpose. In addition, you are now beginning to understand why few people actually do it. It is like getting off a drug, kicking a habit. You now have some idea of the task which is before you.

You are also aware that when the perception of the Reality of your Being is clear enough, it is easier to give up the false sense of individuality for the true experience of Identity. You can, indeed, anticipate a divine adventure, even though it will involve some labor.

Do not expect this to occur overnight, Paul. As a matter of fact, this process began the first night we began our conversations. Be patient and stick with it, and be ready to put your shoulder to the wheel.

I would like for you to type this up and consider it before we speak again.

PAUL   Very well, Raj. I will. And thank you.

RAJ   You're welcome, Paul. I will talk to you later.

April 30, 1982
Friday

PAUL   Good afternoon, Raj.

RAJ   Good afternoon, Paul. I want to begin today with a dissertation on the value of...

PAUL   [Nothing heard.]

Raj, I am not able to hear the next word. Before I delay any longer, I want to express my desire to be of service in any way I can in serving the fulfillment of God's Purpose in my world, rather than simply asking, "What am I supposed to be doing?"

I want to ask the question, "What can I do, what shall I do that will be most fulfilling in the service of the divine Purpose of Being?" I am asking that question of my Self. If you feel like commenting on that, I would enjoy hearing what you have to say. Whether you do or not, my request is of my Being that I be shown what to do to best support the divine Will at this time and place.

RAJ   That is a wise approach. It is only as you are fulfilling the Purpose of your Being that true progress can be made — not by attempting to fulfill the intellectually-developed ideas and concepts which you have come up with.

As you have realized, the theme is "Thy Will be done." I am not going to answer the question for you. But, as you have already planned, I want you to let your desire be known from that Place where you are experiencing your Being as Conscious Being, just as you did when you first contacted me. Patiently await the clarification which will answer your question. Trust that it will unfold itself to you just as clearly as I have communicated with you.

Remember that the whole Universe is the fulfillment of God's purpose. Therefore, do not limit yourself in any way by conceptualizing what might be the fulfillment of God's Purpose. In other words, be totally open. Thus, you will not delay your perception of the answer by the presence of preexisting concepts.

As long as you are in need of the answer to this question, I would suggest that you meditate at least three times a day. Once having arrived at that Place, let your request be known. Continue to do this until you get the answer.

You can rest assured that the answer is close at hand, since the need is extremely definite. Therefore, do not in any way attempt to justify the idea that the answer will take a long time in coming. Remember also, that one's experience of time is relative to the intensity with which a desire is felt. Remember, too, that although it only took two weeks for us to make contact in the beginning, those two weeks seemed to be quite extensive and protracted. It was as though there were a delay. Looking back, you can see that two weeks was not long at all.

Drop the concept of time as you request and desire the answer to your need. Stay fixed on the desire. Do it gently. Do not push it. Do not be overly intense. On the other hand, be genuine, sincere, and consistent. Realize that it is your very own Being to which the desire is being expressed, knowing as you do, that every answer and every demand arises out of your very own Being. As I have said before, trust Your Self. Lean on It. Depend on It.

It should be clear to you by now that any attempt to manipulate arises out of the limited three–dimensional frame of reference. Therefore, do not contemplate or express this desire when you know you are not in that Place. It will be a total waste of time and energy.

You certainly should be aware that the need arises out of your Being, because the fulfillment of that desire *is at hand* to be consciously perceived and lived, rather than unconciously lived as separate and apart from the totality of your Being.

You are getting the picture, I see.

Be alert to the fact, Paul, that sloppy questions beget sloppy answers. Learn to be more precise in your requests and your desires. An ambiguous question begets an ambiguous answer. If you want to know something, be sure to ask a question that begets a specific answer.

As you are aware, James said, "Ye ask and receive not because ye ask amiss."[1] If you are not getting an answer to the need, it is because the question does not address itself to that specific answer. You will find that when you have the right question, you will spontaneously and effortlessly know the answer. You can depend upon it.

You certainly know that, because you exist, you have purpose or intent — there is a design to your Being. You should also know that every single event which is unfolding in and as your conscious experience of being is in perfect harmony with that design. They are all part of the intent of your Being to fulfill Itself specifically and flawlessly, both individually and Universally, since all of you is always unfolding all of Itself with total success.

Paul, you are on the right track. You are very fortunate that your concepts of right and wrong, good and bad, goal or purpose, are not coming to fruition because, when they do, they continue to support the false sense of ego, thus keeping hidden your true Identity. You see, it was your desire to no longer have what *you* think is right, and what *you* ought to be able to do, that opened the Door of your Being to allow your Identity as Fourth-dimensional Man to begin to flow through as your conscious experience of Being.

As long as we hold dear our concepts of righteousness, education, and highly-developed ability to reason, our conscious experience of Being is so full of the "noise" of our ego that we cannot hear the "still, small voice" of our true Identity — the still, small voice of God, as it is called. This is why we are cautioned to "Be still, and know that I am God."[2] You are really beginning to see this point, and are really beginning to feel that it is a valid point — valid enough to trust yourself to completely.

This truly is your task from this moment forward. As I said before, any attempt to avoid the fulfillment of your Being will result in discomfort far greater than you can imagine. It will be far greater than you care to experience, because you have graduated into the Fourth-dimensional frame of reference. Although you may attempt to ignore it at times, you cannot succeed in moving backwards. Growth only moves in one direction, and it moves inexorably and irreversibly.

PAUL   Thank you, Raj. I will get back with you later.

RAJ   You are welcome, Paul. Good-bye.

---

1   James 4:3.

2   Psalms 46:10.

May 1, 1982
Saturday

PAUL I have had a difficult day today.

RAJ I know you have. It would not have been necessary for you to have had a difficult day if you had been willing to remain with the ideas which we have discussed in the last few days, since it would have been clear to you that everything is functioning in perfect order and harmony, and is totally and completely constructive. I reminded you of the necessity of staying with this Fact and cultivating It.

PAUL I know you did, but it is difficult when there is no evidence of income and no evidence of ongoing income–generating employment. Our needs certainly are being met, but they are being met because we are selling things that we own, and not because gainful employment has been found. Sooner or later we will run out of things to sell.

RAJ Paul, "sooner or later" doesn't matter. You cannot deal in the future at the present time. Therefore, you should not govern your feelings on the basis of a future that you imagine may be.

The reason you find yourself feeling challenged is because you are not yet totally secure with the ideas which your Being is unfolding to Itself, and which appears to be a conversation between yourself and myself. The result, inevitably, will be a strengthening of your standpoint through experience — that is, as long as you continue to remain in contact with your experience of your Self as Conscious Being.

I reiterate: Do not be discouraged. You are not lost, and you should not indulge in the imagination that you can somehow get outside the infinitude of your own Being and become isolated from your Good.

As you already know, you have two tasks before you. One is the conscious relinquishment of your sense of ego in preference to your Identity. The second is to get into that Place where you're experiencing your Being as Fourth–dimensional Man, and be conscious of your desire in the form of a specific question. This is to be done at least three times a day. Do not let your objective experience keep you from fulfilling those tasks. Do not let yourself become discouraged, as you almost did tonight, to the point where you would be willing to retire for the night without fulfilling those two objectives.

Trust in your Self is the key here, and steadfastness is the method by which your success will be assured. Do not allow the anxiety or impatience of those around you to cause you to feel that you must push things along more rapidly. This will keep you bound in the three–dimensional frame of reference — a frame of reference from which nothing can be initiated.

We are going to "hang in here" on these points until the answer to your employment becomes clear. In the meantime, I want you to remain as calm and clear as you can. Anxiety is a reaction not to be used as a basis for manipulation of things as they appear three–dimensionally.

I want you to stop now, do your meditation, and contemplate your request for specific direction before you go to bed this night.

PAUL   I will, Raj. Thank you very much.

RAJ   You are welcome, Paul. Good night.

May 2, 1982
Sunday

PAUL   Good evening, Raj.

RAJ   Good evening, Paul. Today was a very pleasant day for you. As I mentioned, the music by Steven Halpern was exceptionally beautiful, and I enjoyed it very much.

It is becoming clear to you that when you are feeling better, it does not mean that things are going better — any more than when you are feeling bad, that things are not going well. Emotional responses have very little to do with Reality. In either case, Reality is unfolding Itself perfectly. The only thing that happens when you are feeling good is that it's easier to take than when you are feeling bad.

It is important to begin to see that Being is unfolding Itself successfully, with absolutely perfect precision, no matter how you feel. Emotional responses are illusions, having no relationship to the Actuality of Being. Thus, if you are wise, you will not let your emotional responses signify anything to you regarding Reality.

If at the end of the day you say you are feeling bad, you should in the same breath be able to acknowledge that you have had a very good day, since the Universe has unfolded Itself with Absolute Perfection — regardless of how *you* feel. The trick is in where the emphasis is being laid. You can be aware of how you may feel, but it is what you *Know* about the Nature of the Universe and your Being which should get the emphasis. That should be what you base your interpretation or understanding of things upon. It doesn't really matter whether you feel good or bad. It really doesn't.

You will find that as ego fades away, so will feeling good and bad. This is because in the long run, feeling good or bad depends upon how much "ego" has been fed or not fed. This is why so few individuals are able to make the transition from the three-dimensional frame of reference to the *being* of Fourth-dimensional Man, because in the process, ego is on its way out and that's b-a-a-a-d news.

PAUL   I am especially grateful for these conversations, because I don't see how this transition could be made without some guidance, since it is spontaneously natural to avoid feeling bad.

RAJ   I understand, and I agree that it is incredibly difficult to do so without some guidance. I appreciate having the opportunity to work with you on this.

Being aware that it is late for you, and being aware that I want you to get into that Place one more time before you retire and contemplate your desire one more time, I am going to keep this conversation short this evening. As a word of encouragement, I will say that the answer to your request is in the process of unfolding to you, although you may not be aware of it at the moment. And with that, I will say good night.

PAUL   Thank you, Raj. Good night.

May 3, 1982
Monday

PAUL   Good morning, Raj.

RAJ   Good morning, Paul. I can see you are definitely in that Place this morning, and that is a wonderful way to start out your day. I would like you to not attempt to take on anything today in the sense of being responsible for it — no matter what you do. I do not mean for you to do nothing, but I mean for you to do it with no sense of personal responsibility. I mean for you to do it from exactly that Place wherein you find yourself at this very moment.

You feel somewhat too relaxed to type accurately, but you have already found out to some degree that, as you are very relaxed and not attempting to maintain control over your fingers, your fingers are more accurate and speedier than when control is attempted. You do not have to be concerned that you will become too relaxed. The more relaxed you are, from a three-dimensional standpoint, the more all of You is available to respond to the demands and needs of the moment, and the fulfillment of these will become more simultaneous with the perception of the need.

You can see that it truly, completely, means getting yourself out of the way. This is the grand lesson. Do not be afraid of being "out of control." So many times people feel that if they are out of control, they will be wide open to being controlled by other entities, forces, or powers. But the omnipresent I Am — the infinite, divine Mind that constitutes the Being of every being that be's — is the only Presence and

253

Power which can exert and manifest Itself, and *be* the center and circumference — the Alpha and Omega. Therefore, such concepts or beliefs are groundless, and one need never be afraid to let go and say and *be* the statement, "Thy Will be done."

Before you begin today's work, be sure and start with your meditation, your consideration of your need, and your specific request. Then proceed with the necessities of the day, and I will talk with you later on.

PAUL   Thank you, Raj. Good-bye.

May 7, 1982
Thursday

PAUL Good evening, Raj.

RAJ Good evening, Paul. You are aware of having felt nervous or tense, with an uneasy feeling in the pit of your stomach, all day today. You have not made the distinction between you as Fourth–dimensional Man, and you as a three-dimensional conglomeration of thoughts, concepts, physical reactions, emotional reactions, et cetera. You are going to have to be very alert now, because more often than not, the mythical structure called "ego" is going to be in the process of dissolving. Much like *HAL*, the computer in the film *2001*, there will be subtle, insistent, plaintive pleas. There will be an even seemingly human capacity to imply that it is capable of truly fearing its own demise.

You must realize that ego is a fraud from the beginning, and you must learn to properly identify your Self as Being, Itself, and not as "ego."

So that there is no confusion, whatsoever, about this process, it had better be clear to you that you will have to listen to, and even seemingly experience, whatever charade is attempted by this false sense of individuality as it gives up the ghost. You will have to remain unmoved and steadfast in the proper identification of your Being.

Ego is what Jesus referred to as "the devil," being a liar and the father of it. It is imperative that you understand that there is no other evil. The only sin there is is the misidentification of one's Self as "ego" rather than Being, as Conscious Being.

You have been concerned in the last few days that you are not making the connection between what I have been discussing with you and your daily experience. The simple fact is that you have been trying to relate infinite ideas to finite beliefs. There is no connection. There is no connection *between* Mind and Its manifestation. They are one.

It is only from the standpoint of ego — of finite, three-dimensional misperception — that there can seem to be a "connection." Since ego separates itself from what it sees, it divides things into subject and object, "in here" and "out there," me and thee, and all the rest of the dualism. This prompts the attempt to manipulate all of these disconnected aspects, so that they will harmonize in such a way as to not destroy the basic illusion of the existence of "ego." Thus, from the three-dimensional standpoint, it seems obvious that the misidentification of Identity called "ego" must become, do, initiate, manipulate, and achieve.

One cannot bring these endeavors into that Place where Self is properly identified and experienced as Conscious Being or Fourth-dimensional Man, since the basic illusion of separateness has no existence there.

It is apparently new territory for you, Paul, although you could say it is your "native land." Nevertheless, as the shift is made from the finite to the infinite view, you are going to have to be a stranger in a strange land, a babe in a new world. Although there will be no aspect of danger involved, it will be necessary to patiently explore, sense, perceive, and understand how to *be,* rather than *do.*

You see, Paul, whether you have misidentified your Self as "ego," or whether you have correctly identified your Self as Fourth-dimensional Man, your Being has effortlessly been being Itself totally, perfectly, and successfully by *being* rather than "doing." Anything ego has thought it has done was pure nonsense.

You are afraid that if you let go and stop "doing," everything will fall apart. This is because you are still caught in the belief that what you have "done" in the past has succeeded in getting you where you are. This is foolishness, and you are beginning to see this. You haven't gotten anywhere, because Infinity has no place to go. Nevertheless, Infinity — your

Being — has unfolded Itself in spite of what you thought you were "doing," and where you thought you were getting to.

An early teacher of Christian Science said, "Be, and by being heal the sick."[1] Being is the only thing that makes anything happen, and It makes it happen by being the "Happening." From the standpoint of Being, everything is already done.

You must beware of the withdrawal symptoms, since the "ego habit" is going to demand another "fix" — and another, and another, and another. It will do so with less and less strength, but it will do so, nevertheless. I am forewarning you of this, so that you may understand the method of its operation, and will not take it seriously.

Your opportunity for activity is as infinite as your Being. You do not need to concern yourself about the ability of your Being to fulfill Itself completely as that which will be recognizable to you as the meeting of your every need — unless, of course, you wish to indulge in the misidentification of your Self as "ego." Such misidentification will not affect the Reality of your Being in any way, but, as you know, it will seem to engage your conscious awareness in an ongoing blindness to the Reality and an uphill climb which is really downhill all the way.

This conversation is, perhaps, one of the most important ones we've had. I would suggest that you make an extra copy, which you can keep separate from the rest and refer to a number of times each day. You may not seem to feel particularly comfortable and at ease objectively or three-dimensionally speaking. Therefore, it will be well for you to be able to easily remind yourself that ego is an "android" and, therefore, not even capable of dying. It had no life to begin with. Although it will seem to present itself as the downfall and destruction of your individuality, such will not be the case.

Again, this is a conversation of serious import. It should receive the attention due it, no matter what other demands present themselves.

PAUL   Thank you, Raj. I accept your instructions completely. Thank you, and good night.

RAJ   Good night, Paul.

---

1   Bicknell Young, C.S.B.

May 9, 1982
Sunday

PAUL   Good evening, Raj.

RAJ   Good evening, Paul. I want you to remember what we have been talking about the past few days, because it is extremely important. It constitutes the crux of your experientially crossing over the change line. We spoke of this some time back. You are truly beginning to experience the Fourth- and third–dimensional frames of reference existing side by side. You are able to observe yourself, and actually experience what seems to you to be yourself, being depressed. At the same time, you are able to experience your Self as being totally clear, at peace, in harmony with your Being, and not emotionally vexed in any way.

I would like you to refer back to the conversations we had regarding the apparent simultaneous experience of both dimensions. Observe how it correlates to your actual experience at this time. You will find it very beneficial.

I will warn you that where you have been able to remain clear as ego puts up its struggle, to be very alert not to be sucked in during the next few days.

PAUL   Very well, Raj. I will be alert.

RAJ   Paul, in spite of what Mrs. Eddy says about manipulation, meaning laying on of hands, and in spite of the fact that the end result will be that you will not use your hands for healing, I want you to follow your inner, intuitive leadings for the present. You will learn invaluable lessons. You will be led, from an experiential standpoint, to the understanding of true healing and its methods, as Mrs. Eddy was.

Since you are presently at the point of experiencing the change line, you are finding that the dynamics apparently are greater and somewhat confusing, unsettling, and disorienting. Do not get caught up in any of those points. Allow them. Adjustment is very rapid once the shift has been made, and things will become spontaneously clear to you.

Before we discuss some of the things which are beginning to jell in your thought, I want you to allow them to unfold so that you may be clearer on what you want to know.

I know that you do not yet trust your Self completely, but by the same token, your Self-trust is greatly increased over what it was when we began our conversations. At that point, you were not even consciously aware of the experience of your Self — of your True Identity — as opposed to your concept and experience of yourself as three-dimensional man.

Right now ego is confused — you are not, even though what seems most forcible in your thought at the moment is the feeling of confusion. . .

PAUL   [Tape recorder went haywire.]

May 10, 1982
Monday
(Morning)

PAUL   Good morning, Raj.

RAJ   Good morning, Paul. I see your tape recorder is on the blink.

PAUL   Yes.

RAJ   Let's talk a little this morning about mechanisms. "Mechanism" implies an orderly arrangement of moving parts which work in harmony with each other in order to fulfill a purpose or function. It is usually physical, although there are mathematical functions which are not.

"Mechanism" is something that functions automatically, unthinkingly, and repetitively. The function of the whole mechanism is dependent upon the proper functioning of the parts. Thus, the "parts" constitute the governing aspect of the whole — that is, if we are looking at the function as a mechanism.

You are learning that the One constitutes the Many, the Function constitutes the Mechanism. And, you are finding that when the emphasis is shifted from the particular to the Universal, then the particular — the mechanism, the Many — is seen in its true perspective. Nothing is dependent upon anything else. "Form follows function," and not vice versa.

This is an important thing to understand at this point, because it will help in relating what we are talking about to your daily activities. You cannot afford to approach your day as being mechanical in any way. You cannot afford to narrow your awareness down to a particular set of activities and see them as parts of a combination which, if adhered to, will result in a profitable, productive day.

If "form follows function," then it is imperative that your attention be on the function and not the form. What is the Function which you see as the unfolding of daily activities? It is the unfolding of Your Being, identifying and fulfilling Itself as Itself. Activity, money and profit are *all* aspects of that identification. Money — income — is not the end goal of it all.

Every aspect of your day identifies your Being, and not any one is more important or less important than another. *Work does not generate income.* Being generates work *and* income *and* leisure *and* growth. Yet, not any one of these things exist for their own independent purpose or identity. They identify Being, and Being is the Alpha and Omega — that which *is* and is identifying Itself completely and successfully.

It is the flow of Being which is the Function. It is identified by the forms which constitute your daily activities. Your need is to identify yourself *as* Being and not as form.

Form does not supply Being with anything, whereas Being supplies Itself with all form. It is the initial misidentification of form as function that fouls everything up. Our limited viewpoint, taking itself as the center and circumference, is the flaw.

You see, not any one activity in itself, or even in conjunction with other activities, has any meaning or purpose. The only purpose any of them has is to identify the Function which they identify. In fact, the intent or purpose of "identification" does not spring from the form. Rather, it has its source in the Function.

Being identifies Itself as Itself. The identification fulfills that purpose, but we get things backward when we think the "identification" is fulfilling a purpose *it* has.

Remember that every activity, and every apparent result of that activity in your daily affairs, does not constitute a cause and effect at all. More properly, it is the apparent activities *and* their apparent results that constitute the "effect" or "form" that follows the Function that is You, Your Being.

I want you to consider this as you go through your day today. Then sit back as you do what you have to do. Observe everything from this standpoint. Then I would like to speak to you later this evening, unless you have something in the meantime.

PAUL   Thank you, Raj. I will speak with you later.

May 10, 1982
Monday
(Afternoon)

PAUL You heard the telephone conversation, Raj?[1]

RAJ Yes, I did, and you handled it very well. It was calculated to arouse your personal indignation. The fact that you find yourself shaking inwardly and outwardly is an indication of the ego viewpoint, rather than the Identity standpoint. But, under the circumstances, you remained relatively clear of getting into the three–dimensional, reactive frame of reference, which he hoped you would utilize.

PAUL All right. We are faced with the necessity of being able to pay for our income tax returns and also handle this situation with Household Finance Corporation. At the same time, we have these other bills due. Fortunately, the creditors are working with me on them.

RAJ Paul, do not let your Universe become broken up into bits and pieces, each acting on its own, each attempting to fulfill its own ends. This is exactly what I was talking about this morning. Do not believe any form, organization, or manifestation when it seems to declare that it can demand or cause something, irritate you, et cetera.

Not only should you not identify *yourself* as form, you need to be sure that you don't allow any form to convince you that *it* has a purpose and can successfully act independent from the Whole. It is a trick of ego to suck you into believing that you, among these other forms, are *a form* to be battered about, manipulated, coerced — and that you must defend yourself against them. It is utterly false. Do not buy it for a second.

Stay with the Fact that your Being is totally present. THAT'S FACT. Your Being is totally functioning. THAT'S FACT. Your Being is being totally successful in fully identifying Itself. THAT'S FACT. You are not a small part of the totality of God's Universe. THAT'S FACT. And you are not *part* of God's Universe, because God is the only Identity you have. Therefore, your Being *is infinite* and cannot be contained. Do not let yourself be coerced into accepting the pea-sized concept of Identity called three-dimensional man.

You must stay with the Infinity of your Being, together with Its Omnipresence and Omnipotence. You are *all* of It. It is *all* of You. God is the only thing going on. It is the Happening. Do not buy the hypnotic suggestions being put forth by "ego."

Fortunately for you, ego is not presenting itself in a constructive manner. It is relatively easy for you to see that succumbing to its suggestions would not be constructive for you.

I urge you to remain steadfast during these last days of the attempt of "ego" to convince you that it is *you,* and that everything must be worked out on its basis. I have warned you, so that you will not be taken in, that it is likely to use every dirty trick it knows. "HAL" is very busy now, whining and cooing and remonstrating against its demise. *Do not be moved!*

PAUL   I hear you, but it's not easy.

RAJ   Do not indulge in the mistaken belief that it is going to be anything less than *hard work,* Paul. Accept that right now! Do not look at this "stage" of your growth as being peaches and cream. Do not indulge in self-pity or indignation at it not being easier since you "know the Truth" and are "having these conversations with me."

Realize right now that indignation and self-pity are *ego, ego, ego* right down the line. You've got to not give a damn about whether it's easy, hard, pleasant, unpleasant, quick or slow. These are all three-dimensional, "ego-bound" concepts. Even if they seem to parade as *your* feelings or thinking, do not "connect" up with them.

I reiterate, Paul: *Plan on it being hard work!* Fight the fight!

Follow through to the end wherein "ego's" claims become the nonsense that they are, just as when HAL began reciting nursery rhymes and singing children's songs.

Do not misunderstand. I am not saying there is a real fight. I'm not saying there is a real antagonist. I *am* saying that if you don't behave as though there were one — if you don't come on to this as the victor from the start, if you don't intend to follow through "come hell or high water" — then you will be lazy and slipshod in your approach. One way or another, ego will insinuate itself into and as your self-awareness, because it is a habit through long years of apparent Self-ignorance.

Let's handle that thought right now — that it's not this hard for others. First of all, that's ego whining! It's not You. Secondly, this idea of "others" is another ploy of ego. Only ego divides things into me and thee. *Ego, ego, ego!* Watch out for it!

Realize right now that ego is ego is ego. Consciously or purposely putting it down will evoke the same whining, pleading, pitiful "show," no matter who is putting it down. I told you, Paul, it's a liar! It *lies, lies, lies!*

It is imperative that you be alone with your own Being — *absolutely alone!* Don't compare (that's ego!). Don't try to find affirmation or agreement with your stance from "out there" (that's ego!). Don't — and I say this *especially* — don't let any feeling of pride enter the picture because of what you might have to do, and the fact that you are willing to do it (that's ego!).

This is a dirty fight! Fight it dirty! I say this because you will have a tendency to be "polite," "civilized," "courteous" if you can. Once again, you will be abiding by a set of concepts which drip with "ego."

Only if you are willing to be *alone* with your own Being will you be alone with the Reality of "things." It is the undistorted awareness of the Reality of "things" which will constitute the resolution of the conflict that seems to be going on "out there."

If you try to work it out from the standpoint of the Many, as though It were separate from You, you will be operating within "ego's" bailiwick.

You must remain steadfastly and abidingly with the Fact

that your Being is One and that that One is You. That One, being Omnipresent, is Omnipotently Omniactive as every last little detail of Its Infinitude — including every bill collector, every dollar owed, every process server, and every dollar paid. It is fulfilling Itself perfectly in identifying Its completeness with absolute success. It *is,* Paul! No matter what the three-dimensional insinuation is.

You see, it's the *whole dream* we're talking about waking up from! And you can do it. You are able.

That's not a pep talk, Paul. It's fact! The reason you are able is that you are now experientially aware of being consciously aware *as Conscious Being.* You are doing it right now. At the same time you are aware of ego doing its simultaneous little jig and operating as though it is you — as though it is your conscious experience of being, also. This is why you are able to wake up rather than just lop off another branch of the tree of "mortality" — three-dimensional thinking.

Read this over. Contemplate it. And then get back with me.

PAUL   I will, Raj. Thank you.

---

1   An extremely insulting call was received from one of my creditors.

May 10, 1982
Monday
(Evening)

PAUL Okay, Raj, I'm alone. . .

RAJ Although you caught it, I want to amplify on it. "Alone" is a three–dimensional concept implying that there's everyone else, and then there's "me." *This is ego.* You've got to be alert. Notice that your body is having physical sensations that you recognize as feeling disheartened, worried, or fearful. Notice that it has an intent; it is not just a feeling. It is there to motivate you to "do" something objective. Notice that in observing it, the I that is You that is observing is clear, unmoved, and at peace.

To be alone with one's Being is to be totally Present, Universally Present, without one iota projected "out there." It is to have no other Mind but God. Notice that Its intent is not directed *at* you. Notice that It does not try to coerce you. Notice that you are not aware of a separate selfhood upon which It can act.

Don't try to reason it out or figure it out. Just notice It.

At the present moment, you are not completely free of the inclination to believe that you are what ego says, and that you are in a pickle. On the other hand, you are not buying the story, either. Just notice.

You have never had to go all the way before, so this is new territory for you. But, as long as you don't relinquish any of the territory you have gained so far, you will find yourself moving forward. You will not lose any ground.

Okay, let's get back to your opening statement.

PAUL   I feel really shaky.

RAJ   No, Paul, it is not You. Ego is feeling really shaky right now. That's a positive indicator!

PAUL   I feel as though I'm really going out on a limb here by maintaining the position which you outlined this morning and previously.

RAJ   Why?

PAUL   Because it appears that I might lose something.

RAJ   There it is! Ego. If nothing can get outside the infinitude of your Being, then how can You lose anything? Paul, you must be very strict. If you *can't* lose anything, then you *haven't* lost anything. All of You is still present and functioning, and all of You will continue to be present and functioning.

PAUL   Okay. I know that all of me has to be present and functioning...

RAJ   Don't add that "but." Stay with the simple Fact you have just stated. The "but" is the hooker! "All is infinite Mind and Its infinite manifestation."[1] There aren't any "buts" about it! Being is "neither behind the point of perfection nor advancing towards it. It is at that point and must be understood therefrom."[2] It will never be understood from the standpoint of the three–dimensional frame of awareness (ego). You must stop looking for clues, helpful hints, or reassurances objectively. Being doesn't need them, and "ego" only needs them in order to hook you.

         Remember, as you "do battle," that there is no battle going on at all. It is a process by which you are becoming less slipshod in your self–identification. It seems as though it is an attempt to influence you in the direction of misidentification, but you are at a point where the thrust truly cannot reach you because you are hidden in the Secret Place of the Most High. You *have* experienced It.

         Leave the "split experience" of Reality/unreality alone, as illustrated in the tares and the wheat parable.[3] Let them *appear* to exist side by side. Let them *appear* to cause differ ent consciousnesses. As long as there are two, you are not caught — deluded — into the three-dimensional-only frame of reference. This dual experience of consciousness is an affirmation or proof of your having crossed the change line. You are not in three-dimensional territory, although you can still see it and feel it. Take my word for it.

Now, turn your back on the old territory and begin to look into the depths of your Being as Fourth-dimensional Man. As I said, once you cross the change line, clarification spontaneously begins to occur, and occur more rapidly. This is inevitable.

Paul, your first call for conversation with me set into motion irreversible unfoldments, because you were ready. As I have said before, you will lose nothing in the process. I know that my stating that has helped you move right through some of the tougher times. Do not worry. I know whereof I speak.

PAUL   Okay, Raj.

RAJ   I know you feel like you need help, but no one can help you at this point. There is no other One but You, and you had better be sure that you have no other "ones" before You, Your Self, God. Your entire Being, in all Its infinitude, is harmonizing with You, loving You, and supporting You because of the Integrity of your Being. No one but *You* can relinquish consciously your hold on the false sense of self — the misidentification which feels it can't do it.

At this point I want to terminate the conversation. I will be instantly available if you need to talk, but I want you to be consciously and quietly alone with your own Being and the Reality of things. This is your baby!

PAUL   All right, Raj. Thank you.

1   Eddy, *Science and Health*, 468:10-11.

2   Eddy, *Miscellany*, 242:5-7.

3   Matthew, 13:24-30.

PAUL   Raj?

RAJ   Yes, Paul.

PAUL   Are you a separate individuality from me?

RAJ   Separateness is a three–dimensional concept, Paul.

PAUL   Would I be misunderstanding Reality if I were to let you speak though me *as* me and relinquish my present sense of identification?

RAJ   I understand what you are trying to get at, Paul. As a matter of fact, when I am speaking to you, it is your Being which is speaking to you. That is, unless I am relating some aspect of my experience, as in my work dealing with the return of Maitreya.

You don't believe that, I see.

PAUL   I guess I don't want to believe it.

RAJ   Well, Paul, I would suggest that you test it out and see for yourself.

PAUL   Do you mean that right now, this very instant, I am speaking with my Being? It is my Being revealing Itself to me *as* my conscious experience of being, and not "Raj" at all?

RAJ   That is correct, Paul. Don't misunderstand. I am not a figment of your imagination, as I have told you before. I am here, but I am here as the Door. I am here to facilitate what you did not think you could do, because you did not conceive it as an existing possibility. In a way, it was like getting to your Self through the back door, unobtrusively, without upsetting or exciting the three-dimensional self-thought-processes.

PAUL   Let me ask this, Raj: If I choose to, or want to, or need to think it is you, will I be able to? Or am I now required to let loose of that concept?

RAJ   You may. But you can already see somewhat that you will delude yourself to some degree regarding your own Integrity, and this will weaken you, or seem to. It will not be a weakness as great as three-dimensional-only thinking, but you need to move on. You need to come into the Power of your Being *as your Being!*

Don't rattle your brains about this. As long as you need to see your Self as "me," I will be here. Even after you don't need to see your Self as me, I will be here. Our relationship will apparently change — but it will remain.

PAUL   Okay, Raj. Let me let this sink in.

RAJ   That's fine, Paul.

May 15, 1982
Saturday

PAUL   Raj, I don't understand why there seems to be so much mechanical failure — the car, the dictation machine, the tape recorder, etc. I especially don't understand why we're having trouble with the car, since if we pay to have it fixed, we won't have the money to rent the copy machine for the business. If we get the copy machine and don't have the car fixed, then we have no way to pick up the copy work.

RAJ   Paul, I Am is the Substance of everything that appears. This I Am is the I Am that you recognize as your Self. If you see things as other than the visibility of I Am and think that they exist independently, then you literally pull the plug on them, since separated from what they Are, they have no existence or function. The fact that you are having this difficulty does not imply anything wrong with your thinking, but it indicates that it's time for this point to be clarified with you. You have grown into an appreciation of this fact, and it's time to incorporate it into your consciousness of your Being.

Cars are not inventions of man, but rather they are that which identifies the Omnipresence of Being to some extent. They illustrate the everpresent availability of your Being as conscious experience. Recording devices, likewise, illustrate or demonstrate the omnipresent availability of some part of your "past" — information which is of value to you to have in your present experience. Do not separate them from their Source, conceptually speaking, and they will continually identify the fulfillment of Purpose.

You are beginning to lose sight of the fact that all of You is always present — and that means *right now!* You are letting *some* things depend on *other* things (objectively speaking), and this is fouling up your *perceptions* of these things by seeing them as having independent existence and purpose.

PAUL I will get back to you in a few minutes, Raj. It's time for the kids to go to bed.

RAJ Okay, Paul.

PAUL [I took a short break.]

Okay, I'm back.

RAJ All right, Paul.

PAUL Raj, I am failing miserably at demonstrating or seeing the omnipresence of my Being in terms of supply. It's true that from day to day we have what we need, but it's far from a comfortable way to live. All we're getting are basics. The larger debts we owe are not being met.

RAJ Paul, I want you to be aware that you are beginning to give up your faith, trust, and belief in the validity of our conversations. This is indicated by the flip-flopping back and forth between knowing they are real and doubting they are real. I point out also that the doubting comes into play when you are challenged by opinions or circumstances. This certainly is a natural response, but it is not the consistent vantage point which you will find necessary if you're going to be free from being dangled like a yo-yo or blown to and fro on the breeze of chance.

PAUL Well, if you are wanting me to develop some inner strength which will not yield, no matter what I'm confronted with — and if I'm supposed to do this while it's my family's lack that I'm faced with — then I don't think you should be surprised! Theoretically, intellectually, I can grasp its value. But when it comes down to the nitty-gritty of life, it often seems like nonsense.

RAJ I understand, Paul. I want to refer you to what your Supply told you about how to set the Law in motion. I want you to begin doing this on a regular basis. A word to the wise: Be sure of what you are asking for, because you shall surely get it.

PAUL All right, Raj, I shall forge forward. I will tell you this: It would be much easier if my family's needs were being better met.

RAJ You are right, absolutely right. Now, do something about it! You've got the necessary tools.

PAUL Very well, I will. Good night, Raj.

RAJ Good night, Paul. I am with you and Susan both. Most of all, you are with your Self.

May 17, 1982
Monday

PAUL   Raj, we are trying to understand why this illusion of ongoing interference, lack, and blockage of free-flowing expression and experience of good is appearing in our lives. We are trying to understand the cause of it, so that we can handle the right thing to correct the situation. Can you shed any light on it?

    You say there is no evil presence, force, or power. Yet there certainly appears to be the effect of something opposed to or different from God, Good, Harmony, et cetera.

RAJ   Paul, you are being confused by the process of three-dimensional thinking. It will always suggest some finite cause. It will always suggest that the reason for events comes from either finite objective causes or finite mental causes.

PAUL   Okay, so far.

RAJ   You are at a point where you need to see that there is only One Cause, only One Action, only One Life, Mind, Being, Consciousness. This does not mean that everything you seem to experience is included in that One Mind, Being, Consciousness, but it means that the step that needs to be taken here is to not deal with specific little "causes." It means that it is time to have no other gods but God.

    I don't care what anybody else seems to have to be doing at the present moment, or whether they are seeming to have to learn this, or be faced with what you are being faced with.

YOU HAVE GOT TO HANDLE THIS AS THOUGH YOU
ARE THE ONLY ONE! AND YOU ARE GOING TO
HAVE TO HANDLE THIS AS THOUGH THERE IS
ONLY *ONE* PRESENCE AND POWER! The time is past
to handle anything from the standpoint of "handling" this
or that or the other "thing," — whether it be thought, belief,
object, or circumstance.

PAUL I'm seeing a pink chrysanthemum. Is that part of your communication?

RAJ The pink chrysanthemum stands as the radiant beauty of Itself as though there is no other thing going on. The image,
as you see it, symbolizes the absolute disregard for the supposed existence of any other thing, purpose, or concept outside of Its purpose of radiating Its fullness, Its beauty — the
fact that it is a glorious pink chrysanthemum.

Being is that way. It radiates Itself, and there is no other
than It.

It is the "consideration" of beliefs, the manipulations of objects "out there," the orienting of "position" and "power"
which ties us into the three–dimensional frame of reference.
Religion works in this realm. Economics works in this realm.
Indeed, all of life is "worked" from this realm.

It is time to move out of this realm, and there is no way to
do it half–way. There is no way to keep a little bit of the finite
view to "work with" and yet move into the Fourth-
dimensional experience of Being (Your Being). Being is not
finite (dimensional) in the very heavy, burdensome, sweat-
producing way that three–dimensional things and thoughts
are.

Paul *and Susan,* you are *both* making the transition very
smoothly, no matter how it seems to you. It is because this
transition is being made that you find yourselves not able
to communicate well with those bound by their three-
dimensional-only thinking. Do not be surprised at it, and do
not be offended by it.

The necessity here, and the only choice you have, is to move
forward — or rather, I should say stand still — *as* Being, as
you are both intuitively doing quite well. Do not look for substantiation of the correctness of your position from the finite
frame of reference.

You can count on this: Conceptually speaking, or objectively speaking, you are seeing the appearance of things not working right.

Now, let's clarify that by dropping the last word. You are seeing the appearance of things not working. What is happening here is that you are objectively seeing the fact that things do not work the way you thought they worked when you were seeing three–dimensionally.

What you can count on is: Everything that appears not to be working *is working* right now, right where you are, unchanged in any way from the Actuality of its working. This is an illusion caused by the shifting of the frame of reference from the finite to the infinite view. The illusion will not continue indefinitely.

It is a "reverse landmark" or waymark which, *because* it is reversed, usually stops one from moving forward in the direction of Infinity until he has the kind of guidance, encouragement, and development which provides him with the proper perception of its significance. It is simply to be observed. It is not to be dealt with.

The Kingdom of Heaven is *apparently* guarded by "demons," "evils," "devils," because that is the only way ego can see the impersonal existence of Being. It is *very EVIL* because it means the demise of ego. Ego is the only baggage that cannot go through the eye of the needle. Since it can't go through, it applies fearful images around the eye to ensure that one will not proceed through it.

You may think what has been happening is rugged, but hindsight will show you that you are coming through almost unscathed. This is because of the strength of your perceptions of what's Real, and your conviction in its Reality.

No one can do this for you. That's why you seem to be alone in this — without communication, without understanding of what's happening to you, et cetera.

You have wondered what is going on. Well, *this* is what is going on. You will find that you have not been separated from anything but the *sense* of separation. It was still lingering when you began this journey through the eye.

I can say, "Be patient, everything will be all right," but that will not help you unless *you* believe it. No one can truly convince you of the Reality of Your Being. It's already the Fact of You, and you are having to live this "time" out from that Fact.

In the process, beware of conceptualizing in any way what is happening. Beware of using old "standards" of reasoning and actions. They may not apply, since most standards have finite bases.

I assure you, for whatever it's worth, that you are "weathering the storm" well. You are, figuratively speaking, like a plane landing on instruments, having very low visibility. You are following an inner flight path with no objective evidence to support you. It's up to you whether you choose to continue the landing or postpone it for a better time — but I'll clue you in to the fact that there won't be a better time. There is no "clear," three-dimensional visibility through which to enter the Kingdom of Heaven.

I hope this answers your question. I Know it *is* the answer.

PAUL   Thank you, Raj.

RAJ   You're welcome, Paul.

May 28, 1982
Friday

PAUL   [Today I decided to try having a conversation with my Wisdom.]

[Addressing Wisdom.] Wisdom?

WISDOM   *Yes, Paul.*

PAUL   Can you tell me what is the wisest thing to do in establishing our business and our life here in Spokane?

WISDOM   *Of course. The wisest thing to do is to acknowledge that you are already established Universally at every point of the Infinitude of Your Being. You cannot* become *established in Spokane, because the establishment has been since the Beginning, and it has been and is Universal.*

It is important to realize that the establishment is Universal. You must begin to perceive and experience the fact that Your Being is Universal, and not localized only to that point at which your consciousness is attentively focused.

It will be wise for you to remain in touch with this Universal establishment of Your Being. You need to flow with your whole Being, and not just with what appears to be happening right now in Spokane. In this way, whatever you do in Spokane will identify and illustrate the Universal establishment of your Being. It will keep you from being fooled into believing that you are nothing more than a finite point in the Universe, eking out an existence, struggling, trying to become, and constantly failing.

I am not going to give you specific outward steps to take, because then you will not do the needed thing. That thing is to go within and remain in that Place — in touch with Your Universal Being — and flow with It. The specific, detailed steps which identify the establishment of your Being Universally — as well as specifically in Spokane — will become clear when you follow the directions I have given you.

PAUL   Thank you.

WISDOM *Paul, I would suggest that since you find that you have good communication with me, you avail yourself often of this aspect of Your Being called your Wisdom. In fact, I would suggest to you that it would be very wise to lean on me regularly.*

PAUL   I will do that. Thank you.

[Addressing Raj.] Good morning, Raj.

RAJ   Good morning, Paul.

PAUL   Raj, I would like to hear whatever you might have to share with me this morning, without asking any questions of you at this point.

RAJ   Very well, Paul. I want you to consider the fact that "pedestals" are for show. They exist for the purpose of exhibiting whatever is resting upon them. As a matter of fact, the pedestal itself has become an object of art. I want you to consider the fact that a pedestal is used to set something apart from everything else. It is a divisive structure, three-dimensionally speaking. It is also divisive from an inner standpoint, wherein it equates with "ego" — "a liar and the father of it."[1] It is the liar, in that it holds up that which is not separate and says, "This is separate." It is the father of the lie, in that what it holds up as separate is concocted of its own fantasy. The pedestal, together with what it shows off, is total illusion. One truly does not exist without the other.

As things seem to take on some definition in your life, I want you to beware of the idea that the form which is taking shape is in any way connected with You as a product of *your* intellect, or *your* good sense, or you, yourself, in any way.

You must remain clear in the fact that form is fluid and not fixed, that it serves to identify what your Being is being. You must remember that if the form became "fixed," that your Being would become fixed, static, immovable, and unmoving. And, thus, it would cease to be Being.

Your focal point must remain at that within Point wherein you are constantly aware of being as Conscious Being, not as the operator of a business, or the promoter of a service. You must let the business and the service be what they will, as the ever-fluid manifestation of that living Being which You Are. Do not let what "occurs" become the repository of yourself. This is because Your Self, being infinite, cannot be confined to any manifestation or visibility which It evolves for Its identification.

Yes, in your terms, it would mean a dispassionate, uninvolved experience of what is appearing. You must learn to get your satisfaction from being What You Are as Conscious Being, rather than what you appear to be by virtue of what is done three-dimensionally.

You have slipped in this regard and have allowed yourself to become trapped in the visibility and tangibility of your Being, and it has not been comfortable for you. At the same time, it has not damaged you. It has *illustrated* to you experientially the difference between being as Conscious Being and being three-dimensionally as a finite form among other forms.

I cannot force you to do it, but I would suggest that you get back into that Place as an ongoing state of Being and remain there.

Being out from Mind is the only state of Being in which illusion is absent. Illusion is always distressing and uncomfortable, as you well know.

I am glad you spoke with your Wisdom this morning. I would suggest that you devote equal time to speaking with your Wisdom and me. In fact, the more you can find your answers coming from that which you recognize to be your own Being, without any possibility of imagining that it is coming from someone or something separate from yourself — such as me — the better it will be for you in tying together those aspects of your Being which you have not consciously been aware of as Your Self.

The fact is that it is all You. But, it must become your conscious experience of your Being, without any dichotomy of any kind.

PAUL   I understand, Raj.

RAJ   Paul, when it comes to your family and your living experience, be observant. Watch to see whether you are seeing yourself and the members of your family as isolated bits and pieces — parts of the flotsam and jetsam of life — floating on the currents of who knows what.

This is a three–dimensional–only point of view. It will be constantly frustrating, because it begins with a false concept of man. It sees him as trying to lift himself up by his bootstraps and getting help in doing so from others who may or may not be "more enlightened." It misses the larger fact that Being is unfolding Itself on an infinite basis. It is unfolding Itself successfully.

This means that, rather than trying to figure out what you can do which will be best for your family, you can abide in that Place of observing with understanding that Being is unfolding Itself perfectly as each specific identity in your family. This perfect unfoldment is, because of Its infinity, occurring in a way which appears to be harmonious for all concerned. I say "appears" because, no matter how many It appears to be, It is still One infinite Event.

You give the weight to the Law of Perfection by beginning with the perfect concept. You seem to diminish your awareness of that Perfection unfolding when you begin with a finite concept of what is going on. You cannot actually change the Fact, but you *can* seem to blind yourself to It.

If All is Infinite Mind, *then All is Infinite Mind!* One must live his experience of the infinitude of his Being as though that were the Fact. Not because that will *help* make it so, but because that *is* what is so! And such thinking is, therefore, in line with what is already true.

Each individuality in your family is the One infinite Individuality infinitely individualized and unfolding Itself in absolutely healthy, constructive and integrating ways. This is the Fact. Even when one member or another of your family vehemently claims his ability to act on his own, you can rest assured that the eternal Facts which contradict such a be lief, contradict it in such a way as to turn it to the advantage of the individuality indulging in the belief. Thus, it illustrates experientially why the belief is invalid and a waste of time.

Every single event, whether constituted of Reality or what seems to be a belief about Reality, cannot get outside the realm of serving the One and Only thing going on. This is why "the very circumstance, which our suffering sense deems wrathful and afflictive, Love can make an angel entertained unawares."[2]

Paul, it is imperative that both you and Susan begin to really get this sense that Being is totally positive and totally constructive. Not even a false belief can escape the design or intent of Being to fulfill Itself, and thus serve to enlighten the one indulging in such a belief.

PAUL   Thank you, Raj. I have other questions, but I want to consider what you have said so far before I go into them.

RAJ   That is a good idea, Paul, since I think some of the questions you will find have already been answered.

I will look forward to speaking with you soon.

PAUL   Thanks again.

[1] John, 8:44.

[2] Eddy, *Science and Health*, 574:27-30.

May 29, 1982
Saturday

PAUL [The first part of the conversation was accidently not recorded.]

RAJ You must realize, Paul, that the concept of "irresponsibility" is going to present itself to you until you see that the concept of "responsibility" is invalid — except from the ego standpoint. This is because the concept of responsibility implies Being is not Universal, and is not unfolding Itself Universally with absolute perfection. It implies, therefore, that each tiny, finite mentality must take on responsibility for what needs to be done, and for seeing that it is done in a "principled," "intelligent," and "reasonable" way. Responsibility and irresponsibility both fade out of the picture as being as Conscious Being becomes the Place from which all is experienced.

Do not be afraid to follow the intuitive inner guidance which comes to you regarding your business. You are learning new principles of business here. I encourage you to be willing to let go of this sense of personal responsibility and control, and be willing to flow with the business as the busy-ness or Activity of Being Itself — Your Self.

PAUL Raj, I am going to change the subject here, because I have a question that is demanding attention. The question is: Why does it irk me when Susan asks to speak to you? Why do I feel that her questions will be an imposition upon you, and why does it make me mad that she doesn't contact her own Guide?

284

RAJ   Because you have not learned that Being is truly unfolding Itself infinitely and not according to concepts. It is true that she has a Guide whom she can contact, but you need to learn to flow with what is happening, rather than with what you think *ought* to be happening.

It is no imposition upon me whatsoever, and it is no imposition on you. What do you have to do that is better than allowing a communication between Susan and myself through you? It is a divine activity. The fact that you are irritated by it is nothing less than ego getting in the way. That's poppycock!

You are simply setting up blocks to the effortless unfoldment of your Being by attempting to structure your Being, and you are doing nothing but causing yourself unnecessary distress. You must get back to the fact that it is the infinitude of your Being with which you are confronted. Stop separating It into compartments — dividing It up into "me" and "thee" — and then attempting to organize the bits and pieces according to concepts.

Your problem at this point is truly a matter of attempting to place an overlay of intellectual patterns upon Infinity. Nothing less than the infinite view will do for you any longer.

Remember that letting go of control — letting go of these intellectual thought structures — will not cause disorganization and disorientation of the Universe. Rather, it will reveal from an experiential standpoint the fact that the Universe is already organized and orderly and intelligent in Its Function, whether you are intellectualizing about it or not.

Remember, too, that until you do go ahead and let go, you will not have the opportunity to observe It working in Its absolute perfection and spontaneous and effortless harmony.

It is equally imperative for you to begin to really grasp that your "others" are your Self seen infinitely. Therefore, "competition" is useless and baseless. No one can control you, and you can control no one, because there is only One Thing going on. You must stop challenging Susan, and you must stop seeing Susan as someone separate who is challenging you. This is extremely important, because none of it is happening that way. The necessity here is for you to own all of yourself as your Self. The infinity of your experience is *your Infinitude* identifying the Oneness of your Being.

I want you to contemplate this with all due seriousness, and more than that, I want you to begin to live it as much as possible.

You will remember that, at the beginning of our conversations, we talked about the necessity of being willing to stand at the edge of the Unknown — knowing nothing. And at this point, you are attempting to take what we have been speaking about and using it as the basis for knowing something now.

In Actuality, the necessity still remains, and will forever remain, for you to continue to stand at the edge of the Unknown — knowing absolutely nothing. Let the infinitude of your Being flow though and as your conscious experience *at each and every moment*. This is essential.

Because it is a well–established habit, it is so very easy to attempt to take the infinite unfoldments of our Being and try to channel them into old habits of action. The need is to give up our habits of "doing," and replace them with *being* what the infinity of our Being is being at every moment.

The call for action this evening is for you to consciously relinquish your attempts at control and conceptualization and get back to that Point where you stand as Nothing. Thereby you allow the Somethingness of your Being to become apparent as your conscious experience of being.

PAUL   Thank you, Raj.

RAJ   You are welcome, Paul. Good night.

PAUL   Good night.

June 3, 1982
Thursday

PAUL   Good evening, Raj.

RAJ   Good evening, Paul. You are beginning to notice the limitations you place upon yourself by virtue of assuming that you don't know something or that you can't figure it out, or that it's not the right time, or any of a number of excuses which are totally false, but which you totally believe. You are beginning to discover that you truly do not have to figure a single thing out. You, Paul, person, three–dimensional finite consciousness, do not have the answer! Yet, the answers are available. The answers *are* available because of What You Are when you are standing as the Door. You are really beginning to see this, and this is excellent.

You are also beginning to find more satisfaction from being that which *is* the Answer unfolding Itself, rather than being the one who is figuring out what the Answer is, or being able in any way to claim credit for the Answer. This also is excellent.

What is not excellent is that you are not yet spontaneously choosing to avail yourself of the answers by means of being the Door on a continuous basis. It is as though it were in some way more laborious than figuring the answer out, or simply postponing having the answer. I want you to take some time to examine what this reluctance is, so that you may understand it better. I could tell you, but I want you to learn it for yourself.

PAUL I will have to say that a number of things are beginning to jell and clarify themselves.

RAJ You are correct. This jelling, as you have put it, will continue. The facts will become more meaningful to you as each day goes by. Since you already know that there truly is no process to it, I would encourage you to relinquish this idea that standing as the Door is something "special," and therefore not something to waste your time doing during everyday activities. Nothing exists outside the infinitude of Being. Therefore, what you denominate "everyday activities" in a somewhat demeaning way, needs to be seen as equally worthy of being embraced and perceived from the standpoint of being the Door.

Remember that standing as the Door, at the edge of the Unknown, will become a constant activity or point of observation in your life. You might as well see it in its proper perspective right from the beginning as being totally normal and not "special" in any way.

PAUL Thank you, Raj. I will do that.

RAJ You are welcome, Paul. Good night.

June 10, 1982
Thursday

PAUL   Good afternoon, Raj.

RAJ   Good afternoon, Paul.

Be aware of your reluctance to have this conversation. Simply recognize it. Notice that the reluctance is because you are wanting to glide over the information and understanding which you imagine you are going to be confronted with. You imagine it is going to discredit you in some way.

Realize, further, to what extent this fear or reluctance is manifested physically in terms of strong perspiration, discomfort in the pit of your stomach, and just a general yukkiness.

I am going to suggest that you clean up your act mentally and physically before we continue further. *Go take a bath!* And while you're taking the bath, refresh your consciousness also.

PAUL   Very well, Raj, I shall.

[So, I took a bath.]

Okay, I'm back, and that does feel better. Let's go ahead and take the plunge.

As I observe myself, it seems incredible to me that there is this definite reluctance to get into the subject of Substance, or into the specific answer to the problems we have been faced with over the past number of months. It is extremely strong.

289

RAJ And, Paul, it is entirely operating at the level of belief. It is a totally ignorant experience. That is what makes it *most* incredible.

It simply means that you are going to have to move through it *purposely,* and not hope for some way to get around it.

Are you ready?

PAUL Yes. I can't say that with a whole lot of enthusiasm, but I can say it with determination.

RAJ That is good, Paul. Part of doing this purposely means that I am not simply going to sit here and expound. I want you to ask me specific questions and I will answer your specific questions.

PAUL Very well. My first question is: What is Substance?

RAJ Your first answer is that Substance is infinite, nondimensional, and pure Energy — the Life Force, as it were.

It is Intelligence.

It is Soul.

It is Spirit.

It is Principle.

It is Love.

It is Life.

It is Truth.

It is Mind.

It is, in the final analysis, what is meant by the word God.

It is omnipresent. It is omniactive. It is the nondimensional or Universal "stuff" of which all that is made is made. It is that which constitutes You and your entire experience as Conscious Being, whether you are being "out from Mind" or not.

The Bible says, "Faith is the substance of things hoped for, the evidence of things not seen."[1] This means that no matter how deeply we may seem to be buried in the distortions of a personal, three–dimensional, finite frame of mind, the faith that we find everpresently abiding within us is our ever present "connection" with the Actuality of our Being *as It is really going on.* In other words, it is our Actual experience of Substance, inviolably "held in trust" for us, you might say, so long as we indulge in attempting to experience the Reality of our Being from a partial view. This is why it is "the evidence of things not seen." It is the evidence of Reality, present and undistorted, in spite of the distortions inherent in the partial view.

Faith, intuition, and desire constitute three aspects of our everpresent conscious experience of Reality while we are involved in the deception of existing as a finite mentality.

Now, it does no good to have a lifeline attached to us while trekking around in the foreboding territory of the three-dimensional frame of reference *if we do not use it* to guide ourselves back into the Fourth-dimensional view, wherein perspective returns and there is no foreboding.

In other words, it serves no purpose to *stand* in the finite view and *have* faith, *have* intuition, and *have* desires. From within that frame of reference, the distortion applies equally to those three everpresent perceptions of Reality. It causes them to be experienced as arising out of the *absence* of that which we have faith in, intuition about, and desires for.

One can sit and rot in the illusion of "hell" while tenderly fondling and embracing his intuitions, faith, and desires. Your faith in what is Real, your intuitions about It, and your desire to experience It must be seen for what they are, *and utilized,* no matter how infinitesimal they seem to be from the standpoint of the partial view!

PAUL   How does Substance function?

RAJ   It functions by being the omnipresent omniaction of Being. The substance of Mind is Consciousness. The substance of Truth is Principle. The substance of Principle is Intelligence/Law. The substance of Soul is Love. The substance of Love is Life. And the substance of Life is Mind.

You are wondering what happened to Spirit.

PAUL   You are correct.

RAJ   Spirit is the substance of all of these, both nondimensionally and dimensionally. It is the Light, Itself, which illumines and is illumined. It is That which shines, and That which is shone upon. Spirit is, Itself, the Life Principle, the Life Force, the Initiator and Initiated, the Cause and the Effect.

Law is intelligent Principle — principled Intelligence — and this constitutes the omniactive Nature of Substance. The Light which is divine, intelligent Love is the means by which divine Mind reveals Itself to Itself infinitely as the omnipresently active Experience of Revelation. It allows Soul to respond, "And, behold, it was very good."[2]

Substance is the infinite "recognition" of Reality when we are standing as the Door, since there is no disparity between the perception of Reality and the concrete or substantial experience of It in all of Its completeness.

PAUL   What is the function of Substance?

RAJ   Its function is congruency, integrity, confluency, and inseparable Oneness, the inviolable substantiality of Infinity, of Reality. It is the constituting indivisibility of Conscious Being. It is the Absolute Law of the intelligent, harmonious blending of the infinite manifestations which constitute the experience of *being* as Conscious Being.

Substance is Omnipotence. There is nothing passive, whatsoever, about it. It is the adhesion, cohesion, and attraction which constitute the immutable orderliness of the Totality of Being.

PAUL   I truly don't know what to ask you next, Raj.

RAJ   That's all right. Why don't you consider these things before continuing?

PAUL   I will. Thank you.

RAJ   You are welcome, Paul.

PAUL   [I transcribed the conversation, considered what had been said, and then continued.]

Raj, you really know how to put the screws to me. It isn't easy coming up with pertinent questions, I am finding.

RAJ   That's correct. Learning what questions to ask is half the battle of learning what you need to know. Abstract generalities mumbled in consciousness serve no practical purpose, even though a temporary sense of satisfaction can be gained from such mumbling.

PAUL   In what way does Substance constitute Supply?

RAJ   Let us first be clear that when we speak of Supply we are not speaking from a finite, three-dimensional standpoint.

Supply is not something that comes from one point to another point, such as payment from a client or customer. Supply does not come from one thing to another, such as food value from wheat. Supply is not given or received.

Supply is an Omnipresencing of That Which Is: God, the Life Principle, Divine Mind, Fourth-dimensional Being as Conscious Being. You must remember that Substance is *Activity,* not a static lump of stuff. We have already spoken in regard to the fact that It has intent or purpose.

Substance is Being's Ability to fulfill Itself successfully, Totally. Therefore, it should be clear that Substance is fulfillment — Supply in its truest meaning.

Supply is inescapable, unavoidable, when understood.

PAUL   Thank you. How does Substance relate to health?

RAJ   Health is the constituting Wholeness of Being, the Orderliness, Integrity, Indivisibility and, therefore, the Perfection of all Conscious Being. Being omnipotent in Its ability to fulfill Its Intent or Purpose, there is no delay or obstacle to that fulfillment. It is this unimpeded Omnipresencing of Substance which constitutes Supply in what is called health or Wholeness.

PAUL   Thank you.

RAJ   I reiterate that Supply is not a movement from "here" to "there," not even from God to man — meaning, the infinite to the finite — since in Reality there is no finite realm, only a finite view of the Infinite.

The revelation for you today is not only a clearer understanding of what Substance is, but the specific disclosure that You — as Fourth-dimensional Conscious Being — are this Self-fulfilling, omnipotent, omniactive Substance in exactly the same way that you are the Answer.

When you have been conversing with your Supply or Substance, you have been consciously experiencing the constitutional Universal Substance of Your Being. Substance and Its omnipotent omniaction is in no way separate or apart from that which You Are. It is the All–constituting Spirit Omnipresencing Itself, and is experienced as your conscious experience of Being when you are standing as the Door.

There is only One Substance, no matter how infinitely seen nor how great its diversification. Substance is not an attribute or a manifestation of God, of Being, but is Its Constitution.

Now, you can see that this understanding cannot be used to overcome lack. It reveals unequivocally that it is impossible for there to be lack to overcome. Abide steadfastly in this understanding of Substance — as being that which constitutes Your Being Totally, infinitely, and unfailingly — from that Place where you are experiencing Being as Conscious Being. Joyously observe what unfolds.

PAUL   Thank you, Raj. I have no further questions regarding Substance at this time.

Good night.

RAJ   Good night, Paul.

---

1 Hebrews, 11:1.

2 Gen. 1:31.

June 12, 1982
Saturday

PAUL   Good evening, Raj.

RAJ   Good evening, Paul.

PAUL   I have a number of specific questions for you tonight.

RAJ   That's just fine, Paul. Go ahead.

PAUL   What relation does Substance, as you've described it, have with substance as I experience it every day?

RAJ   Paul, when you ask that question, you are seeing Substance gathered together in clumps, so to speak — objects — which imply that Substance is absent in the spaces between those objects. In other words, you are thinking of Substance three-dimensionally. In fact, Substance is Fourth-dimensional or nondimensional. It constitutes every aspect of conscious experience as Conscious Being.

You must remember that none of what you see, hear, taste, smell, or feel is going on external to the conscious experience of it, even though that is the way it appears. All of it is Consciousness. All of it is Mind's Self-experience.

As I have explained Substance to you, it has only this connection in relation to substance as you experience it every day: It constitutes the Actual conscious experience of every single idea included in the conscious experience of Being *as* Conscious Being. This Reality of conscious experience is what

295

is objectified as the three-dimensional universe, but none of it is happening *in* the objectification.

When you are observing the three-dimensional universe, and you are interpreting it as existing and functioning on its own, then substance, *as you are seeing it,* has absolutely nothing to do with Substance as It Is.

The flaw in your interpretation — the distortion of this partial or finite view — causes what is seen, heard, felt, tasted, and smelled to seem to be capable of sickness, decay, and death. These are dysfunctions which the Actuality of what you see, hear, taste, smell, and feel is totally incapable of.

The shift we have been discussing for the past few months involves a shift of the point of awareness from an objective placement to a subjective placement, wherein each and every Actual idea of Mind is experienced and recognized as being absolutely mental.

PAUL This would mean, then, that man is incorporeal?

RAJ This would mean that the conscious experience of Being is not existent someplace in an objective, three-dimensional universe.

It means that the Universe of Mind *is* peopled with infinite ideas which are perfectly tangible to Consciousness. Therefore, they are not bodiless in the sense of having no visible, tangible outline, form, or colour. It means that everything is identified and identifiable, minus the finite sensation of space and time, minus the sense of separation between subject and object, which is unavoidable in the three-dimensional frame of reference. It is also minus the sense of the beholder being located somewhere *in* that which is beheld.

Man is as incorporeal as God, and yet "all is infinite Mind and Its infinite manifestation." Mind is never minus Its manifestation.

Now, when I said that Substance is Energy, I did not mean that It was energy in the sense that your scientists measure and call electrical or atomic energy. It is Energy in the sense that It is Light. Even so, It is not Light in the sense of It being that energy which emanates from your sun. In terms of the manner in which It is *experienced* Fourth-dimensionally, it is very similar. It radiates, glows, or fluoresces, yet these are very poor words to describe It.

Light, as it is experienced objectively, is seen only as it reflects off of an object. At night, when you look out into the objective universe and there is nothing in the sky to reflect light, the sky appears to be black, except where light is either reflected or generated as planets and stars.

Fourth-dimensionally speaking, the Substance which is Light is illumined, apparently, from within. It is not a reflected light. The apparent space between specific manifestations of Mind will not be found to be dark, because the Fourth-dimensional equivalent of what *appears* to be empty space in the three-dimensional frame of reference, *is* filled with the omnipresent Substance of Being. Therefore, you will find that even "empty space" is filled with that living Illumination of the Universal Substance which is Light.

Further, it must be understood that this Substance which is Light is Love, living Love. You have experienced this already in Illumination, and so I know you understand what I am saying.

PAUL Thank you, Raj. I am going to change the subject now. I want to understand in what way God gave man dominion over all the earth.

RAJ Paul, that statement was made within the illusion of three-dimensional existence. In the first place, there is no man separate from God for God to give anything to. Secondly, it is only from within the finite frame of reference that there can seem to be an "earth" separate from "man" for man to have dominion over. Any apparent success that the human concept (ego) has of being able to exercise dominion over an earth "out there" only succeeds in further deepening the illusion that life is going on objectively.

Fourth-dimensionally speaking, the observer and the observed are One, although they are experienced in infinite variation of qualities, outline, form, and colour — which go beyond anything you have conceived up to this point.

PAUL Will you clarify for me how it is that Jesus appeared to have dominion in raising the dead, healing the sick, et cetera? Will you further explain how I am to understand his statement that "He that believeth on me, the works that I do shall he do also, and greater than these shall he do"?[1] If I were to do them, it would certainly appear that I was exercising dominion over the objective world, conditions, and circumstances.

This question is of importance to me. Since before I began speaking with you, and right straight through to this point, it certainly appears that there is no exercise of dominion in my experience at all... and no healing.

RAJ It is because the time has come to stop manipulating the finite view to improve it according to finite concepts. This does not constitute waking up out of the dream or waking up out of the distortions of the partial view. If you succeed in improving the partial view — in "healing it" — you will find no necessity to involve yourself in the labors necessary to Awaken.

You have been nagged in the back of your mind with the Biblical statement that a time will come when "no sign shall be given."[2] You have felt that your experience is indicating that this is the case for you now, and this is an intuitive perception of the fact. Any sign given three-dimensionally will serve to hold you in the partial view, rather than move you out of it.

To answer your unspoken thought there, I am not responsible for your being in this position. Nor could I be, if I wanted to. I am simply telling you where you are by virtue of your own unfolding Being, and to that extent, at least, you are not in the dark. I have nothing to do with it one way or the other. I cannot hold you to it or relieve you of it, put you in it, or get you out of it.

Being as Conscious Being, and not as three-dimensional man, is the shift which you *are* experiencing at this time. It cannot be altered in any way, just as the three-dimensional, objective delivery of a baby, once begun, is not a matter of choice in any way.

At the apparent "birth" of Christopher, the practitioner related that "Love is the Art of giving." It will be well for you to remember this in your own regard in that you will have to give in to this Awakening and flow with it.

PAUL Thank you, Raj.

RAJ You are welcome, Paul. Good afternoon.

[1] John 14:12.

[2] Mark 8:12.

June 14, 1982
Monday

PAUL   Good morning, Raj.

RAJ   Good morning, Paul. You are beginning to grasp that there truly is a more infinite and accurate view of what you are experiencing, and yet you feel you have no basis upon which to wake up to that larger, more accurate perception. You recognize the demand for something, and I have told you that the three–dimensional situation will not be relieved until you wake up. Thus, you find yourself in a bind from which you see no escape. The fact is that Being has no dead ends. It is only the finite view which would make Infinity appear to be blocked off.

You are sitting, right now, as the Omnipresence of infinite Good, actively, omnipotently unfolding and fulfilling Itself without exception.

It is the intuitive perception — it is the desire, faith, and intuition of there being something to wake up *into* — which must remain the focal point of your conscious experience, regardless of the illusion of being boxed in. Then you must *desire* to wake up. Do not waste any energy in attempting to overcome any facet of the dream, since the way things appear is imaginary. It, therefore, cannot be dealt with in any way other than waking up!

I mentioned in our last conversation that the Awakening is already occurring. I will add to that that because you are waking up, the dream seems to be coming to an end — even the "good" aspects of the dream seem no longer to be good, to

299

be functioning properly, to be dependable, and so forth. For this reason it is imperative that you not react to the appearance of "ending" and attempt to keep it going. You will not be able to do it anyway. Even if you could, you would end up with only a further dream.

In the process of desiring to Awaken, keep in mind what we have been discussing about Substance. In fact, keep in mind everything we have discussed because these Facts are substantial and are constituted of the Substance which is Light. Allow this Light to illumine your way, no matter how abstract this may seem to you.

Keep more in touch with the Fourth–dimensional Actuality of your family experience, and of any activity which you are involved in during the day. If necessary, remind yourself of the Facts of which we have spoken. Measure your daily experience according to these Facts, rather than the way the day *seems* to be appearing or what it seems to be claiming.

The simple fact is that you need to proceed as though the divine Facts were Facts — which They are. And, on the basis of these Facts, you must be alert with a sense of active expectancy to see Them become apparent in and as your conscious experience.

PAUL   Thank you, Raj. I shall do that. I will get together with you again tomorrow morning.

June 19, 1982
Saturday

RAJ I think you can see that unfoldment is really a matter of how quickly or slowly we are willing to let go of limitations, rather than the presence or availability of something to expand into, since Infinity is the Actuality of every moment of conscious experience. This is important to understand, because we often feel that we are held back by the limitation as though *it* had the ability to influence or deprive us of our Good. Not true! *There is never anything holding us!*

It is always *us* that is holding onto some comfortable sense of limitation with which we feel some sense of familiarity. The active agent which holds us back is actually our own refusal to let go of the known for the Unknown.

This reluctance is entirely due to an adopted belief that we are what we appear to be — finite, separate, an independent "intelligence" that exists "inside" this finite object called a body, a potential victim of an unpredictable environment. Yet, the finiteness, separateness, independence, and unpredictability are entirely inherent in the partial view of the Actual conscious experience of Being which *is* going on. If it weren't going on, there couldn't be a misinterpretation or misidentification!

Essential to being able to break the partial view, is the shifting of the "point of awareness" from being *within* that which is observed to that subjective Place wherein It *is* that which is what is observed — the all-inclusive, infinite experience of being as Conscious Being.

It is only *the intuitive perception* of our Infinity *as* Conscious Being — prior to our "expansion" — which gives us the guts to expand. That intuition gives us the perspective to see that we are expanding into what we already *Are,* and that we are not expanding into the unknown at all! True, we may not know the details of our Infinity, but it's the details that we cannot see until the Universal Nature of our Self becomes an accepted Fact and basis from which to *be.* This is so essential to understand, and you are beginning to see this. Excellent!

PAUL   You realize, of course, that you interrupted the transcript that I was in the middle of!

RAJ   I can't always wait until you *think* you're ready, Paul. In fact, I didn't interrupt you at all. You have maintained an open link with your Being all day, which is excellent. This is when the revealing occurred. It is well that you flowed with it.

Now, return to your transcript.

PAUL   Thanks, Raj.

[I resumed work for about five minutes, and then. . .]

RAJ   Whenever you are faced with a demand to give specific attention to some part of your infinitude and it presents itself as being "problematic," it is simply the time and place for this aspect of You to be consciously incorporated into and as your conscious experience of being *as* Yours!

You say you don't want to be bothered, that this is not a good time because of other more pressing demands. But, Paul, your Being unfolds Itself *as* You according to divine Intelligence, Universal order and priorities. Every problem is your opportunity to be the Christ — that accurate perception of Reality (Your Being) that is not deluded in any way — and for that perception to become irrevocably "incorporated" into and as your Self-awareness. There is no more pressing need than that, because when seen, it becomes apparent that pressing needs are illusions of the partial view. They never existed as anything for you to sweat over and tense yourself up about.

PAUL   Thank you, Raj.

RAJ   You are welcome, Paul. You may continue.

June 21, 1982
Monday

PAUL   Good morning, Raj.

RAJ   Good morning, Paul.

PAUL   I am feeling some confusion this morning about things. I feel a sense of pressure, and also of being up against the wall. It is not a comfortable feeling. I can conceive of the fact that this sense of pressure and of being up against a dead end is an illusion. But this theoretical knowledge isn't helping me, at the moment, to know what to do and which way to go in order to see the illusion dissolve.

We are down to $2 in our pocket. We have a payment due on the copy machine, and we have $400 owed to us currently which cannot be paid until approximately two weeks from now. Yet, we have a substantial amount of business coming in. It's the same old story.

RAJ   Paul, it *is* the same old story, but let us be clear about what the story is. Do not be fooled into believing that what you see, hear, taste, smell, and feel is what the story is. You are allowing a three–dimensional means of being conscious determine what is real for you, based upon its limited, partial ability to perceive the Actuality which is going on. Thus, you compound the problem.

It is one thing to see anything from the partial view. It is entirely another thing to believe what you see on that basis, and then base your thoughts and responses upon what you see as though it were accurate.

The same old story which *is* going on is that Reality, the Actuality, Fourth-dimensional Conscious Being, is what is going on and is what has always been going on in Its Totality. You must be very strict in your observance of what you know Actually to be true. Be willing to act, think, and respond from that standpoint.

The need is to see the Actuality, not to respond or react to the partiality. Right now you are geared to spontaneously react to the way things appear. You are beginning to perceive that the necessity is to spontaneously respond to the Actuality as though *that* were the urgent need, rather than the limited, finite, three-dimensional view.

I realize what I am telling you is not something new, but it is, nevertheless, the step that needs to be taken. It is the needed thing.

Now, I do want to deal with some of these issues which are confusing to you at the moment. First of all, it is an accurate perception on your part that your allegiance, your trust, and your energies need to be placed unequivocally where they have been for the past six months — in other words, in your direct perception of your Self as Fourth-dimensional Conscious Being. You will be foolish to use any external source as a gauge or measuring stick by which to know whether you are on the right track.

It would be a backward step for you to allow the writings of Mary Baker Eddy, or any other author, or the current point of unfoldment of any group or organization to become in any way the authority for what you are to think or do. These sources most certainly have their place when one seems to be unable to consciously perceive the Divinity of his own Being directly as his very own conscious experience. But, this is not where you are. Therefore, you cannot afford to place the authority for what you think, believe, or do at any point external to that direct perception of your Conscious Being.

PAUL   Thank you, Raj.

RAJ   You do not need to feel that you will in any way be deprived of anything worthwhile by relinquishing external authorities, concepts, or organizations, no matter how beautifully they may have served to identify your unfolding perceptions of Reality as your Conscious Being.

PAUL   I shall remember that, Raj.

RAJ   Now, as to another point with which you are having difficulty. I will point out to you that this is a difficulty similar in nature to others that you will be confronted with as those with whom you speak become aware of the manner in which our conversations occur — the fact that an individuality called Raj is speaking with you. You must be willing to stand with things the way they are unfolding in and as *your* conscious experience of Being.

Reality does not exist to fit into or coordinate with partial views of Reality. As long as you are expressing clear explanations of Reality, you must fully expect those seeing with a partial view to attempt to discredit Truth if It doesn't agree with or come in the form that they conceive that It must come.

It is a fact that from the three-dimensional frame of reference, conscious identity must come to that point where it recognizes itself as being the Door. Then, it must actively and consciously *be* the Door. This, then, allows the Reality of Fourth-dimensional Conscious Being to "break through" into and *as* that apparently finite conscious experience of Being called three-dimensional man. This reveals the eternally accurate conscious perception of what is Really going on — the Christ-consciousness. This break-through is what has been perceived as the statement, "Behold, I stand at the Door and knock."[1]

However, it must become clear that the apparent relationship of a three-dimensional consciousness becoming the Door and then the Christ-Truth — the direct perception of Reality *as It is* — flowing through that Door as the conscious experience of a three-dimensional, finite man, does not then become the new "norm." Man, as he conceives himself to be three-dimensionally, does not simply forever remain the "conduit" for Reality to flow through.

The fact is that the more consistently he is willing to stand as the Door, the more consistently he will begin to experience himself less and less as "a three-dimensional man standing as the Door." He will become consciously aware of himself as *that conscious experience of Reality which includes no distortions of any kind* — the Christ-consciousness, the means by which God, or Conscious Being, experiences Its Infinity.

Therefore, those in your experience who are attempting to "help" you see that what is unfolding here in your experience *is* the Christ-consciousness revealing Itself, are correct to that degree. However, they are incorrect in attempting to "help" you see that an individuality by the name of Raj is an illusory part of this experience.

Their view is still so limited — in spite of the grandness and infinity of the view they see currently, as opposed to what they saw originally — that you would be foolish to use their vantage point as your own.

It is true that you are not participating in spiritualism. You are not communicating with a soul that has "passed on." You are not speaking to an individuality still befuddled by the three-dimensional illusion of birth and death who thinks that he was ever born or ever died.

I am not the medium through which the Christ-consciousness is revealing Itself as your conscious experience of Being. But, I do exist, as does every other individualization who has existed as an infinite aspect of Fourth-dimensional Conscious Being.

There *is* infinite progression, even beyond the partial, three-dimensional-only view. It is simply ignorance — the inability to see infinitely — which would make one think that once the "mortal dream" is grown out of, there does not continue to be the infinite unfolding of Being as Conscious Being. This is true before or after the experience called death.

It is quite accurate that it is not possible for those who believe that they have been born to communicate with those who *believe* that they have died. These are two different states of the three-dimensional-only frame of reference. It is part of the distortion of that finite view which makes it seem as though some part of one's infinitude (those who have "passed on") is not available to him as his conscious experience.

There are infinitely more individualizations of Being who are Awake than there are those who are "asleep." It is ridiculous to believe that communication with them is impossible.

Be very wise, and do not bother to waste your time trying

to accommodate the three-dimensional viewpoints of those around you. Do not allow yourself to give authority to anything outside of your own demonstrated conscious experience of Reality, of Fourth-dimensional Being, under any circumstances.

PAUL   Thank you very much, Raj.

RAJ   You are welcome, Paul. Good-bye.

---

1   John 10:9.

Afterword

Thus, a journey has begun. Not just Paul's, but yours — not a journey in space or time, not even an *inner* journey toward something which you are not yet. Rather, it is a journey of undoing, of stopping the movement away from What You Are — into a personal, private, individualistic sense of yourself. It is an inevitable journey because you cannot ignore your Self indefinitely. Who and What You Are will keep stepping up and confronting you, slapping you in the face to get your attention, because it is insane to function as though *you* are out of your Mind — the conscious experience of your Fullness.

The "journey" constitutes a *return* to the primitive and ultimate conscious experience of your Being, and therefore constitutes an "unjourney." In its simplicity, it is effortless. Indeed, all effort is ego and constitutes the act of separation. Thus, you must *allow* yourself into the Kingdom of Heaven — the unadulterated, undistorted Conscious experience of Being.

To have an ending to this book would be to *give* you the answer, when the fact is that you *are* the answer, and you will write your own book in the language of your own conscious experience. It is your Self which you must come face to face with and agree to be. It will not be easy, but it need not be hard; and, as I said, it is inevitable.

You are not, and will not be, alone in this journey, although it will be absolutely individual. You are on it, whether you are consciously engaged in it or not, because of What You Really Are. Your success is assured because you began your journey from your destination, and Actually never left it except in the illusory ego sense.

It is so simple!

Rajpur
Bellingham, Washington
May 20, 1985